*SPIRITUAL ASSESSMENT IN SOCIAL WORK
AND MENTAL HEALTH PRACTICE*

# Spiritual Assessment in Social Work and Mental Health Practice

*David R. Hodge*

 COLUMBIA UNIVERSITY PRESS    NEW YORK

COLUMBIA UNIVERSITY PRESS
*Publishers Since 1893*
New York    Chichester, West Sussex

cup.columbia.edu

Library of Congress Cataloging-in-Publication Data

Hodge, David R.
  Spiritual assessment in social work and mental health practice / David R. Hodge.
    pages cm
  Includes bibliographical references and index.
  ISBN 978-0-231-16396-5 (cloth : alk. paper) — ISBN 978-0-231-53881-7 (e-book)
  1. Spiritual care (Medical care). 2. Social service—Religious aspects.
  3. Mental health counseling—Religious aspects. I. Title.

  BL65.M4H626  2015
  361.3—dc23

                                                         2014018942

Columbia University Press books are printed on permanent and durable acid-free paper.
This book is printed on paper with recycled content.
Printed in the United States of America


Cover design: Rebecca Lown
Cover image: © Shutterstock

References to websites (URLs) were accurate at the time of writing.
Neither the author nor Columbia University Press is responsible for URLs
that may have expired or changed since the manuscript was prepared.

TO OUR CLIENTS AND THE PRACTITIONERS
WHO HELP THEM REALIZE THEIR STRENGTHS
AND ACHIEVE THEIR GOALS

# CONTENTS

IT IS INCREASINGLY RECOGNIZED THAT spirituality plays an important role in service provision. For many clients, spirituality is intrinsically connected with health and wellness. To optimize services for such clients, it is necessary to take spirituality into account during service provision (Koenig, 2013).

This recognition has resulted in healthcare professionals seeking to address spirituality in practice settings, a process that begins with the administration of a spiritual assessment. Spiritual assessment can be defined as the process of gathering, analyzing, and synthesizing information about spirituality into a multidimensional framework that provides the basis for future clinical decisions (Hodge, 2013a). Understood in this sense, assessment provides the foundation for all subsequent practice interactions.

The resulting information may be used to assist clients in overcoming obstacles, preventing relapse, and promoting well-being. Interventions designed to enhance coping, ameliorate problems, and aid recovery flow from the data obtained during assessment. Barriers that inhibit effective service delivery can be removed, and assets that facilitate successful outcomes can be operationalized.

How information obtained from a spiritual assessment is used in a specific clinical context varies from case to case, depending on factors such as the practice setting, the practitioner's theoretical orientation, and the client's interests and needs (Canda & Furman, 2010). For example, adapting services for clients from vulnerable populations, for whom spirituality is often particularly important, can play an instrumental role in achieving positive outcomes. Although applications vary, it is the assessment that provides the necessary information to optimize the services delivered. Put differently, the failure to administer a spiritual assessment can impair clinical effectiveness and, in some cases, exacerbate problems.

Different types of spiritual assessments exist (Holloway & Moss, 2010; Draper, 2012). Broadly speaking, these different methods can be classified into two categories: qualitative and quantitative. Although quantitative assessments can be productively employed in many practice settings, they are characterized by significant limitations, particularly when used with subjective constructs such as spirituality. These shortcomings limit their validity but do not preclude their use, as will be discussed in further detail in chapter 11.

To obtain clinically valid information, spiritual assessment is best conducted with qualitative assessment approaches (Narayanasamy, 2010). These approaches tend to be individualistic, ideographic, holistic, open-ended, and process oriented (Hodge, 2001a). As such, they are particularly appropriate for exploring clients' spiritual reality. The depth, quality, and richness of information that these approaches tend to produce effectively position practitioners to optimize service provision in an ethical manner that is consistent with disciplinary norms. Consistent with this understanding, a qualitative frame is assumed throughout most of this book.

### A TRANSDISCIPLINARY APPROACH

Contemporary work on the topic of spiritual assessment can be traced back at least as far as Pruyser (1976), a clinical psychologist at the Menninger Clinic. Seminal scholarship on spiritual assessment has also been conducted in fields other than psychology, including nursing (Stoll, 1979), pastoral care (Fitchett, 1993), and social work (Bullis, 1996). More recently, work on this and related topics has appeared across the helping professions.

Previous scholarship, however, has been criticized for its disciplinary focus (Fitchett, 2012; Praglin, 2004; Ross & McSherry, 2010). These commentators have noted that much of the extant scholarship has tended to be conducted in distinct professional silos. To advance the field, these writers suggest a more cross-disciplinary approach.

In keeping with these recommendations, this book incorporates content from a wide variety of fields. It draws heavily from the social work literature, but this literature is integrated with scholarship from other disciplines to help clarify and disseminate best practices in the assessment of spirituality in a wide variety of practice settings.

As a result, practitioners from a number of disciplines may benefit from the book. Helping professionals who may find the text useful include social workers, marriage and family therapists, counselors, and psychologists. Nurses, chaplains, and physicians who are working in hospitals and other healthcare settings that require spiritual assessments might also benefit. Other professionals who might profit include those who work in areas where spirituality is often a salient dimension of practice, such as addictions, gerontology, and hospice.

In line with this transdisciplinary approach, the word practitioner is typically used as a proxy for helping professionals more generally. This term is commonly used in social work but also has applicability in other fields. Likewise, the philosophical perspectives that inform the text are also transdisciplinary in nature.

## UNDERLYING PHILOSOPHICAL PERSPECTIVES

The approaches to spiritual assessment presented in the book are informed by two broad philosophical perspectives. These related movements are labeled differently in various disciplines. The first stresses the role of assets and resources in the promotion of health and wellness; the second affirms the social construction of reality and is commonly referred to as constructivism.

The importance of assets and resources in service provision has been noted in social work (Saleebey, 2013), marriage and family therapy (DeFrain & Asay, 2007), counseling (Smith, 2006), psychology (Snyder, Lopez, & Pedrotti, 2011), nursing (Cederbaum & Klusaritz, 2009), and other disciplines. This movement, which encompasses the *strengths perspective* in social work and *positive psychology* in psychology, seeks to reorient the helping process. Instead of focusing on deficits and pathologies, the movement aims to help clients deal with challenges by concentrating on their capabilities. In counseling, for instance, the therapeutic process centers on exploring, unearthing, and marshaling clients' strengths to help them overcome their challenges. In almost any practice setting, identifying and operationalizing strengths helps clients cope with, if not overcome, the obstacles they face.

Constructivism refers to a way of knowing that has its roots in postmodernism (Denzin & Lincoln, 2013). This epistemological framework posits that people construct their worldviews. Human beings, individually and corporately as social groups, construct their realities in unique, individualistic manners. Various factors inform the creation of these worldviews, one of which is spirituality. As a result of this process, it is assumed that everyone has a limited understanding of the world. No one has a completely objective understanding of reality.

Spiritual assessments are perhaps best administered using a constructivist theoretical framework. A number of assumptions about the nature of the helping relationship flow from this perspective. These suppositions are largely shared by the strengths perspective, which affirms similar notions about how best to operationalize practitioner/client interactions (Saleebey, 2013).

Specifically, hierarchical relationships that privilege practitioners' status are avoided in favor of egalitarian relationships in which clients are considered to be experts on their own situations. Treatment goals are co-constructed, and clients' strengths, as opposed to deficits, are understood to be central to the helping process. Also stressed is empathic respect for divergent constructions of reality and a belief in the power of the clinical dialogue to engender empowering narratives (Slife & Williams, 1995).

Informed by these assumptions, spiritual assessments are organized around understanding how spirituality shapes functioning (Shafranske, 2005). The aim is not to determine the correctness of clients' beliefs, values, and practices but rather how they influence functioning related to service provision. Put differently, assessment focuses on the *viability*, as opposed to the *validity*, of clients' worldviews. In turn, this understanding lays the foundation for tailoring service provision to assist clients in achieving their goals. As implied above, these two philosophies—the strengths perspective and constructivism—provide the philosophical foundation for operationalizing the approaches to assessment contained in the book.

Another important influence that informs the work is the evidence-based practice movement (Thyer & Myers, 2010). Originating in the field of medicine, this evolving transdisciplinary movement emphasizes the provision of effective services. Key concepts in evidence-based practice are client preference, clinical expertise, and cultural competency, in tandem with an evaluation of relevant research (Hodge, 2011b). Although research on the topic of spiritual assessment is limited, practice-oriented research is incorporated into the text to the fullest extent possible (Jordan & Franklin, 2011).

## THE FORTHCOMING TERRAIN

People have different backgrounds, experiences, and interests. Just like there is no single, perfect approach to spiritual assessment, there is no one correct way to get the most out of a given book. Some readers may wish to skim or skip certain content or chapters relating to concepts with which they are already conversant. Others may want to focus on a chapter featuring an assessment approach that is particularly germane to their situational context. Readers should approach the book in a manner that maximizes their ability to get the most out of it.

Chapter 1 begins by discussing how spirituality and religion are commonly understood, both in professional discourse and among potential clients. Chapter 2 asks the question: why should practitioners administer spiritual assessments in light of the many time constraints they typically encounter in clinical settings? Six intertwined rationales are offered in response: (1) to ensure compliance with professional ethics codes, (2) to respect clients' basic human rights, (3) to honor client autonomy, (4) to identify and operationalize spiritual strengths, (5) to provide culturally relevant services, and (6) to adhere to professional standards for good practice, as articulated by various accrediting bodies and professional organizations.

With this foundation in place, chapter 3 introduces the concept of a two-stage assessment, in which a brief assessment is followed, if clinically warranted, by a comprehensive assessment. A number of different brief assessment approaches are reviewed—including the newly developed iCARING model—and process suggestions are offered to facilitate a successful brief assessment. Chapter 4 offers guidelines to help decide if a brief assessment is sufficient or if the administration of a comprehensive assessment is clinically warranted.

To move beyond a one-size-fits-all approach to assessment, chapters 5 through 9 present five modally different approaches to comprehensive assessment: one completely verbal approach (spiritual histories) and four diagrammatic methods (spiritual lifemaps, spiritual genograms, spiritual eco-maps, and spiritual ecograms). To assist readers in understanding the various tools, each chapter includes a conceptual overview of the method, a case example to help practitioners understand and operationalize the assessment in practice settings, and a discussion of the method's respective strengths and limitations. Chapter 10 features an alternative method—referred to as an implicit assessment—for use when the previous approaches may be ineffective. The chapter concludes by presenting a model to integrate an implicit assessment with the other approaches, resulting in a comprehensive framework for thinking about assessment, from a brief assessment through to the use of various comprehensive methods.

The idea is to develop an assessment toolbox that comprises these various methods. Both practitioners and clients have a variety of needs and interests that vary from case to case, including the nature of the presenting challenge, the amount of time available for assessment, and clients' cultural backgrounds. Having a toolbox allows practitioners to select the approach that best suits the needs of their clients.

Chapter 11 provides additional suggestions on conducting a comprehensive assessment. Guidelines are presented for selecting among comprehensive approaches, using quantitative instruments in clinical settings, and dealing with spiritual countertransference and what might be called faux spiritual direction. The chapter ends by discussing the benefits that flow from collaborating with clergy. The concluding chapter reiterates the book's major themes and offers ideas for building on the themes in the areas of research, practice, and education.

This journey begins, however, with a discussion of spirituality. To effectively administer spiritual assessments, it is necessary to understand what is commonly meant by the term *spirituality*. This is important because the conceptualizations people employ serve to guide and direct their inquiries. Common conceptualizations are presented in chapter 1. More specifically, the chapter discusses the relationship between spirituality and religion, reviews common understandings of these constructs among both scholars and the American public, and provides a working template to think about spirituality and religion in the context of conducting spiritual assessments.

*SPIRITUAL ASSESSMENT IN SOCIAL WORK*
*AND MENTAL HEALTH PRACTICES*

# 1

# Understanding Spirituality and Religion

DEFINITIONS ARE IMPORTANT. They help us understand the landscape of a given phenomenon (Holloway & Moss, 2010). Definitions highlight areas that should be examined while simultaneously functioning to exclude certain other themes that are implicitly deemed irrelevant. Indeed, communication—the lifeblood of practitioner-client interactions—depends on a shared understanding of the concepts discussed (Ai, 2002). If practitioners and clients conceptualize an entity differently, effective communication may be hindered, even though both participants might believe that mutual understanding occurs since the same terminology is used.

Few topics, however, are more controversial in academic discourse than conceptualizations of spirituality and religion (Pattison, 2013). Also highly contested is the nature of the relationship between these two constructs. No consensus exists among either academics or potential clients, with conceptualizations of spirituality being the subject of particularly intense debate.

This chapter explores these topics. The goal of the chapter is not to posit definitive definitions of spirituality and religion. Rather, the aim is to sketch out various understandings, in tandem with some of the arguments for and against various conceptualizations. By developing a sense of the various views affirmed by scholars and members of the public, practitioners are better positioned to explore and identify the diverse understandings of spirituality and religion affirmed by clients (Fitchett, 2012). In keeping with this goal, the chapter begins by reviewing the traditional view of spirituality and religion.

## TRADITIONAL VIEW OF SPIRITUALITY AND RELIGION

The academic study of spirituality and religion can be traced back at least to William James's (1902/1985) seminal work at the turn of the prior century. Historically, James and other academics have understood spirituality as a dimension within religion (Koenig, 2011). In other words, religion is viewed as the broader, more encompassing concept. It includes individual and social dimensions, as well as subjective and objective dimensions (Pargament, Mahoney, Exline, Jones, & Shafranske, 2013).

In keeping with this understanding, religion has been defined "as a culturally shared system of values, beliefs, and rituals which include spiritual concerns" (Praglin, 2004:74). Put simply, religion is a spiritually animated culture characterized by certain ideals, principles, and practices that have a spiritual purpose.

In the traditional view, the term *spiritual* refers to a subset of individuals who are invested in, or committed to, their religious tradition, often in a deeply experiential manner (Koenig, 2011). James (1902/1985), for instance, understood religion to consist of an external, communal dimension manifested in forms such as church services, as well as a solitary, individual dimension manifested in the experience of the divine. This personal manifestation of religion was understood to encompass a dynamic, subjective, emotional element in a manner akin to contemporary understandings of spirituality. In essence, spirituality is a form of devout religion.

In a similar manner, Allport and Ross (1967) posited the existence of a construct they called *intrinsic religion*. For intrinsic individuals, religion is hypothesized to provide adherents with an internalized "master motive" that serves to guide and direct life. This conceptualization is congruent with many current conceptualizations of spirituality, as illustrated by the fact that the intrinsic measure has been used as a proxy for assessing individual spirituality in a variety of settings (Hodge, 2003b; Reinert & Koenig, 2013).

What about individuals who express their spirituality outside of traditional religious settings? Within the traditional framework, newer, postmodern forms of spirituality are viewed as representing new religions. Thus the New Age or syncretistic spirituality movement might be referred to as a new religious movement. Established but less common religions, such as neo-paganism, are commonly referred to as alternative religions (Canda & Furman, 2010).

In the past few decades, the traditional view of spirituality and religion has been largely supplanted in many academic circles (Swinton, 2010). The reasons behind the emergence of this new understanding of spirituality and religion are complex. One contributing factor was the success of the Enlightenment, and the attendant modernist metanarrative, in successfully delegitimizing religion among societal elites (Gellner, 1992). Another factor is the recent ascendance of postmodernism, with its emphasis on individualized ways of knowing, which includes individualized knowing in the non-material, metaphysical realm (Gray, 2008). Together with other influences, these factors have led to new conceptualizations of spirituality and religion.

## CONTEMPORARY VIEW

In the contemporary understanding, spirituality and religion are typically defined as distinct, unique concepts (Pargament et al., 2013). Spirituality is usually understood as an individualistic, relatively subjective construct. Religion tends to be conceptualized as a socially shared set of beliefs and practices that can be related to spirituality (Derezotes, 2006).

In contrast to the traditional understanding, it is spirituality, rather than religion, that is typically viewed as the broader, more encompassing concept (Swinton, 2010). Spirituality may or may not be expressed within a religious framework. As an individually oriented construct, it is hypothesized to exist separate from religion, which is viewed as a more communal entity. Thus, while understandings of religion in the traditional and contemporary view are somewhat similar, conceptualizations of spirituality have changed substantially.

Indeed, the terrain encompassed by the term spirituality has expanded markedly (Paley, 2008). In the contemporary framework, spirituality is commonly defined in universal terms. That is, everyone is understood to be spiritual (Canda, 2008). For instance, spirituality has been defined, in brief, as "lived experience that gives meaning to life and death" (Catterall, Cox, Greet, Sankey, & Griffiths, 1998:163); "an inner life of personal development" (Chandler, 2012:578); "aspects of human life relating to experiences that transcend sensory phenomena" (World Health Organisation [WHO], 1990:50); "the wholeness of what it means to be human" (Canda, 1997:302); and "what we do to give expression to our chosen worldview" (Moss, 2005:2).

Such definitions tend to implicitly frame spirituality as a positive construct. In contrast, religion is often depicted in more negative, institutionally oriented terms (Wolfer, 2012). Individually oriented spirituality is a positive, intrinsic dimension of human experience, which organized religion may facilitate or hinder.

This broad understanding of spirituality offers at least two advantages. First, the universal understanding ensures that no unique manifestation of spirituality is inadvertently overlooked or excluded. Since everyone is assumed to be spiritual in some sense, practitioners are implicitly encouraged to understand how this spirituality is manifested in each person's life (Crisp, 2010). Clinically relevant aspects of clients' lives that might have otherwise been overlooked may be identified as a result.

Second, this conceptualization of spirituality may resonate with a certain segment of the general population. Depending on the data source and question phrasing, roughly a quarter of the population self-identifies as "spiritual but not religious" (Ellison & McFarland, 2013). In many cases these individuals have effectively decoupled spirituality from traditional understandings of religion in pursuit of an individualized spiritual path. Theoretical frameworks that also reflect this decoupling may represent a particularly good fit for such individuals, enabling practitioners and clients to readily identify issues of relevance to service provision. In addition to these important advantages, some limitations also exist.

## LIMITATIONS OF THE CONTEMPORARY UNDERSTANDING

A number of shortcomings regarding contemporary understandings of spirituality and religion have been noted. For example, defining spirituality as a universal facet of human experience effectively imposes this construct on people who may not wish to be described as spiritual (Paley, 2008). Approximately 10 percent of the American population rejects the term spiritual as a self-descriptor (see tables 1.3 and 1.5). Applying terms to individuals that they personally deny is ethically problematic and can impede the therapeutic relationship (Saleebey, 2013).

Another limitation is the capacity of broad definitions to assist practitioners in identifying spiritual content. The purpose of definitions is to distinguish one entity from another (Koenig, 2011). If spirituality is defined in broad universal terms, it can be difficult to distinguish it from other aspects of human experience (Canda, 1997). Practitioners may have trouble identifying the unique spiritual dimension of existence (Doherty, 2009).

In addition, some spirituality definitions confound outcomes with the underlying construct (Swinton, 2010). It is arguable that a sense of meaning, to cite one example, is an outcome or an effect of spirituality rather than its essence. Defining spirituality in terms of outcomes is problematic in both research and practice settings (Koenig, 2011). Clients who are depressed and lack a sense of meaning and purpose are essentially precluded from being spiritual. Deeply spiritual Catholic saints experiencing a "dark night of the soul" cannot be spiritual based on certain definitions.

Another potential limitation relates to the decontextualization of spirituality from its larger social context (Pargament et al., 2013). Like other human phenomena, an individual's spirituality is shaped and informed by other people—usually those who share similar understandings of spirituality. This process occurs in traditional religious settings, such as the Catholic Church, as well as in newer and alternative religious environments, such as the syncretistic movement (Doherty, 2009). The tendency to conceptually decouple spirituality from religion can result in neglecting the important social context in which spirituality is formed. Indeed, for people in many cultural contexts, the separation of spirituality from religion makes little sense ontologically or epistemologically (Wong & Vinsky, 2009). As such, understandings that frame spirituality as a personal, private, interior construct can inhibit practitioners' ability to work effectively with people for whom religion is the central, overarching dimension in their lives.

Racial bias has also been cited as a problem with the decoupling of spirituality from religion (Wong & Vinsky, 2009). Spirituality, with its positive connotations, is typically associated with people who are white. Conversely, religion, with its more conflicted connotations, is frequently ascribed to groups such as African Americans and Latinos (Henery, 2003). This can foster a form of "spiritual colonialism" that privileges the spiritual understanding of groups with power while simultaneously delegitimizing the views of traditionally disenfranchised groups (Swinton, 2010). Such discourse can reinforce larger discriminatory patterns and inhibit the ability of practitioners to work effectively with members of such groups (Sue & Sue, 2013).

An additional limitation is that contemporary views of spirituality do not typically reflect common understandings of spirituality among clients (Pargament et al., 2013). Although contemporary conceptualizations are congruent with a certain segment of the population, they are not widely affirmed more generally. Privileging such definitions is often considered to be problematic (Saleebey, 2013). Using conceptualizations that are congruent with clients' views tends to enhance collaboration (Wolf, 1978). Indeed, a central precept of the strengths perspective is the use of definitions and theories that resonate with clients. In turn, this raises the question as to how members of the general public understand spirituality and religion.

## SPIRITUALITY AND RELIGION AMONG THE GENERAL PUBLIC

As Wuthnow (2007) observes, the term spirituality is typically used in American society to talk about a person's relationship with God. According to Gallup data, 90 percent of the public believes in God (Newport, 2012). The percentage has remained relatively stable across decades, supported by elevated levels of theistic belief among the rapidly expanding Latino population (Jones, Cox, & Navarro-Rivera, 2013).

Understandings of God are diverse and are held with varying degrees of confidence (Suarez & Lewis, 2013). This is illustrated by data in table 1.1, which portrays perceptions about God's existence (Smith, Marsden, Hout, & Kim, 2013). Confidence in the existence of God varies along the nature of this existence. For example, some people reject the notion of a personal God but believe in a higher power of some kind. Others believe in God but have doubts about God's existence. Although it is important to keep this variation in mind, a majority of the general public (60 percent) report they know God really exists and have no doubts about God's existence.

Most people believe God is actively involved in human affairs. When asked in the 2008 GSS if there is a God who is concerned with every human being personally, most people concurred (Smith et al., 2013). Indeed, 71 percent of public believe God takes a personal interest in human welfare; only 16 percent disagree.

Furthermore, for a certain subset of the general population, this involvement is manifested in very personal and often dramatic ways (Hood & Francis, 2013). This is illustrated by a nationally representative study conducted by Baylor University in collaboration with the Gallup organization (Stark, 2008). When queried about their spiritual experiences, approximately two-thirds of the public report some type of personal, experiential encounter with God or a guardian angel (see table 1.2).

TABLE 1.1   Beliefs About God's Existence Among the General Public

| OPTIONS | % |
| --- | --- |
| I know God really exists and have no doubts about it. | 59.7 |
| While I have doubts, I feel that I do believe in God. | 15.7 |
| I find myself believing in God some of the time but not at others. | 4.1 |
| I don't believe in a personal God, but I do believe in a Higher Power of some kind. | 11.7 |
| I don't know whether there is a God, and I don't believe there is any way to find out. | 5.5 |
| I don't believe in God. | 3.3 |

*Source*: 2012 General Social Survey (GSS)
*Note*: Excludes 0.9 percent of respondents who did not know or refused to answer.

TABLE 1.2   Experiences of the Supernatural Among the General Public

| OPTIONS | % |
| --- | --- |
| I was protected from harm by a guardian angel. | 55 |
| I felt called by God to do something. | 44 |
| I heard the voice of God speaking to me. | 20 |
| I witnessed a miraculous, physical healing. | 23 |
| I received a miraculous, physical healing. | 16 |

*Source*: Stark (2008)
*Note*: Percentage of public reporting an affirmative response.

Affirmative responses to the five mystical experiences delineated in table 1.2 are highly correlated (Stark, 2008). Just over a quarter (27 percent) of adults indicate they have had at least three of these experiences; an additional 18 percent have had two. Thus close to half the population (45 percent) report what might be called mystical experiences with God. Women and African Americans were more likely than, respectively, men and European Americans to report multiple supernatural encounters. It should also be noted that many other types of mystical experiences are also commonly reported (Mack & Powell, 2005).

Like human relationships, people's relationships with God are not static but dynamic, changing over time (Exline, Park, Smyth, & Carey, 2011). People may feel close to God in certain circumstances. At other times they may be angry with God, and even reject God entirely. Their attachment to God varies over time as it is shaped by various life events (Granqvist & Kirkpatrick, 2013).

One factor that molds people's relationship with God is religion (Wuthnow, 2007). According to Gallup data, approximately 80 percent of Americans have a religious identity (Newport, 2012). Roughly 55 percent report that religion is very important in their daily lives. As implied above, religion is related to gender, race, ethnicity, age, and socioeconomic status. Specifically, women, African Americans, Latinos, older adults, and people who are poor are disproportionately likely to affirm the importance of religion.

The intertwined nature of spirituality and religion among the public is illustrated by questions that ask individuals to describe their level of spirituality and religion. Table 1.3 features the responses to the following question: To what extent do you consider yourself a spiritual person? The same question was asked to determine people's level of religiousness. These two questions provide a window on the intensity of people's spirituality and religion.

Two-thirds of the population consider themselves to be at least moderately spiritual, while almost 60 percent consider themselves to be at least moderately religious. The correlation between these two variables is 0.58,

TABLE 1.3   Self-Ascribed Levels of Spirituality and Religion Among the General Public

| LEVEL OF SPIRITUALITY | % | LEVEL OF RELIGIOUSNESS | % |
|---|---|---|---|
| Very spiritual | 29.2 | Very religious | 18.8 |
| Moderately spiritual | 37.2 | Moderately religious | 39.5 |
| Slightly spiritual | 22.6 | Slightly religious | 21.6 |
| Not spiritual | 11.0 | Not religious | 20.1 |

Source: 2012 General Social Survey

Note: Level of spirituality excludes 2.1 percent of respondents who did not know or refused to answer. Level of religiousness excludes 0.9 percent of respondents who did not know or refused to answer.

TABLE 1.4    Interrelationship of Spirituality and Religion Among the
General Public

| | VERY RELIGIOUS | | MODERATELY RELIGIOUS | | SLIGHTLY RELIGIOUS | | NOT RELIGIOUS | | |
|---|---|---|---|---|---|---|---|---|---|
| *Very* *spiritual* | 50.5% | 78.0% | 30.4% | 22.5% | 7.9% | 10.5% | 11.2% | 16.2% | 100% |
| *Moderately* *spiritual* | 10.0% | 19.8% | 64.8% | 61.6% | 14.7% | 25.3% | 10.4% | 19.3% | 100% |
| *Slightly* *spiritual* | 0.9% | 1.1% | 24.3% | 14.0% | 52.8% | 54.9% | 22.0% | 24.7% | 100% |
| *Not* *spiritual* | 1.9% | 1.1% | 7.1% | 2.0 | 18.4% | 9.3% | 72.6% | 39.7% | 100% |
| | | 100% | | 100% | | 100% | | 100% | |

*Source*: 2012 General Social Survey

*Note:* Excludes 2.4 percent of respondents who did not know or refused to answer.

a value that is commonly considered to represent a strong association
between the self-described intensity of spirituality and religion (Cohen &
Cohen, 1983).

Table 1.4 depicts a cross-tabulation of these two self-descriptors. This
allows one to see the interrelationship between the two variables. For
instance, the first italicized row provides the religious breakdown for 100
percent of respondents who self-identify as very spiritual. Of these, 50 percent also self-describe as very religious, while an additional 30 percent self-
describe as moderately religious. Only 11 percent of those who identify as
very spiritual indicate they are not religious.

An even greater degree of overlap occurs when looking at those who
self-describe as very religious. Some 78 percent of those who self-describe
as very religious also report they are very spiritual, and only 2 percent
self-describe as slightly or not at all spiritual. A similar degree of overlap
exists among those who exhibit little interest in spirituality or religion.
For example, among those who indicate they are not spiritual, approximately 73 percent also indicate they are not religious. In short, these data
suggest that spirituality and religion are closely related in the lives of most
Americans, regardless of whether they are interested, or uninterested in
spirituality and religion.

TABLE 1.5    Spirituality and Religion Profiles Among the General Public

| OPTIONS | % |
| --- | --- |
| A. I follow a religion and consider myself to be a spiritual person interested in the sacred and the supernatural. | 41.0 |
| B. I follow a religion but don't consider myself to be a spiritual person interested in the sacred and the supernatural. | 24.2 |
| C. I don't follow a religion but consider myself to be a spiritual person interested in the sacred and the supernatural. | 23.5 |
| D. I don't follow a religion and don't consider myself to be a spiritual person interested in the sacred and the supernatural. | 11.4 |

*Source*: 2008 General Social Survey

*Note:* Excludes 3.2 percent of respondents who did not know or refused to answer.

A slightly different perspective emerges from a question that asks individuals to select from one of four possible spiritual and religious profiles. Instead of providing a graduated response scale, as with the questions regarding self-described levels of spirituality and religion, this question asks individuals to select the one option that best describes them. As can be seen in table 1.5, a plurality report that they follow a religion and consider themselves to be a spiritual person. Roughly a quarter affirm each of two alternative profiles: follow a religion but don't consider themselves to be spiritual, or consider themselves to be spiritual but don't follow a religion.

Taken together, these data provide some sense of common understandings of spirituality and religion among the American population. It is important to note that survey data are always subject to a variety of qualifications. For instance, question wording can influence how individuals respond. To cite one example, many religious traditions consider humility to be a virtue. Describing oneself as spiritual might be taken as an indication of pride, leading to a reluctance to self-identify in this manner.

Figure 1.1 summarizes the data discussed above in a pictorial illustration. For most people, spirituality and religion are interconnected, overlapping constructs. These individuals self-identify as spiritual and express their spirituality in religious settings. Put differently, their spirituality is mediated by religion (Geppert, Bogenschutz, & Miller, 2007).

Others, however, express their spirituality outside of traditional religious frameworks. In some cases individual spirituality is also mediated

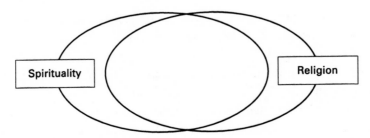

FIGURE I.I  Pictorial view of the relationship between spirituality and religion among the general public

by engagement with others in the syncretistic spirituality movement or alternative religious settings (although the term religion may be rejected in favor of alternative phrasing such as spiritual tradition, community, or group). In a few cases a completely individualistic spirituality is personally constructed apart from any social influences.

Finally, another group of individuals privilege religion. In some instances these individuals have a relationship with God but subsume this relationship under a religious rubric, in a manner analogous to the traditional understanding of religion as the broader, more encompassing concept. In other instances people may attend religious functions for cultural, social, or other reasons.

Some scholars have offered definitions of spirituality that may be relatively congruent with common understandings of spirituality among potential clients. For example, spirituality has been defined as a person's "existential relationship with God (or Ultimate Transcendence)" (Hodge, 2005d:343); a "capacity to experience a transcendent relationship with someone or something" (Gilbert, 2000:68); "engagement with, or experience of, the transcendent" (Ellison & McFarland, 2013:22); "movement of the heart towards God" (Clark, 2009:1668); and as an individual's "search for the sacred" (Pargament, 2013b:259). As with other definitions, these conceptualizations can also be critiqued on various grounds. For instance, they are all likely nonuniversalistic and thus may fail to highlight certain manifestations of spirituality that universalistic definitions might do a better job of identifying.

In keeping with the strengths perspective, this book refers to spirituality in terms of an individual's subjective relationship with God, or, more broadly, the transcendent or the sacred. It is important to emphasize, however, that this usage is, in effect, a proxy for the diverse understandings of spirituality that exist among the general population. Indeed, all the understandings reviewed above, supplemented by many other views, exist among the general public (Ammerman, 2013; Gall, Malette, & Guirguis-Younger, 2001; Gallup & Jones, 2000; Hodge & McGrew, 2006).

In this book the term spirituality is generally used to refer to both spirituality and religion. This is a text about assessment at the level of an individual or family. Since both scholars and the general public widely understand spirituality to be an individually oriented construct, it seems appropriate to refer to a spiritual assessment (Gallup & Jones, 2000). Accordingly, the phrase *spiritual assessment* should be understood as shorthand for a spiritual and religious assessment. In other words, at a conceptual level, a spiritual assessment includes an exploration of both spirituality and religion in whatever manner the client conceptualizes these two constructs to exist.

In practice settings the aim is to understand clients' definitional frameworks and then work within those parameters. Attempting to fit clients' views into predetermined definitional categories is typically unhelpful (Chandler, 2012). Nor is it likely even possible given the diverse array of conceptualizations that exist among the general public. While having some understanding of commonly held views aids in the process of conducting assessments, the process is best served by allowing clients' conceptualizations to shape practitioners' understanding, rather than the converse. Among the benefits of this approach is that it helps establish an ethic of tailoring service provision to reflect clients' values, which is a key reason for conducting an assessment.

In the following chapter, six rationales are posited in support of conducting spiritual assessments. These rationales are not necessarily dependent on how spirituality is defined. Regardless of how broadly spirituality is conceptualized, the rationales are designed to support the concept of a universally administered spiritual assessment.

# 2

# Rationales for Conducting a Spiritual Assessment

WHY SHOULD PRACTITIONERS CONDUCT SPIRITUAL assessments? Helping professionals are typically busy and face numerous time constraints. Why should they attempt to carve out the time needed to inquire about clients' spiritual beliefs and practices? This is a significant question. Since support for the concept of spiritual assessment is still questioned in some professional circles, it is important to understand the philosophical basis for assessment (Paley, 2009; Timmins & Kelly, 2008).

Accordingly, this chapter reviews a number of practical reasons in support of administering spiritual assessments as a routine component of service provision. These rationales can be summarized as follows: (1) to ensure compliance with professional ethics codes, (2) to respect clients' basic human rights, (3) to honor client autonomy, (4) to identify strengths that can be used to ameliorate problems or facilitate coping, (5) to provide culturally relevant services, and (6) to adhere to professional standards for good practice as articulated by various accrediting bodies and professional organizations.

Although discussed individually in the following sections, these six rationales are intertwined. For instance, honoring client self-determination is a central ethical component in most, if not all, ethics codes throughout the helping professions. As such, the rationales serve to reinforce one another and together provide a basis for conducting an assessment of spirituality in diverse practice settings.

## COMPLYING WITH PROFESSIONAL ETHICS

Ethics play a critical role in service provision (Reamer, 2006). Professional codes of ethics delineate normative standards for the provision of care. They are quasi-legal documents designed to guide practitioners' conduct in practice settings (Yarhouse & Johnson, 2013). In other words, a professional code of ethics specifies what is considered appropriate professional conduct (Dolgoff, Harrington, & Loewenberg, 2012).

For example, the Code of Ethics for the National Association of Social Workers (NASW) (2008) states that its overarching purpose is to "guide social workers' conduct." The code states that professional ethics represent the core of the social work profession. Accordingly, the code is relevant to all social workers, regardless of their status, function, or employment setting, or the population they focus on serving. The code enumerates a specific set of ethical standards to guide social work practice.

The NASW Code of Ethics refers to religion in numerous ethical standards, either directly or indirectly. In accordance with some other ethics codes, the NASW code does not mention spirituality but implicitly follows the traditional understanding of the relationship between spirituality and religion. Religion is assumed to be a broader concept that includes spirituality. Understood in this manner, the code provides ethical standards that deal with both spirituality and religion (Vogel, McMinn, Peterson, & Gatherecoal, 2013).

Religion is explicitly mentioned in four standards in the code. For example, under the rubric of diversity (1.05c), the code instructs social workers to seek to understand religious diversity, as well as the oppression people of faith encounter. In a related standard (4.02), social workers are enjoined not to practice, condone, facilitate, or collaborate with any form of religious discrimination. In addition, the code mentions religion in a macro context. For example, in the area of social and political action (6.04c), social workers are called on to prevent and eliminate religious discrimination directed toward people of faith.

Furthermore, the ethical standards enumerated in the NASW Code of Ethics are not unique to American social work. In the broader social work profession, the most influential ethics code may be the Statement of Ethical Principles (2004) developed by the International Federation of Social Workers (IFSW). The IFSW statement explicitly mentions spirituality in two locations (but does not mention religion, implicitly subsuming devout religion under spirituality). Specifically, social workers are called to uphold and defend each person's spiritual integrity and well-being (4.1). In the area of social justice, social workers are enjoined to challenge the discrimination people experience that stems from their spiritual beliefs (4.2.1), a form of discrimination that is a substantial problem globally (Grim & Finke, 2010).

Social work is not unique in terms of articulating ethical standards that address spirituality. Many professional ethics codes in the helping professions mention spirituality or religion in a similar manner, including ethics codes in counseling, marriage and family therapy, psychology, and nursing (Hodge, 2013a; Miller, 2003). For instance, the American School Counselor Association's (2010) ethical standards state that school counselors should advocate for and affirm students' religious/spiritual identities (preamble), alleviate bias directed at students because of their religion (E.2.b), and work effectively with students with respect to their religious/spiritual identities (E.2.d).

The widespread acknowledgment of spirituality across professions suggests that some type of broad consensus exists regarding the importance of spirituality. The professional agreement underscores the significance of attending to spirituality. To be congruent with the vision of practice depicted in professional ethics codes, practitioners must address spirituality in practice settings.

For instance, to comply with the NASW Code of Ethics, social workers are implicitly called to conduct a spiritual assessment with each client (Hodge, 2013a). It is difficult to understand how practitioners can respect diverse expressions of religious beliefs and alleviate religious discrimination without administering an assessment. To respect clients' religious beliefs and avoid discriminatory practices, it is necessary to have some understanding of those beliefs. Indeed, without such information, practitioners may inadvertently engage in offensive or discriminatory practices (Hodge & Limb, 2010a).

Similarly, supporting clients' spiritual integrity and spiritual well-being, as called for by the IFSW, requires social workers to gather information about clients' spirituality. It is difficult to understand how practitioners can support clients' spiritual well-being without familiarizing themselves with clients' spiritual beliefs, values, and experiences. A spiritual assessment provides a vehicle for collecting such information. As such, it provides the necessary information to help ensure ethical compliance (Plante, 2009). In a manner analogous to professional ethics, assessment plays a foundational role in respecting clients' basic human rights.

### RESPECTING BASIC HUMAN RIGHTS

Another rationale for administering a spiritual assessment is to respect human rights. Human rights can be defined as those characteristics that are necessary for people to live as human beings (United Nations Association in Canada, 1995). They are commonly understood to be universal (Dershowitz, 2004). In other words, human rights theoretically apply equally to all human beings, regardless of their recognition in law. They transcend national law, cultural norms, and organizational policies. Like ethics codes, they serve to guide and direct human interactions.

The provision of services that take clients' human rights into account is widely seen as an ethical necessity. Indeed, the ethics codes of many professions explicitly endorse practice that respects and affirms basic human rights, such as those enumerated in the United Nations' (1948/1998) Universal Declaration of Human Rights. Included among these are the codes of the IFSW, the American School Counselor Association (2010), and the American Psychological Association (2002). In this sense, professional ethics and human rights are intrinsically linked. Furthermore, professional organizations that do not explicitly include the affirmation of human rights in their ethics code, such as NASW, often endorse the affirmation of basic human rights in other professional documents (Reichert, 2003).

Globally, the most authoritative understanding of human rights is the United Nations' (1948/1998) Universal Declaration of Human Rights. Developed in the aftermath of the Second World War and the persecution of Jewish people, the declaration represents the international community's attempt to prevent future tragedies by articulating the fundamental human rights that provide a lasting foundation for freedom, peace, and justice. The declaration was adopted without dissent by the UN General Assembly in 1948 (Gil, 1998) and is widely viewed as a major accomplishment in human history (Reichert, 2003). Virtually every nation endorses the fundamental rights articulated in the declaration.

The declaration mentions religion in a number of places. For example, it prohibits religious discrimination (art. 2, 16). More importantly, it also lists religious freedom as a basic human right and then maps the terrain of this right in article 18. In slightly paraphrased form, article 18 states that everyone has the right to freedom of religion; this right includes the freedom to change one's religion, and freedom, either alone or in community with others, and in public or private, to manifest one's religion in teaching, practice, worship, and observance. Forum 18, a Norwegian human rights organization, summarizes this multifaceted right as (1) the right to believe, worship, and witness; (2) the right to change one's belief or religion; and (3) the right to join together and express one's beliefs (Nesvag, Diesen, Solheim, de Jimenez, & Osttveit, 2001).

A spiritual assessment helps practitioners respect people's basic rights. Assessment provides a mechanism to identify situations in which clients' rights may be violated. For instance, students in public school settings, patients in hospitals, and older adults in long-term care facilities may have their right to practice their religion infringed on. The information obtained through an assessment can be used to address such human rights violations and to proactively deliver services that honor clients' rights. In sum, a spiritual assessment plays a foundational role in assisting practitioners ensure compliance with the basic human rights articulated in the Universal Declaration and the standards articulated in professional ethics codes that speak to spirituality, not to mention standards that refer to client self-determination.

### HONORING CLIENT SELF-DETERMINATION

A third rationale for addressing spirituality is related to client self-determination. The concept of self-determination is widely affirmed in ethics codes across the helping professions. For instance, the NASW Code of Ethics (2008:1.02) enjoins social workers to respect and promote clients' right to self-determination.

In addition to being a central ethical principle, honoring self-determination plays a critical role in successful practice. Tailoring service provision to incorporate clients' desires leads to better outcomes. The importance of client preference is underscored by the evidence-based practice movement, which emphasizes the importance of incorporating clients' preferences into practice decisions (APA Presidential Task Force on Evidence-Based Practice, 2006). Effective therapy is predicated on the creation of a noncoercive atmosphere in which clients' desires are respected. Accordingly, practitioners are encouraged to foster the basic precept of self-determination as much as possible (Hepworth, Rooney, Rooney, & Strom-Gottfried, 2013).

In keeping with the fact that over 90 percent of the general population believes in God, many people want their spiritual values integrated into service provision (Newport, 2012). Not everyone, including some people for whom spirituality is very important, wants to have spiritual values incorporated into service provision. Many people, however, do want practitioners to consider their spiritual beliefs and practices, as illustrated by the following study.

Using a national sample of likely voters, the American Association of Pastoral Counselors (AAPC) and the Samaritan Institute examined respondents' attitudes about the role of spirituality in the treatment of mental and emotional problems (Boorstin & Schlachter, 2000). Seventy-five percent believed it was important to have their spiritual beliefs and practices incorporated into the counseling process. In addition, almost half (47 percent) said it would be very important to them to integrate their spirituality into the process of working to overcome a serious problem.

What underlies these perceptions? Respondents reported that spirituality is closely linked to health and wellness. Eighty-three percent reported that their spirituality was closely tied to their mental and emotional health. Furthermore, 55 percent reported that spirituality and psychological wellness were *very closely* related. This finding is consistent with Gallup data, which indicate that approximately 60 percent of the general population believe that religion can answer all or most of life's problems (Newport, 2012).

The importance of incorporating spirituality into counseling was even more pronounced among traditionally disenfranchised populations (Boorstin & Schlachter, 2000). African Americans, women, and older adults were all more likely to affirm the importance of having their spirituality incorporated into therapeutic conversations. This finding is consistent with the fact that these three groups are disproportionately more likely to affirm the importance of religion (Newport, 2012). Populations for whom spirituality and religion tend to be more important are more likely to prefer having their spiritual values integrated into the therapeutic conversation. For instance, 97 percent of African Americans reported that spirituality was closely tied to mental and emotional health (Boorstin & Schlachter, 2000).

Consequently, it is unsurprising that African Americans were more likely than European Americans to report that it was very important to integrate their spirituality into service provision.

Research using diverse samples of clients has yielded similar results (Arnold, Avants, Margolin, & Marcotte, 2002; Larimore, Parker, & Crowther, 2002; Rose, Mathai & North, 2003; Westefeld, & Ansley, 2001, 2008; Solhkhah, Galanter, Dermatis, Daly, & Bunt, 2008). In such studies, a majority of clients often report interest in incorporating their spiritual values into service provision. For instance, in one therapeutic community devoted to helping people overcome various forms of chemical dependency, 84 percent of clients reported wanting more emphasis on spirituality in treatment (Dermatis, Guschwan, Galanter & Bunt, 2004). Similarly, among patients dealing with advanced cancer, over 80 percent reported that practitioners should consider patients' spiritual needs and concerns as part of their care (Balboni et al., 2013).

Ignoring spirituality when clients desire to have it addressed violates their autonomy (Nelson-Becker, 2005). As noted above, practitioners have an ethical obligation to respond to clients' desires to integrate their spiritual values into service provision. Unfortunately, research suggests that client autonomy is often compromised in this area. Many clients want to have their spirituality incorporated into service provision, yet their desires are overlooked or ignored (Koenig, 2013).

Administering a spiritual assessment as a routine component of care helps ensure clients' preferences and concerns in the area of spirituality are not disregarded. Such an assessment provides a vehicle for ascertaining clients' desires regarding incorporating clinically relevant spiritual beliefs and practices into service delivery (Leach, Aten, Wade, & Hernandez, 2009). It demonstrates responsiveness to clients' desires and aids in identifying strengths that might be used to ameliorate problems.

### IDENTIFYING SPIRITUAL STRENGTHS

A fourth rationale for conducting a spiritual assessment is to identify clients' spiritual strengths. Ascertaining assets, resources, and strengths is a fundamental component of the larger assessment process (Hepworth et al., 2013). Once identified, these assets can often be operationalized to enhance wellness, foster coping, and ameliorate problems (Koenig, 2013).

The significance of the emerging strengths movement is evidenced by the fact that at least one ethics code has been revised accordingly. The NASW Code of Ethics (2008) posits that strengths exist in all cultures. In turn, the code enjoins practitioners to recognize these strengths in their work with clients (1.05a).

For most people spirituality is an important asset, and for many it is their most important strength (Koenig, 2013). According to data from the General Social Surveys, seven of every ten adults believe that God is personally concerned with human beings (Smith et al., 2013). Essentially half of all adults (49 percent) report finding strength in their spirituality or religion at least once a day. Just over one in ten (12 percent) report that they never or almost never find strength in their spirituality or religion.

. This helps explain why most individuals prefer to have their spiritual beliefs and values integrated into service provision. As noted in the previous section, most people believe that spirituality is closely related to health and wellness (Boorstin & Schlachter, 2000). The data on strengths help to explain this relationship. Spirituality is viewed as a source of strength that engenders salutary outcomes.

Empirical research provides support for these perceptions. A relatively large and growing body of research on spirituality has emerged over the course of the past few decades. Thousands of studies have linked spirituality with a wide variety of mental and physical health outcomes (Koenig, King, & Carson, 2012; Koenig, McCullough, & Larson, 2001).

Table 2.1 summarizes the research on spirituality and wellness. Despite the positive relationships featured in the table, the association between spirituality and health is not universal. In some cases the linkages are unclear. Some individual studies report no relationship, or even an inverse relationship, between spirituality and health.

However, in aggregate, higher levels of spirituality tend to predict better mental and physical health across a diverse array of outcomes. Indeed, the state of the present research is such that it is no longer a question about whether spirituality predicts better health. Rather, the relationship between spirituality and wellness is so well established that research tends to focus on understanding the mechanisms that explain the relationship, with various theoretical explanations being posited and tested (Pearlin, 2002; Smith, 2003b).

TABLE 2.1　Empirical Outcomes Commonly Associated with Spirituality and Religion

| MENTAL HEALTH OUTCOMES | PHYSICAL HEALTH OUTCOMES |
|---|---|
| *Positively associated with* | *Positively associated with* |
| Adjustment and coping (e.g., adaptation to bereavement) | Endocrine functioning (stress hormones) |
| Altruism | Immune system functioning |
| Compassion and gratefulness | Longevity |
| Forgiveness | Self-rated health (highly correlated to objective measures of physical health) |
| Happiness and joy | |
| Hope and optimism | *Inversely associated with* |
| Internal sense of control | Alzheimer's disease and dementia |
| Life satisfaction | Cancer and cancer prognosis |
| Martial stability (increased satisfaction, commitment; decreased infidelity, abuse, and divorce) | Cerebrovascular disease (stroke) |
| | Coronary heart disease |
| | Hypertension |
| Purpose and meaning in life | Mortality |
| Quality of life (typically when facing major life challenges) | |
| Recovery from depression | |
| Self-esteem | |
| Social capital | |
| Social support | |
| | |
| *Inversely associated with* | |
| Alcohol and drug use or abuse | |
| Anxiety | |
| Delinquency and criminal activity | |
| Depression | |
| Loneliness | |
| Positive attitudes toward suicide | |
| Risk-taking, hostility, and anger | |
| Suicide | |

*Source*: Adapted from Koenig, McCullough, & Larson (2001); Koenig, King, & Carson (2012)

One mechanism that may accentuate the personal salience of spirituality is encountering major life challenges (Soenke, Landau, & Greenberg, 2013). Spirituality frequently becomes more significant during times of stress or difficulty, which may help explain why it tends to play a more pronounced role in the lives of traditionally disenfranchised populations (Newport, 2012). For instance, people often turn to spirituality when coping with general medical illnesses, chronic pain, cancer, vision problems, HIV/AIDS, care-giving burdens, psychiatric illnesses, bereavement, or end-of-life issues. Individuals wrestling with such problems tend to report that spirituality enhances their ability to cope and adapt (Pargament, 1997, 2007).

This is important since practitioners typically encounter people when they are facing major life challenges. To help clients deal with these challenges, they have an ethical obligation to identify all assets that may be relevant to this task. In many cases spiritual assets can be marshaled to assist clients overcome challenges.

To identify these spiritual strengths, a specific exploration of potential assets is needed. The emotional weight of challenges can overwhelm clients, causing them to overlook important personal and community assets and resources (Saleebey, 2013). Unless an assessment is conducted, it is difficult to see how clients' assets can be identified in such circumstances. A spiritual assessment helps practitioners and clients uncover spiritual strengths that might otherwise lie dormant. It is only when strengths are identified that they can be operationalized, a process that may be facilitated by understanding clients' overarching spiritual worldviews.

### PROVIDING CULTURALLY RELEVANT SERVICES

A fifth rationale for assessment is to understand clients' spiritual worldviews so that services can be tailored to increase their cultural relevance. The growing cultural diversity of Western societies has underscored the importance of ensuring that service provision is congruent with patients' beliefs, values, and customs, or, more simply, their cultural worldviews (Sue & Sue, 2013). For interventions to be successfully implemented, it has long been recognized that a given intervention must be congruent with the client's value system (Wolf, 1978).

The importance of developing an empathetic understanding of a client's cultural worldview is mentioned in numerous professional ethics codes.

For instance, social workers are instructed to develop their knowledge of clients' cultures and provide services that are culturally sensitive (NASW, 2008:1.05b); school counselors, to respect and affirm students' values, beliefs, and cultural backgrounds (American School Counselor Association [ASCA], 2010:A.1.c, E.2.d); nurses, to provide care that is sensitive to the values, customs, and beliefs of all people (ICN, 2006:5); and psychologists, to be aware of and respect cultural differences based on religion (American Psychological Association [APA], 2002: principle E).

The United States is among the most religiously diverse nations in the world (Eck, 2001). Over the past few decades, many new groups have supplemented the nation's existing religious mosaic. Among these are Asian Muslims, Hispanic Catholics, Indian Hindus, Korean Presbyterians, Latino Pentecostals, European American New Age adherents, Punjabi Sikhs, and Soviet Jews (Melton, 2009; Smith, 2002). These groups supplement existing subcultures in America, such as traditional Catholics, evangelical Christians, Latter-day Saints, and hundreds of American Indian tribes.

These various religious cultures all affirm distinct value systems (Koenig, 1998; Pargament, 2013a; Richards & Bergin, 2014; Van Hook, Hugen, & Aguilar, 2001). Drawn from these and other sources, box 2.1 lists some of the areas in which beliefs and practices are shaped by these value systems.

BOX 2.1    AREAS IN WHICH CLIENTS' SPIRITUAL VALUES MAY INFORM BELIEFS AND PRACTICES

| | |
|---|---|
| Animals | Finances |
| Burial practices | Gender interactions |
| Celebrations | Grieving |
| Childbirth | Healing |
| Child care | Health |
| Clothing | Marital relations |
| Communication styles | Medical care |
| Coping practices | Military participation |
| Death | Recreation |
| Diet | Schooling |
| Emotional expressiveness | Wellness |

As an examination of the list suggests, clients' spiritual values can affect service delivery in many areas of significance to practitioners (Hamilton & Levine, 2006).

The degree to which service provision incorporates these values can have a dramatic effect on outcomes. Interventions that are congruent with clients' value systems typically enhance client buy-in (Sue & Sue, 2013) and are more likely to be adopted and faithfully implemented, including after treatment termination (Hodge, 2011a). They can aid recovery, wellness, and the prevention of relapse.

Conversely, interventions that are incongruent with clients' spiritual values can lead to detrimental outcomes (Gardner, 2011). For instance, many Muslims are uncomfortable with intimate interactions with members of the opposite sex, medicines containing pork or alcohol, and accommodations that do not allow for daily prayers (Husain & Ross-Sheriff, 2011). Failure to adapt service provision to account for these values can lead to negative outcomes. Alternatively, modifying services so that they are sensitive to these values increases the likelihood of obtaining better results with Muslim clients.

A spiritual assessment provides a window into clients' culturally unique value systems (Richards & Bergin, 2005). Learning how clients construct their spiritually animated worldviews assists in developing an empathetic understanding of the beliefs and values that inform clients' actions. The information gathered helps practitioners build rapport, identify strengths, respect autonomy, and design culturally relevant practice strategies. By constructing culturally sensitive interventions, clients' sense of ownership is enhanced, increasing the likelihood that they will implement and follow through with treatment recommendations (Pearce, 2013).

In short, a spiritual assessment helps ensure that service provision engages with, rather than conflicts with, clients' values. Put differently, an assessment helps to ensure that service delivery is culturally competent. This typically results in better outcomes, an issue of concern to accrediting bodies and other professional organizations.

## ADHERING TO PROFESSIONAL STANDARDS

The final rationale for addressing spirituality is to adhere to professional standards for good practice, as articulated by various accrediting bodies and professional organizations (Wolfer, 2012). These entities are typically invested in creating professional standards that promote good practice. In a manner analogous to ethics codes and human rights protocols, these standards serve to guide professional practice with the aim of ensuring that clients receive optimal services.

For instance, the Joint Commission, formerly known as the Joint Commission on Accreditation of Healthcare Organizations (JCAHO), is the largest healthcare accrediting organization in the United States. It accredits most of the nation's hospitals as well as thousands of other healthcare organizations (Hodge, 2006). The mission of the Joint Commission (2010) is to encourage healthcare organizations to provide safe and effective care of the highest quality and value.

Toward this end, the Joint Commission highlights the importance of identifying and addressing clients' spiritual needs. In the Joint Commission's (2010) Roadmap for Hospitals, it recommends administering an assessment to identify spiritual, religious, or cultural beliefs and practices that may influence care. Consistent with the previous section, the roadmap notes that patients' beliefs and practices can affect perceptions of illness and medical care. The information obtained during the assessment is to be used to accommodate patients' unique needs and desires to the extent possible.

In keeping with these recommendations, the Joint Commission's (2012) Hospital Accreditation Standards mandate the administration of spiritual assessments. More specifically, patients receiving treatment for emotional, behavioral, or substance abuse problems should receive an assessment. The same requirement also exists for patients receiving end-of-life care.

The National Cancer Institute (NCI) (2013) at the National Institutes of Health is the federal government's principal vehicle for cancer research and training. The NCI is responsible for disseminating state-of-the-art cancer treatments in clinical practice. As part of this wider mandate, the NCI (2012) recommends the administration of spiritual assessments. The organization notes that over 90 percent of the general population believes in God, many clients want their spiritual needs and desires taken into account during service provision, and spirituality is often a vital strength that helps clients cope with cancer. Citing the importance of spirituality to clients, the NCI states that integrating a systematic assessment of clients' spiritual needs into medical care, including outpatient care, is crucial.

Similarly, the NASW (2005) Standards for Social Work Practice in Health Care Settings affirms the importance of a bio-psycho-social–spiritual perspective. These standards note the fundamental role that assessment plays in service provision and recommend an assessment that examines the spiritual factors and needs of clients and their families. Among the rationales cited in support of these policies is the strengths perspective.

The articulation of such standards is not limited to organizations in the United States (Furness & Gilligan, 2010; Ross, 2008). The World Health Organisation (1990) expert committee on cancer pain relief recommends an assessment of clients' spiritual and religious beliefs and practices. WHO grounds this recommendation in the human right of religious freedom articulated in the Universal Declaration.

In the United Kingdom, the National Institute for Clinical Excellence (2004) endorses the administration of a spiritual assessment with people diagnosed with cancer. Similarly, the Royal College of Psychiatrists (Cook, 2011) counsels that the exploration of clients' spirituality should be a routine component of clinical assessment. These recommendations are variously justified by referring to the fact that many clients want to have their spiritual values incorporated into service provision and that spirituality is an empirical strength that can assist clients deal with problems.

Such justifications illustrate the interconnected nature of the six rationales discussed in this chapter. An exploration of clients' spiritual worldviews provides the information required to help ensure ethical, nondiscriminatory practice that affirms clients' basic human rights. In turn, this knowledge equips practitioners to respect client autonomy, identify spiritual assets, build therapeutic rapport, and design interventions that are congruent with clients' value systems. Developing interventions that resonate with clients' spiritual values enhances clients' sense of ownership, increasing the likelihood that clients will implement and follow through with treatment recommendations. In recognition of these realities, accrediting bodies and professional organizations invested in good practice also highlight the need for procedures to identify and address client spirituality to help ensure optimal service provision.

As such, these six rationales are interlinked and mutually reinforcing. Together they provide a comprehensive foundation for services that address spirituality. If one accepts the merit of this argument in favor of a universally administered spiritual assessment, this implicitly raises the issue of how to conduct such an assessment. In the next chapter, the concept of a brief spiritual assessment is discussed, and models are presented for conducting such assessments.

# 3

# Brief Assessment

HOW DOES ONE GO ABOUT assessing spirituality in practice settings? What options exist for conducting a spiritual assessment, and how does one administer such an assessment? In response to these questions, this chapter introduces a two-stage approach to spiritual assessment.

The chapter begins by providing a conceptual overview of the two-stage model in which a brief spiritual assessment is administered to all clients. Arguments against a universal assessment are presented along with counterarguments. A number of approaches are reviewed, including the newly developed iCARING model. The chapter concludes by offering process suggestions to help ensure a successful assessment.

## CONCEPTUAL OVERVIEW

Spiritual assessment is typically conceptualized as a two-step process: a brief preliminary assessment followed, if clinically warranted, by an extensive comprehensive assessment. Initially a brief assessment—sometimes called a preliminary or screening assessment—is administered to all clients. Its purpose is to determine the clinical relevance of spirituality and to ascertain whether a subsequent comprehensive assessment is appropriate.

This brief assessment is conducted as part of a larger bio-psycho-social evaluation. Time is limited during this evaluation process. Issues commonly explored include the nature of the presenting problem; psychological, social, and physical histories; risk factors and strengths; and treatment goals (Pargament & Krumrei, 2009). Spirituality is just one variable among many that is explored during this assessment.

Nevertheless, this broad initial assessment often plays a pivotal role in shaping the direction of service provision (Leach et al., 2009). Client/ practitioner rapport is established (or hindered). An emotional tone is developed, and the foundation for future interactions is often laid. Consequently, it is especially important to include an exploration of spirituality.

A brief assessment provides a mechanism to ensure that spirituality is addressed during this initial evaluation. As noted in the previous chapter, spirituality often intersects service provision. In such cases a comprehensive assessment is generally warranted. Such an assessment allows practitioners to fully understand clients' spiritual needs and desires, and to tailor service delivery accordingly.

In some instances, however, spirituality plays a limited role in clients' lives. In other cases it is important to clients but unrelated to their presenting challenges. In such instances a brief assessment may be all that is required. Indeed, as soon as it becomes clear that spirituality is unrelated to service provision, practitioners should consider redirecting their attention toward more clinically relevant content (Plante, 2009).

In sum, a brief universal assessment is administered to everyone to assess whether spirituality is pertinent to service provision. Although such an assessment requires a relatively minor expenditure of time, this approach is not without controversy. Some commentators have questioned the notion of administering a universal brief assessment.

## ARGUMENTS AGAINST A UNIVERSAL BRIEF ASSESSMENT

At least two arguments against a universally administered assessment have appeared in the literature (Pearce, 2013). These concerns are related to the time involved and the potential for coercion. Each concern is examined below along with mitigating factors.

### Time Constraints

Since spirituality is not relevant to all clients, some individuals favor dispensing with a brief assessment to conserve time. While acknowledging the importance of spirituality to some clients, these observers suggest waiting until clients bring up the topic. Once the topic has been broached, then relevant spiritual issues can be explored.

The difficulty with this perspective is that many clients are reluctant to initiate a conversation about spirituality, which is a delicate subject for many people (Wolfer, 2012). Some clients may believe that such topics are inappropriate to discuss in practice settings; others may acknowledge the importance of spirituality to service provision but be concerned about practitioners' response.

Hesitancy to raise the topic may be accentuated by the power differential between practitioners and clients. Spirituality plays a substantial role in the lives of many African Americans, American Indians, Latinos, older adults, women, people who are poor, and recent immigrants (Newport, 2012). These are the very populations that typically experience a power imbalance in practice settings. Members of such vulnerable populations may be particularly hesitant to initiate a discussion about their spiritual needs and desires. Older adults, for instance, may not mention spirituality unless directly asked (Nelson-Becker, Nakashima, & Canda, 2007).

A brief assessment creates a safe space where spirituality can be discussed (NCI, 2012). In other words, it helps legitimize the topic in practice settings. It sends an implicit message that the practitioner believes spirituality can be an important issue in service provision and is open to discussing the topic. It validates the importance of spirituality in the eyes of clients.

### Potential Coercion

A second argument leveled against brief assessment relates to coercion. Some individuals worry that raising the topic of spirituality may be experienced as subtly coercive by some clients. Clients who are not spiritual may, for example, feel that practitioners expect them to be spiritual. Given the power differential between practitioners and clients, some secular clients may feel pressured to affirm spirituality. Likewise, others for whom spirituality is important but who do not wish to discuss their spirituality may experience a brief assessment as intrusive and distressing. Such coercion, it is argued, can be avoided by allowing clients to broach the topic when, and if, they feel it is appropriate.

Although such respect for client autonomy is commendable, there is little evidence that clients experience a brief assessment as intrusive (NCI, 2012). Even clients who are not interested in spirituality do not appear to experience assessment as a distressing event (Kristeller, Rhodes, Cripe, & Sheets, 2005). In fact, some research suggests the opposite—that even those who are uninterested in discussing spirituality appreciate being asked about the topic.

For instance, Williams and associates (2011) examined satisfaction with service provision among a sample of patients who initially expressed no interest in discussing their spiritual concerns during hospitalization. These researchers found that patients who subsequently had an opportunity to discuss their spiritual concerns reported higher levels of satisfaction with service provision. Further, this positive association between discussing spirituality and overall satisfaction existed across all four measures of satisfaction used in the study. For example, those who discussed their spiritual concerns were 70 percent more likely to rate the overall care received during hospitalization as excellent compared to those who did not have such a discussion. These results are consistent with related research suggesting the administration of a brief assessment strengthens the therapeutic bond between clients and practitioners (Hamilton & Levine, 2006; Kristeller et al., 2005).

This research suggests that even those who initially show little or no interest in spirituality appreciate being asked about their spiritual needs and desires. There is no doubt that some individuals dislike such questions, just as some people dislike being asked about other areas that are routinely assessed during an initial evaluation. On balance, however, clients appreciate being asked about their spiritual needs and desires, regardless of whether they are personally interested in discussing them with practitioners.

In addition, research has linked the administration of brief assessments with a number of positive outcomes. Included among these are enhanced client satisfaction, coping, and well-being immediately following assessment and three weeks later (Kristeller et al., 2005), as well as increased appointment attendance after three months (Huguelet, Mohr, Betrisey, Borras, & Gillieron, 2011). This underscores the importance of administering a spiritual assessment to all clients, a practice that may also help mitigate disparities in spiritual care that have been identified with African Americans (Williams et al., 2011). Once the decision has been made to administer such an assessment, practitioners are faced with the question of which brief assessment approach to select and administer.

## BRIEF ASSESSMENT MODELS

A number of brief assessment models have appeared in the literature (Canda & Furman, 2010; Hodge, 2004b, 2013a; Pargament & Krumrei, 2009; Plante, 2009; Shafranske, 2005). Although these various approaches employ different questions, they are all animated by the same underlying goal: to develop a preliminary understanding of clients' spiritual worldview and the degree to which their spiritual values may be relevant to subsequent treatment.

Some brief approaches use acronyms to aid memorization of the key domains that are typically addressed during assessment. Among such approaches is the FICA model (Puchalski, 2001). FICA stands for Faith, Importance, Community, and Action (table 3.1). Within these four areas, questions are provided to flesh out each domain.

More specifically, clients are invited to self-identify regarding their faith, manifested in spirituality, religion, or secular forms of meaning (Borneman, Ferrell, & Puchalski, 2010). The self-ascribed importance of spirituality is examined, including its potential influence on service provision. Participation in a spiritual or religious community is explored, along with potential actions that might be taken to address any spiritual needs or concerns that clients may report.

A similar acronym approach is employed by the HOPE model (Anandarahah & Hight, 2001). HOPE stands for sources of Hope, meaning, strength, peace, comfort, love and connection; Organized religion; Personal spiritual practices; and Effects of spirituality on service provision. Various existentially oriented questions are used to understand the role of

TABLE 3.1   FICA Brief Spiritual Assessment

| | ATTRIBUTE | SAMPLE QUESTION |
|---|---|---|
| F | Faith | Do you consider yourself spiritual or religious? |
| I | Importance | What importance does your faith or belief have in your life? |
| C | Community | Are you part of a spiritual or religious community? |
| A | Action | How would you like me to use this information to enhance service provision? |

*Source*: Adapted with permission from Borneman, Ferrell, & Puchalski (2010)

TABLE 3.2   Potential Areas to Explore in a Brief Spiritual Assessment

| AREA EXPLORED | QUESTION TO BE ANSWERED |
| --- | --- |
| Metaphysical worldview | What is the client's metaphysical worldview (e.g., theistic, pantheistic, naturalistic)? |
| Childhood affiliation | What were the client's childhood religious affiliation and key spiritual experiences? |
| Current affiliation | What is the client's current religious affiliation and level of spirituality or devoutness? |
| Related to problem | Are the client's spiritual beliefs and practices related to the presenting problem (e.g., bullied at school because of spiritual beliefs)? |
| Spiritual concerns | Does the client have any spiritual concerns or needs? |
| Use of interventions | Degree of openness to exploring spiritual issues and using spiritual interventions? |
| Strength and support | Are personal spiritual beliefs and practices or the client's religious community viewed as sources of strength and support? |

*Source*: Adapted with permission from Richards & Bergin (2005)

spirituality, religion, and secular sources of meaning in clients' lives and their potential impact on service provision.

Another approach to brief assessment is featured in table 3.2. This model consists of a series of broad questions to which practitioners seek answers in the manner with which they are most comfortable. These areas might be explored with clients verbally in the form of a semistructured interview, for instance, as typically occurs when using the FICA and HOPE models.

Alternatively, these broad questions could be operationalized in written form (Richards & Bergin, 2005). In direct practice or counseling settings, it is common for clients to complete an intake history questionnaire after they have completed the necessary paperwork to begin counseling (e.g., insurance forms, release of medical records, informed consent). The intake history questionnaire typically elicits information about a variety of topics, including basic demographics, history and nature of the presenting problem; counseling history; career trajectory; physical health; social and developmental factors; and family, marital, and sexual history. A set of questions dealing with spirituality can be incorporated into the questionnaire. Some examples of this approach are presented in Plante (2009) and Richards and Bergin (2005), as well as in the next section.

### ICARING BRIEF ASSESSMENT

Table 3.3 depicts another model for conducting a brief assessment. This approach draws from the works listed above, as well as others who have contributed to the literature on brief assessment (Canda & Furman, 2010; Hodge, 2004b, 2013a; Pargament & Krumrei, 2009; Plante, 2009; Shafranske, 2005). Each model is characterized by a certain set of strengths and limitations. No approach is optimal in every situation (Ross & McSherry, 2010). With this caveat in mind, the iCARING approach represents an attempt to synthesize the strengths of existing models.

To assist recall, the acronym iCARING is used, which is pronounced *I caring*. This mnemonic stands for Importance, Community, Assets and Resources, Influence, Needs, and Goals. Each term represents a specific domain that is explored: the Importance of spirituality and religion; participation in religious or spiritual Communities; the degree to which spirituality functions as Assets and Resources; the Influence of spirituality in shaping understanding and response to the issue at hand (e.g., presenting problem);

TABLE 3.3 iCARING Brief Spiritual Assessment

| DOMAIN | QUESTION TO OPERATIONALIZE DOMAIN |
| --- | --- |
| Importance | I was wondering how important spirituality or religion is to you? |
| Community | Do you happen to attend a church or some other type of religious or spiritual community? |
| Assets and resources | Are there particular spiritual beliefs and practices you find especially helpful in dealing with challenges? |
| Influence | I was curious how your spirituality has shaped your understanding of and response to your current situation? |
| Needs | I was also wondering if there are any spiritual needs or concerns I could address? |
| Goals | Looking ahead, I was wondering if you were interested in incorporating your spirituality into our work together? And if so, what would that look like? |

the existence of spiritual Needs or concerns; and the role that spirituality might play in shaping future treatment Goals, or service provision more broadly. Sample questions are provided to help operationalize the model in practice settings.

### Administering a Brief Assessment using the iCARING Model

IMPORTANCE

The first question examines the relevance of spirituality with the following item: "I was wondering how important spirituality or religion is to you?" Given that many people subsume spirituality under religion, it is advisable to use both the terms—spirituality and religion—until clients' inclinations become clear. Once clients' preferences regarding terminology become evident, practitioners should attempt to use this language in their responses and subsequent questions.

Using the terms spirituality and religion to begin the assessment also helps to legitimize the topic (Mutter & Neves, 2010). As noted above, some models begin with very broad, existentially oriented questions, asking clients about hope, meaning, and so forth. Such questions can elicit responses about secular sources of meaning or, alternatively, spiritual or religious sources. Given the dominance of the secular culture, many clients assume that spirituality and religion are unacceptable topics in practice settings (Smith, 2003a). Spiritually committed clients may therefore respond to existentially oriented questions by providing answers that reflect secular sources of meaning, hope, strength, and so on.

Follow-up questions inquiring about spirituality and religion by name can place such respondents in a subtle ethical bind. Spiritually motivated clients have already provided secular responses, in keeping with their perception of acceptable conversational norms in professional practice settings. When queried specifically about spirituality and religion, it becomes apparent that answers of a completely different metaphysical nature may be acceptable (i.e., answers that involve mention of God or the transcendent). Clients cannot, however, retract their previous answers without the risk of appearing duplicitous. Yet if clients provide answers that reference the role of spirituality and religion as sources of hope, meaning, strength, and so on, they may feel that such answers suggest their earlier secular responses were dishonest. Alternatively, if they decline to answer the questions about spirituality, continuing to adapt their language to conform to secular norms, they risk personal incongruence with their value system.

To avoid placing clients in this ethical bind, it is usually wise to use the terms spirituality and religion initially. This is not to say that existentially oriented questions have no place in the assessment process. Indeed, these questions are instrumental in administering an implicit spiritual assessment, a topic discussed in some detail in chapter 10. Rather, the point is that using the terms spirituality and religion helps to legitimize these topics in practice settings, communicating to clients that it is safe to discuss sacred content (Mutter & Neves, 2010).

The first and many subsequent questions in the iCARING model employ tentative phrasing. Such language aids in the creation of an emotionally neutral environment that is both inviting and noncoercive. This creates emotional room for people who are not spiritual to respond as such.

Prompts and follow-up questions can be used to flesh out responses (e.g., "Yes," "I was wondering if you could unpack that some more for me?") (Shafranske, 2005). Practitioners might employ a scaling question to understand the degree of importance ascribed to spirituality (i.e., "On a scale of 0 to 10, in which 0 represents the complete absence of interest and 10 represents the most important thing in your life, I was curious how important is spirituality to you?").

### COMMUNITY

The second domain explored in the iCARING assessment is participation in spiritual or religious communities. This domain can be explored with the following question: "Do you happen to attend a church or some other type of religious or spiritual community?" Initially it is often helpful to use common terms to aid understanding of the concept being assessed (i.e., church). Widely used terms can then be followed with very broad phrases to ensure as much inclusivity as possible (i.e., spiritual community).

As alluded to above, if the first question on the self-ascribed importance of spirituality indicates the client is affiliated with a certain religion (e.g., Hinduism), the second question would employ culturally appropriate terminology (temple). Affiliation with a specific religion, in tandem with regular participation, raises the possibility that clients may see the world through a distinct cultural worldview (Koenig, 2013; Richards & Bergin, 2014; Van Hook et al., 2001). In turn, this worldview can shape interactions with practitioners and expectations about service provision.

### ASSETS AND RESOURCES

The third domain—assets and resources—is explored with the question, "Are there particular spiritual beliefs and practices you find especially help-ful in dealing with challenges?" This item provides insight into the use of spirituality as a means to cope with and ameliorate problems. Instead of focusing on present challenges, the query is phrased broadly on challenges more generally. Since clients can become overwhelmed by the problems they currently face, causing them to overlook important personal and com-munity resources, this phrasing opens up more terrain (Saleebey, 2013). If clients have used spiritual assets to help them deal with problems in the past, practitioners may be able to leverage previously used strategies to address current obstacles.

### INFLUENCE

The fourth domain examines the influence of spirituality in shaping cli-ents' understanding and response to the issue that precipitated the client/ practitioner interaction (e.g., the presenting problem). This domain is explored with the query, "I was curious how your spirituality has shaped your understanding of and response to your current situation?" This question sheds light on the relationship between the presenting problem and spirituality. How clients respond helps practitioners understand the role and salience of spirituality in clients' lives as it relates to the chal-lenges at hand.

### NEEDS

The fifth domain investigates the issue of spiritual needs or concerns, using the question, "I was also wondering if there are any spiritual needs or con-cerns I could address?" Spiritual needs often manifest in practice settings (Koenig, 2013). These needs often pertain to (1) barriers that may inhibit standard service protocols or (2) strengths that help clients cope with the challenges they face.

Addressing such needs in healthcare settings has been associated with a variety of salutary outcomes. Included among these outcomes are lower medical costs (Balboni et al., 2011) and depression (Ganatra, Zafar, Qidwai, & Rozi, 2008; Pearce, Coan, Herndon, Koenig, & Abernethy, 2012), as well as higher levels of spiritual meaning and peace (Pearce et al., 2012), quality of life (Balboni et al., 2007; Balboni et al., 2010; Kang et al., 2012), quality of care (Astrow, Wexler, Texeira, He, & Sulmasy, 2007), and overall satisfaction with service provision (Astrow et al., 2007; Clark, Drain, & Malone, 2003; Williams et al., 2011). Accordingly, it is important to identify any extant spiritual needs or concerns so that they might be addressed in one form or another.

### GOALS

The final domain in the iCARING model examines clients' expectations regarding incorporating spirituality into treatment goals or service provision. The item used to assess this area is, "Looking ahead, I was wondering if you were interested in incorporating your spirituality into our work together? And if so, what would that look like?" This question is similar in nature to the spiritual needs question but asks respondents to adopt an explicitly futuristic orientation. This can provide insights into client interest in the use of spiritual interventions and other spiritual strategies.

These questions may be asked in a loose sequential manner in the form of a semistructured clinical interview (Plante, 2009). Alternatively, the items might be integrated into other domains covered during the intake process. For example, the first two questions, concerning importance and community, might be integrated into other content areas examining clients' roles and identities (e.g., occupation, family status). The third question, on assets and resources, could be woven into content exploring clients' strengths, and the fourth question, on influence, might be incorporated into content exploring the impact of the presenting problem on other psychological, social, and physical systems. The fifth and sixth questions, on, respectively, needs and goals, might be incorporated into content dealing with expectations for service provision (Pargament & Krumrei, 2009).

Another option is to operationalize the iCARING assessment in written form so that it can be included as part of the written intake history questionnaire. The iCaring Assessment Form provides one example of such an approach. After clients complete the form, it may be helpful to review the written answers together with the client to flesh out various answers (Richards & Bergin, 2005).

## ICARING ASSESSMENT FORM

1.  How important is spirituality or religion to you? Please circle the appropriate number.

    0 1 2 3 4 5 6 7 8 9 10

    Not at all important / Moderately important / Most important thing in my life

2.  Would you like to discuss spirituality and religion when it is relevant to service provision?

    Yes ___ No ___

    If you answered no, you may skip the remaining questions.

3.  Do you attend a church or some other type of religious or spiritual community?

    Yes ___ No ___

    If you answered yes, please list the group you are affiliated with_____ and indicate your level of involvement.

    Low ___ Moderate ___ High ___

4.  Are there particular spiritual beliefs and practices you find especially helpful in dealing with challenges?

    Yes ___ No ___

    If you answered yes, could you briefly describe them?

5.  How has your spirituality shaped your understanding and response to your current situation?

6.  Are there any spiritual needs or concerns I could address?

    Yes ___ No ___

    If you answered "yes," could you briefly list them?

7.  Looking ahead, are you interested in incorporating your spirituality into our work together?

    Yes ___ No ___

    If yes, can you briefly describe what that would that look like?

It is important to reiterate that no single brief assessment model is ideal for every setting. The validity of the information provided by a given approach is contingent on the population, the setting, and other factors (Hodge & Limb, 2010c). Practitioners are encouraged to adapt and tailor the iCARING model to develop unique tools that represent appropriate approaches for their practice settings and the populations they commonly encounter. Regardless of the brief assessment model used, however, the ultimate success of the assessment depends on the manner in which the assessment is administered.

### PROCESS SUGGESTIONS

Spirituality is often a very sensitive and private matter. For many clients, it is the most sacred dimension of their being. As a result, their relationship with the transcendent is often guarded and protected with the utmost caution.

Clients are frequently hesitant to trust practitioners—who are often assumed to be secular—with this sacred content (Boorstin & Schlachter, 2000). The situation is analogous to others whose experiences are frequently misunderstood in the dominant culture. A person who is African American or gay, for example, may experience similar concerns around issues of race or sexual orientation, particularly when interacting with a heterosexual, European American practitioner (Griffith & Griffith, 2002).

Accordingly, practitioners' emotional posture is critical to the assessment process. Exhibiting courtesy, etiquette, and respect for the personhood of the "other" is essential. Such characteristics help create an emotional space where clients can risk sharing. It may be helpful to implement some of the strategies discussed in the spiritual competence section in the next chapter, especially if practitioners are unfamiliar with the client's spiritual value system.

To help create an open and accepting environment, some commentators recommend removing spiritual artifacts from offices and other public spaces. Thus, for example, New Age practitioners might ensure their offices are devoid of crystals, books, and other objects that may denote affiliation with the syncretistic movement. It is posited that the removal of such artifacts will help make adherents of other traditions feel more comfortable and accepted.

While this approach may achieve the desired outcome in some instances, it is problematic in at least four ways. First, it reinforces the dominance of the secular worldview, which is often perceived to be hostile to spirituality. Thus some clients may be less, rather than more, inclined to trust practitioners. Second, it may infringe on the religious rights of practitioners. Sikhs, for instance, may be required by their faith to dress in a manner that clearly identifies them as members of Sikhism.

Third, it is arguably deceptive. Although different opinions exist on the topic of self-disclosure, it is possible to contend that some information about practitioners' spiritual orientation should be disclosed to assist clients in making an informed choice. Fourth, it deprives clients of a point of contact that may enhance the therapeutic relationship. In the same way that African American clients may feel more comfortable interacting with black practitioners, clients from a particular religious tradition may appreciate interacting with practitioners from the same, or similar, tradition.

This implicitly raises the issue of self-disclosure. To assess the level of safety that exists, clients may ask practitioners about their personal spiritual beliefs. For instance, a client might inquire, "Are you a charismatic Christian?" (or born-again, LDS, Pentecostal, traditional Catholic, etc.). Although there are no universally affirmed methods for handling such inquires, a number of options are commonly recommended (Canda, Nakashima, & Furman, 2004).

As implied above, self-disclosure is frequently the most advisable choice (Fife & Whiting, 2007). In situations where practitioners hold the same beliefs as clients, self-disclosure can enhance rapport. It also helps reassure clients that the services they receive will be aligned with their spiritual values and treatment goals. In the same way that clients may wish to see someone who shares their belief in the efficacy of cognitive behavioral therapy (CBT), they may want a counselor who shares their belief in the value of their spirituality.

If practitioners do not share their clients' spiritual beliefs, self-disclosure can still be beneficial. This approach offers the advantage of authenticity and transparency, which can enhance the therapeutic alliance (Pargament, 2007). After declaring their personal beliefs, practitioners might relate their desire to work within the parameters of clients' spiritual worldview. This might be followed by an offer to facilitate a referral to other practitioners within the client's tradition if any problems emerge.

In some situations practitioners may wish to avoid disclosing their personal beliefs. Indeed, this is the traditional view in counseling (Richards, Rector, & Tjeltveit, 1999). In such cases practitioners might explore the reasons behind a client's inquiry (e.g., concern about the practitioner's ability to respect the client's beliefs) and convey their interest in providing services that address the latent concern (affirm their belief in the importance of spirituality and their commitment to working within a client's spiritual value system). As was the case above, this can be followed by expressing a commitment to refer clients to practitioners within their tradition if they have concerns at any point during service delivery.

Regardless of the method chosen to respond to inquiries about one's spiritual beliefs, it is clients' interests that should be prioritized (Yarhouse & Johnson, 2013). Self-disclosure is for clients, not practitioners. Clients' needs should drive decisions about self-disclosure during the administration of a brief assessment and throughout the course of subsequent service provision.

As noted above, the overarching aim of a brief assessment is to determine whether a comprehensive assessment is warranted (Shafranske, 2005). In some situations the assessment may suggest that spirituality is not clinically relevant. In other situations the assessment may imply that spirituality is related to service provision, in which case a comprehensive assessment may be necessary. The next chapter is devoted to helping practitioners determine whether to proceed with a comprehensive assessment.

# Guidelines for Moving to a Comprehensive Spiritual Assessment

HOW DOES ONE KNOW WHEN to transition from a brief assessment to a comprehensive or in-depth assessment? Are there situations in which a comprehensive assessment may be inadvisable or contraindicated? This chapter discusses a number of guidelines to help practitioners decide when it is appropriate to conduct a comprehensive assessment.

Specifically, at least four factors bear on the decision to transition from a brief to a comprehensive assessment. These four guidelines are often held in tension with and inform one another. In brief, they are related to clients' interest, practitioners' level of spiritual competence, the salience clients attribute to spirituality, and the degree to which clients' spiritual values intersect service provision.

### CLIENT INTEREST

One of the reasons for administering a brief assessment is to gauge clients' interest in the topic of spiritually as it relates to service provision (Pearce, 2013). As noted in chapter 2, self-determination is a key ethical principle. Effective service provision is predicated on client engagement (Hepworth et al., 2013).

Before proceeding with a comprehensive assessment, it is important to obtain clients' consent. Although research suggests that many, if not most, clients want to integrate their spiritual values into service provision, these same studies also indicate that some clients believe discussing spirituality is inappropriate (Koenig, 2013). Such clients may be willing to answer the relatively few questions involved in a brief assessment even though they are uncomfortable with the notion of a comprehensive assessment.

Consequently, it is typically advisable to discuss the prospect of a comprehensive assessment and secure clients' consent before proceeding (Pargament, 2007). Take, for instance, a situation where the brief assessment suggests that spirituality is an asset that might help ameliorate the presenting challenge. Practitioners might begin the informed consent process by observing that spirituality might be an important resource in dealing with the presenting problem and then follow up by tentatively asking if interest exists in exploring how spirituality might be used to address the challenge. Once verbal agreement has been obtained, practitioners might share some of their beliefs regarding the incorporation of spirituality into practice.

Informed consent should be viewed as a dynamic, ongoing process (Canda & Furman, 2010). In many practice settings, this process begins with an informed consent document. In counseling settings, this document typically includes information about confidentiality, the practitioner's background and theoretical orientation, referral and treatment options, fee structure, and other pertinent information. This helps orient clients to the counseling process while sketching out the parameters of what can be expected in future sessions. Including reference to spirituality and religion in the informed consent document helps to establish a trusting, spiritually safe atmosphere.

The consent document shown in box 4.1 features an example of how one might be constructed in two areas that are especially germane to the integration of spirituality into clinical work: the description of the practitioner and the approach to therapy. Information about spirituality and religion is woven into both areas. This provides potential clients a sense of the practitioner's beliefs about spirituality and religion and what they can expect in counseling sessions. The information implicitly conveys the practitioner's intention to create a safe zone in which clients are free to incorporate their spirituality into the clinical conversation if they so desire.

The example depicts just one approach to informed consent that might be used in a private practice setting. Informed consent documents vary depending on practitioners' personal values, theoretical orientations, and work settings. Additional examples of such documents that incorporate spirituality are available elsewhere (Leach et al., 2009; Miller, 2001; Richards & Bergin, 2005). In all cases, however, the choice of what to include or exclude conveys important information about a practitioner's value system.

BOX 4.1   **EXAMPLE OF A SPIRITUALLY INCLUSIVE INFORMED CONSENT DOCUMENT**

### Description of the Practitioner

I am a licensed clinical social worker, with psychotherapy privileges, in the State of New York (LCSW-R). I received my Master of Social Work (MSW) from Washington University in St. Louis in 2010. I keep my knowledge and skills current by attending continuing education workshops and professional conferences. I also subscribe to a number of academic databases to keep abreast of the latest research on intervention effectiveness. In addition, I have specialized training in dealing with spiritual and religious issues in psychotherapy. I have obtained this training by reading professional journals, participating in training sessions at professional conferences, and consulting with colleagues who have expertise in spiritually informed therapeutic strategies.

### Therapeutic Approach

My counseling orientation is strengths-based: I seek to build on people's assets and resources to assist them deal with the challenges they face. In developing treatment strategies, I frequently draw on cognitive behavioral therapy, one of the most effective evidence-based therapeutic modalities. I may also use therapeutic techniques from other helpful modalities such as solution focused, existential, psychodynamic, client-centered, and family systems therapies.

In the early stages of therapy, I will invite you to share information to help me understand the challenges you currently face, as well as some of your strengths and assets. During this process, I may inquire about a number of aspects of your life, such as family, work, relationships, employment, and health.

As part of this broader assessment, I typically include an assessment of spirituality and religion. In my work with clients, I have found that spirituality and religion are often important—but frequently neglected—dimensions of human experience. Consequently, if spirituality and religion are important to you, I am comfortable including these dimensions in therapy. For example, I may suggest spiritual or religious interventions that are consistent with your value system if they might assist you in dealing with problems. You are always free, of course, to accept or reject such suggestions. You are under no pressure to reveal any information about spirituality or religion with me, and if you choose not to disclose such information, it will not be a part of any therapy or practice suggestions.

From this initial contact, the informed consent process continues on throughout service provision. Practitioners should continuously monitor clients' responses to ensure that they remain fully supportive of continuing the conversation about spirituality. During the assessment process, practitioners should be alert for verbal and nonverbal cues that indicate clients remain comfortable with the dialogue.

Such monitoring plays a critical role in maintaining client engagement and safeguarding clients' rights. This can be particularly important for practitioners operating in government-funded settings. The establishment clause of the First Amendment of the U.S. Constitution—popularly known as separation of church and state—requires government actors, such as school counselors, to remain neutral regarding religion (Wolf, 2004). Concurrently, the free exercise clause guarantees people the right to freely express their spiritual beliefs, in keeping with the internationally recognized human right of religious freedom. In other words, practitioners should neither disparage nor promote any specific forms of spirituality but should create an environment that allows individuals to freely express their spirituality if that is their wish.

As implied in chapter 2, an important reason for administering a spiritual assessment is to protect clients' constitutional and internationally recognized human rights. For clients to freely incorporate their spirituality into service delivery, coercion must be absent. Consequently, it is critical to monitor clients' responses throughout the assessment process to ensure they wish to continue discussing the intersection between spirituality and service delivery.

Clients may change their mind at any point during the assessment for any number of reasons. For example, clients may initially agree to a comprehensive assessment but later reconsider their consent if practitioners exhibit culturally insensitive behaviors. Alternatively, clients may be unwilling to discuss spirituality until they have determined their practitioner is trustworthy. Change can occur in both directions. Thus it is important to remain open to the possibility of a comprehensive assessment even if the initial assessment suggests clients are uninterested in spirituality. This also underscores the importance of spiritual competence in the decision-making process.

## SPIRITUAL COMPETENCE

A second factor to consider is practitioners' level of spiritual competence with clients' religious cultures and associated value systems (Pearce, 2013). Spiritual competence is a form of cultural competence that deals with spirituality and religion—specifically clients' spiritual worldviews. In a manner analogous to cultural competence, it is characterized by three interrelated dimensions. These dimensions, originally developed by Hodge and Bushfield (2006), draw on the seminal work of Sue, Arredondo, and McDavis (1992) (see box 4.2).

The first dimension is to develop an understanding of one's own value informed worldview. Everyone views reality through the prism of a distinct worldview (Kuhn, 1970). These worldviews serve important functions, such as helping adherents understand and interpret life experiences (Soenke et al., 2013). In keeping with the constructivist perspective, however, they also serve to refract reality in ways that adherents are not always fully conscious of; hence the need to develop awareness regarding the values, limitations, and biases of one's own worldview (Gilligan, 1993).

Religions often function as worldviews (Pargament, 2013a). Common examples in the United States include traditional Catholicism, evangelical Christianity, Mormonism, American Indian tribal cultures, Islam, and, in certain manifestations, the New Age or syncretistic movement. These cultural belief systems provide adherents with a unique value system, as will be illustrated in subsequent chapters.

BOX 4.2  THE THREE DIMENSIONS OF SPIRITUAL COMPETENCE

An increasing or growing
1. awareness of one's own value-informed worldview along with its assumptions, limitations, and biases
2. empathic, strengths-based understanding of the client's spiritual worldview
3. ability to design and implement interventions that resonate with the client's spiritual worldview

Secularism serves a similar function. Comprehending the influence of secularism, however, can be difficult. As the dominant worldview in Western societies, secularism serves as the cultural default (Smith, 2003a). As a result, it can be hard to ascertain its effects as it is implicitly assumed to reflect what is normative, appropriate, and "right" (Sue & Sue, 2013). In keeping with this line of thought, some adherents attempt to frame secularism as a neutral, rational, unbiased worldview (Hodge, 2009). This worldview is posited to stand in contrast to religious worldviews, which are framed as value animated.

No worldview, however, is neutral (Lyotard, 1979/1984). An unbiased worldview is a philosophical impossibility (Slife & Williams, 1995). Secularism stems from the Enlightenment, which originated in eighteenth-century continental Europe. Enlightenment thinkers explicitly rejected transcendent worldviews. In their place they affirmed worldviews characterized by naturalistic value systems that privileged the notion of the autonomous individual (Gellner, 1992).

Table 4.1 depicts values that are commonly affirmed in Western secular discourse. Since secularism is culturally dominant, practitioners are likely familiar with most of these values. Indeed, they permeate educational programs in the helping professions. In such forums they are also implicitly associated with healthy functioning (Jafari, 1993). For example, practitioners are frequently socialized to accept the assumption that explicit communication that clearly expresses individual opinion fosters beneficial interactions between adults (e.g., "I statements"). While this may be true among many adults in Western societies, it is not a universally affirmed value in all cultural contexts (Yarhouse & Johnson, 2013).

In addition to developing an awareness of one's own worldview, practitioners should also seek to develop an empathic understanding of their client's spiritual worldview (Hodge & Bushfield, 2006). Table 4.1 also lists values commonly affirmed in Islamic discourse. Not all self-identified Muslims will affirm all, or even most, of these values (Crabtree, Husain & Spalek, 2008). However, in the same way that helping professionals commonly affirm secular values, many Muslims endorse the values featured in the table (Husain & Ross-Sheriff, 2011). Religious worldviews are perhaps best envisioned as malleable templates that suggest, but do not prescribe, the existence of a certain set of culturally distinct values among adherents (Pattison, 2013).

TABLE 4.1    Commonly Affirmed Values in Western Secularism and Islam

| WESTERN SECULARISM | ISLAM |
| --- | --- |
| Material/naturalistic orientation | Spiritual/eternal orientation |
| Individualism | Community |
| Separateness | Connectedness |
| Self-determination | Consensus |
| Independence | Interdependence |
| Self-actualization | Community actualization |
| Personal achievement and success | Group achievement and success |
| Self-reliance | Community reliance |
| Respect for individual rights | Respect for community rights |
| Self-expression | Self-control |
| Clothing used to accentuate individual beauty and sexuality | Clothing used to operationalize modesty and spirituality |
| Sensitivity to individual oppression | Sensitivity to group oppression |
| Identity rooted in sexuality and work | Identity rooted in culture and God |
| Egalitarian gender roles | Complementary gender roles |
| Pro-choice | Pro-life |
| Sexuality expressed based on individual choice | Sexuality expressed in marriage |
| Explicit communication that clearly expresses individual opinion | Implicit communication that safeguards others' opinions |
| Spirituality and morality individually constructed | Spirituality and morality derived from the *shari'a* |
| Food consumed in accordance with individual tastes and preferences | Food consumed in accordance with Islamic values to honor God and community |

*Sources*: Adapted from Hodge (2005c) and Husain & Ross-Sheriff (2011).

What does an empathic understanding look like? Take the value of modesty in attire, which many Muslim females over the age of puberty operationalize through the practice of veiling or hijab. From within the vantage point of Western secularism, it can appear that this value is oppressive to women, restricting their ability to express themselves. Conversely, from within the vantage point of an Islamic worldview, many Muslim women believe that it is Western secular values that lead to the oppression of women. These Muslims point to the commodification of women as sexual objects in Western societies, in tandem with elevated levels of eating disorders, high levels of physical violence against women, and popular music that extols the humiliation of women. Such degradation of women is comparatively rare in Islamic communities, where, it is argued, women are treated with respect and dignity.

As the NASW Standards for Cultural Competence in Social Work Practice (2001) state, it is not necessary to personally affirm the values of culturally different worldviews. It is essential, however, to understand and appreciate clients' value systems as legitimate constructions of reality; to understand their internal logic, and why adherents find them so compelling. It is at this point that practitioners are able to tailor service delivery so that it resonates with clients' value systems.

Given the potential difference in worldviews between many practitioners and clients, it is important to consider one's ability to work with clients in a spiritually competent manner in light of the knowledge obtained from the brief assessment. Interactions that are incongruent with clients' worldviews can damage the therapeutic relationship and have a detrimental effect on service provision (Sue & Sue, 2013). For instance, assuming an egalitarian framework in marriage counseling is often offensive to Muslims, Latter-day Saints, and couples from many other traditions in which complementary relationships are commonly affirmed.

In some instances spiritual insensitivity can harm clients. For instance, asking American Indians about particular spiritual rituals or ceremonies is often culturally inappropriate and can engender negative affect (King & Trimble, 2013). In some tribal cultures, spiritual rituals are understood to be instrumental to health and wellness but can be discussed only with other tribal members. Inquiries about such rituals, even in the context of service provision, are often experienced as stressful and can result in clients terminating services.

Information from the brief assessment can help practitioners determine whether to proceed with a comprehensive assessment. In making such determinations it is helpful to recall the symbiotic, reciprocal relationship between spirituality and religion (Loewenthal, 2013). Brief assessment typically provides some insights into clients' membership in a discrete religious community. This suggests the possibility that clients may affirm a particular value system in keeping with the norms of their religious tradition.

Formalized religious value systems, however, are rarely adopted without qualification. Rather, they are typically individualized to some extent. People's unique desire to connect with the transcendent affects the specific religious values that are incorporated into their personal spiritual worldview.

Other factors that shape the parameters of clients' personal spiritual worldviews include geography, ethnicity, and the degree of assimilation to the dominant secular culture. For example, Muslims from Asia tend to express their spirituality differently than Muslims from the Middle East. The same can be said about southern Baptists who are African American compared with those who are European American. Similarly, the degree of acculturation to the dominant secular culture functions to mold clients' spiritual worldviews. In short, clients' religious values and personal spiritual values interact with each other and in turn are reciprocally influenced by clients' ethnic and cultural values and degree of acculturation (Hodge, 2011a).

It is important to consider all these possible influences in making a decision about working with clients. In situations where insufficient levels of spiritual competence exist, consultation or referral should be considered. Indeed, termination or referral is widely viewed as an ethical requirement when practitioners cannot provide effective services (APA, 2002; ASCA, 2010; NASW, 2008).

In some contexts, strategies might be implemented to help counter marginal levels of spiritual competence. For example, practitioners with high levels of spiritual competence may not be available in a given geographic area, or such practitioners may not have expertise in the client's presenting problem. In such situations, it may be advisable for practitioners with marginal levels of spiritual competence to implement the strategies listed in box 4.3 when working with clients. These strategies can often bridge the competence gap, enabling practitioners to provide more effective services.

BOX 4.3   **STRATEGIES FOR ADDRESSING MARGINAL LEVELS OF SPIRITUAL COMPETENCE**

Acknowledge that spiritual beliefs and practices are frequently very personal.

Explain why it is helpful to gather spiritual and religious information.

Indicate how the information may be used in service provision.

Explicitly acknowledge one's lack of knowledge about the tradition.

Proactively ask forgiveness for questions or responses that might inadvertently be offensive.

Clarify that clients are free to refuse to answer any or all questions.

Create space for clients to express discomfort or unease and to raise questions at any time.

As indicated in the list, practitioners might acknowledge that spiritual beliefs and practices are very personal, explain why it is helpful to gather spiritual and religious information, and indicate how the information will be used in service provision. It can also be helpful to proactively ask forgiveness for questions or responses that might inadvertently be offensive, and clarify that clients are free to refuse to answer any or all questions. Creating space for clients to express discomfort or unease and to raise questions can also be beneficial (Hodge & Limb, 2010a).

In sum, explicitly acknowledging one's lack of knowledge and adopting the posture of a humble student can effectively mitigate lower levels of spiritual competence. Given the increasingly diverse religious mosaic that characterizes American society, it is difficult, if not impossible, to be spiritually competent with every group. Cultivating an attitude of cultural humility can often assist practitioners in bridging cultural differences (Ortega & Faller, 2011).

With some clients, it may also be beneficial to implement these strategies during the administration of the brief assessment. For instance, if clients' apparel suggests they are from a tradition that practitioners have minimal familiarity with, then practitioners might proactively address the situation to set the stage for the administration of the brief assessment.

Afterward practitioners might reassess the situation in light of the information obtained from the broader bio-psycho-social evaluation.

As this suggests, spiritual competence is not a static entity. Rather, it is a dynamic set of attitudes, knowledge, and skills regarding various worldviews, which can be developed over time (Sue & Sue, 2013). A number of resources exist to assist practitioners in developing their level of spiritual competence with clients from different religious cultures (see chapter 12). By reading these and other resources, especially those written by cultural insiders and sympathetic outsiders, practitioners can develop spiritual competence regarding the various groups commonly encountered in their catchment areas.

Understood in this manner, spiritual competence is a continuous construct. Practitioners have different levels of competence with clients from different cultures. A practitioner may be highly competent with Muslims but less so with members of the Assemblies of God. Questions that may be appropriate with one tradition may be culturally inappropriate with another. For example, asking clients if they can describe their image of God may be suitable for mainline Christians but not for Orthodox Jews, who are proscribed from constructing such images (Griffith & Griffith, 2002).

To proceed with a comprehensive assessment, it is necessary to ensure that a sufficient level of competence exists to provide ethical and professional services that help clients achieve their goals. If this is not the case, referral should be considered. Another closely related factor that should be assessed is clients' degree of spiritual motivation.

### SPIRITUAL SALIENCE

The importance clients ascribe to their spirituality is another factor that practitioners should consider (Shafranske, 2005). Some clients affirm the mainstream tenants of their religious tradition but exhibit little enthusiasm about their faith. Many people engage in spiritual activities for cultural or social reasons. If clients are not particularly spiritually committed, then a spiritual assessment may not represent an appropriate use of practitioners' time.

The converse is true if clients are spiritually motivated (Johnson, Elbert-Avila, & Tulsky, 2005). For example, if clients are highly committed, the potential for worldview conflicts is accentuated. In situations where a difference in worldviews exists between practitioners and clients, the importance of spiritual competence increases in direct proportion to the level of importance clients place on their spirituality. Spiritually committed Muslims, for example, may be more uncomfortable receiving services—particularly those that address intimate issues in which modesty is a factor—from practitioners of the opposite gender than are less committed adherents of Islam (Smith, 1999).

Certain spiritual needs are also likely to manifest more acutely among people for whom spirituality is very important. Table 4.2 depicts the results of a qualitative metasynthesis of eleven studies that sought to identify and describe spiritual needs among clients. In keeping with the qualitative methodology, the study focused on patients' perceptions of their spiritual needs. The table features the diverse array of interconnected spiritual needs that commonly manifest among patients who are hospitalized or are facing hospitalization.

It should be noted that the perceived importance of many of the needs listed is likely driven by the existential issues associated with hospitalization. Examples might include experiencing a need to get over asking "Why me?" or a need to reduce the frustration associated with reduced capabilities. The felt importance of such needs is not necessarily contingent on one's spiritual motivation.

Many other needs, however, are directly tied to patients' level of spirituality (Soenke et al., 2013). For instance, compared to their more secular counterparts, spiritually motivated African Americans may be more likely to experience a need to read the Bible or listen to devotional music. In keeping with their interconnected nature, tailoring treatment to address such needs helps clients cope with the challenges they encounter, including the existential challenges caused by reduced physical capabilities (Hamilton, Sandelowski, Moore, Agarwal & Koenig, 2013).

Similarly, spiritually committed clients may be disproportionately likely to draw on their spiritual beliefs and practices to help them deal with challenges (Pargament, 1997). For such clients, it is often possible to leverage these strengths to address difficulties. Practitioners can operationalize this spiritual motivation to collaboratively ameliorate problems by, for example, developing spiritual interventions that harness this motivation (Propst, 1996). Spiritually modified CBT, which is an empirically supported treatment, is one example of such an intervention that may be more effective with spiritually motivated clients (Tan, 2013).

TABLE 4.2 Common Spiritual Needs Among Patients Hospitalized or Facing Hospitalization

| UNDERLYING SPIRITUAL NEED | SPECIFIC MANIFESTATIONS OF NEED |
|---|---|
| Meaning, purpose, hope | Finding explanation for why the illness/death occurred<br>Getting over asking "Why me?"<br>Reducing the frustration associated with reduced capabilities<br>Recognizing that others are worse off<br>Sensing the reason for one's present existence<br>Becoming aware of the positive things in one's situation<br>Counting one's blessings<br>Focusing on the good in life<br>Conducting a life review<br>Trying to make the world a better place |
| Relationship with God | Questioning, blaming, pleading with, and/or wrestling with God<br>Getting right with God<br>Knowing, accepting, and/or trusting God's will in the current context<br>Understanding God's plan<br>Believing God for healing<br>Being reassured of God's presence and care<br>Knowing that God is in control and watching over me |
| Spiritual practices | Prayer<br>Scripture reading<br>Meditation<br>Meditation on scripture<br>Reflection<br>Attending religious services<br>Listening to inspirational tapes/messages<br>Hearing devotional music<br>Reading spiritually themed books<br>Receiving the sacraments |
| Religious obligations | Kosher or Halal food (Jews and Muslims)<br>Avoidance of blood transfusions (Jehovah's Witnesses)<br>Respect for modesty and complementary gender roles<br>Respect death and burial practices |
| Interpersonal connection | Visiting with family members<br>Conversing with people who share one's spiritual values<br>Receiving prayer from others<br>Seeking forgiveness from people one wronged in the past<br>Processing events with others who had similar experiences<br>Receiving tangible expressions of support and encouragement<br>Being appreciated and loved by other people<br>Enjoying someone's simple, physical presence |

TABLE 4.2  (*continued*)

| | |
|---|---|
| Professional staff interactions | Using friendly facial expressions, words, and body language |
| | Conducting interactions that communicate dignity and respect |
| | Exhibiting empathy and caring |
| | Giving complete and accurate medical information |
| | Offering opportunity to discuss treatment options and ramifications |
| | Showing trust, integrity, and a willingness to go to bat for clients |
| | Praying with clients |
| | Seeking to mobilize resources to address clients' spiritual needs |

*Source*: Adapted from Hodge & Horvath (2011)

Spiritual salience also affects client autonomy. The more vital spirituality is to clients, the more important it may be for them to have their spirituality integrated into service provision. This is another factor that should be assessed when deciding whether a comprehensive assessment is warranted.

During the brief assessment it is helpful to look for concrete indicators of spiritual salience. In addition to relying on clients' self-report, practitioners can also look for other indicators, such as the degree to which clients practice the norms of their religious tradition. For instance, relative to others within their respective traditions, Protestants who attend a midweek Bible study, Catholics who attend mass weekly, Muslims who practice most or all of the five pillars, and Hindus who consistently perform morning puja may be more spiritually committed.

As will be discussed in more detail in chapter 11, short quantitative instruments can also be used to assess spiritual engagement. For example, the six-item Intrinsic Spirituality Scale (ISS) measures spiritual motivation (Hodge, 2003b). The ISS is designed to be valid with members of numerous theistic and nontheistic traditions, regardless of whether they express their spirituality within religion. Similarly, the ten-item Religious Commitment Inventory measures commitment across a number of religious traditions (Worthington et al., 2003).

Regardless of the indicators used, if the initial assessment suggests that spirituality functions as an organizing principle in clients' lives, then a more extensive assessment is likely appropriate. A couple of caveats should be mentioned. For some devout clients, spirituality may be unrelated to their problems and, in some cases, even solutions. It is also important to note that spiritual issues may be relevant among some clients who are uninvolved or disengaged. Such clients may be experiencing spiritual struggles that are related to their psychological problems, which implicitly raises the next guideline (Exline et al., 2011).

### INTERSECTION OF SPIRITUALITY AND SERVICE PROVISION

The final factor that should be considered in deciding whether to proceed with a comprehensive assessment is the degree to which client spirituality intersects service provision (Hathaway & Ripley, 2009). Practitioners typically encounter clients when they are dealing with some type of challenge. Spirituality can be related to problems in at least four possible manners. Specifically, spirituality can be (1) related to the solution but not to the problem; (2) unrelated to the solution but related to the problem; (3) related to both the problem and the solution; or (4) unrelated to both the solution and the problem. In the latter case there is little need to administer a comprehensive assessment. In the first three instances, however, a comprehensive assessment should be considered.

Spirituality is often related to solutions. For example, in hospitals and other healthcare settings, addressing patients' spiritual needs can help patients cope with the challenges associated with illness, isolation, and loss. Depending on the nature and complexity of the need, a comprehensive spiritual assessment may or may not be warranted.

Similarly, in counseling settings, spiritual assets can often be operationalized to ameliorate problems. For example, spirituality may be an asset that was insufficiently marshaled to bring about solutions, either by getting rid of problem behavior or eliciting new alternative behaviors. Practitioners' theoretical orientation is also relevant. For example, practitioners who adhere to solution-focused, strengths-based, or brief therapeutic modalities will typically benefit from exploring how the spiritual assets of devout clients can be operationalized to ameliorate problems. Similarly, within the context of CBT, a comprehensive assessment can help practitioners identify important spiritual beliefs and practices that can be incorporated into CBT protocols to enhance their effectiveness (Hook et al., 2010).

Spirituality can also be related exclusively to problems. Students in public schools may be picked on and bullied because of their spiritual beliefs and practices (Hodge, 2005b). Healthcare organizations may restrict patients' ability to express their spirituality or impose treatment plans that conflict with patients' value systems. Clients' anger at God may contribute to their depression, resulting in withdrawal from religious activities, further isolation, and increased despair (Exline et al., 2011).

In many situations the nexus between spirituality, problem, and solution is complex. As the *Diagnostic and Statistical Manual of Mental Disorders, 5th Edition* (American Psychiatric Association, 2013) acknowledges, the symptoms of psychopathology are often culturally contingent. Beliefs, experiences, and practices that are normative in religious cultures can, when seen from the vantage point of the dominant secular culture, be understood as indicators of pathology.

For example, the emphasis on selflessness, detachment, and dharma in Hinduism may result in some Hindu clients appearing to have an "underdeveloped ego" from a psychodynamic perspective (Roland, 1997). In many American Indian cultures, hearing the Creator's voice is a normative experience, as opposed to an indicator of mental illness. In such cases a comprehensive assessment may be necessary to determine if clients' beliefs and practices represent a manifestation of mental illness or are conventional expressions of faith.

During the brief assessment, practitioners should be alert to various indicators that might suggest a connection between spirituality and service provision. When it appears that spirituality intersects clients' problems, a comprehensive spiritual assessment may be appropriate.

The four questions in box 4.4 summarize the guidelines discussed in this chapter. Ideally the brief assessment provides sufficient information to allow practitioners to answer these questions. While administering the assessment, in tandem with assessing their own degree of spiritual competence, practitioners should seek to determine clients' interest in additional assessment, the importance they ascribe to spirituality, and the potential intersection of their spirituality with service provision.

As the framing of the questions implies, it may be helpful to think of each guideline as existing along a continuum, in a manner analogous to spiritual competence. Thus it is typically not a question of whether a given guideline has been satisfied. Rather the question is where a particular client falls along the continuum in terms of, for example, degree of interest in transitioning to a comprehensive assessment.

BOX 4.4    **QUESTIONS TO HELP DETERMINE WHETHER TO PROCEED WITH A COMPREHENSIVE ASSESSMENT**

> How interested is the client in transitioning to a comprehensive assessment?
> To what extent can I work with the client in a spiritually competent manner?
> How important is spirituality to the client?
> To what degree is spirituality related to service provision?

Accordingly, each guideline should be considered in light of the others. For instance, if clients are very interested in integrating their spirituality into service provision and the level of spiritual salience is high, then a comprehensive assessment may be warranted, even though practitioners have a moderate level of spiritual competence with the religious culture and the intersection between spirituality and service provision is initially somewhat vague.

The overarching goal of the brief assessment is to make a preliminary determination about the potential clinical relevance of spirituality. If the information obtained during this assessment suggests that spirituality is relevant to service provision, then it is appropriate to proceed with a comprehensive assessment. The next few chapters present various options for conducting such assessments.

# 5

# Comprehensive Assessment and Spiritual Histories

THE CENTRAL AIM OF A comprehensive spiritual assessment is to obtain a more detailed understanding of clients' spiritual beliefs, practices, and experiences and how these variables can be incorporated into service provision to help clients achieve their goals. To accomplish this overarching aim, practitioners seek a variety of information. For example, depending on the results of the brief assessment and a multiplicity of contextual factors, practitioners may seek to determine how normative clients' spiritual lives are in comparison to their religious reference group; the degree to which social, psychological, or physical problems impair clients' spiritual functioning; and how clients' spiritual beliefs and practices may serve as assets to ameliorate challenges or constitute barriers to service provision (Hathaway & Ripley, 2009).

As this suggests, both practitioners and clients have a variety of needs and interests. Factors that can vary from case to case include the nature of the presenting challenge, the amount of time available for assessment, the physical environment, communication styles, and clients' cultural background. This implies that no single comprehensive assessment approach is ideal in all situations (Ross & McSherry, 2010). The unique factors surrounding each client call for different approaches.

The following chapters present six conceptually distinct comprehensive assessment approaches, methods, or tools. The first tool, described in this chapter, consists of a completely verbal approach: spiritual histories. Four diagrammatic approaches are explored in chapters 6–9: spiritual lifemaps, spiritual genograms, spiritual eco-maps, and spiritual ecograms.

Chapter 10 discusses an alternative method—referred to as an implicit assessment—for use when the previous approaches may be ineffective. The chapter concludes by presenting a model to integrate an implicit assessment with the other tools. The end result is a comprehensive framework for thinking about assessment that moves from brief through to comprehensive assessments.

Ideally practitioners should select a comprehensive assessment approach that provides the best fit for each clinical setting (McSherry, 2010). Developing familiarity with a variety of methods enables practitioners to develop an assessment toolbox. Practitioners can then draw from this toolbox to provide more client-centered, clinically effective services. In the next section a particularly important approach is discussed.

## SPIRITUAL HISTORIES

Spiritual histories are perhaps the most widely used method of conducting a comprehensive assessment. In addition, practitioners often draw from this approach to help operationalize the other assessment tools discussed in subsequent chapters. For these and other reasons, spiritual histories represent an important and foundational approach to spiritual assessment.

The notion of a spiritual story is widely affirmed across religious traditions (Pargament et al., 2013). As people move through life, they create narratives about their existence. These broader narratives usually include reference to the transcendent. Over time, people develop an account of their relationship with God. Furthermore, in many cases it is this sacred story that serves to inform and direct the broader narrative of people's existence.

To explore clients' spiritual stories, spiritual histories typically employ a semistructured clinical interview. The process is very similar to operationalizing the iCARING brief assessment. In a manner analogous to conducting a family history, practitioners elicit clients' spiritual narratives in a face-to-face setting. A series of open-ended questions are commonly employed to flesh out clients' spiritual stories in the context of an empathic dialogue.

A number of approaches have appeared in the literature to assist practitioners unpack clients' spiritual stories (Canda & Furman, 2010; Fitchett, 2012). These approaches are frequently organized in a loose chronological format, in keeping with the idea that information is stored and organized narratively in the mind. This allows the spiritual assessment to proceed in an autobiographical format that clients typically experience as comfortable and natural.

### Chronological Spiritual History

One example of this approach (box 5.1) uses three main question sets to guide the conversation in a chronological manner: past, present, and future. These items provide practitioners with options to help clients tell their spiritual stories, typically moving from childhood through to the present and, if clinically warranted, on into the future.

As is generally the case with all qualitative approaches, the questions are not meant to be asked in a rote, sequential, word-for-word manner. Rather, the intent is to adapt the questions to fit the client's cultural worldview and seamlessly integrate them into the flow of the clinical dialogue (Starnino, Gomi, & Canda, 2012). Similarly, the expectation is that practitioners will select certain questions and ignore others to facilitate a dialogue that feels natural to clients while also eliciting clinically relevant information. It is the ability to tailor questions, as well as the larger assessment itself, that enables qualitative approaches to yield more clinically useful information.

The first set—past spirituality—is designed to explore the role spirituality plays in clients' past, with an emphasis on their family of origin. Understanding how spirituality was experienced and expressed in the past provides the context for understanding how the sacred functions in clients' current situation.

Although this question set may have limited utility with some clients, the questions from this set often play a critical role in understanding clients' present spiritual strengths. For example, well-established spiritual assets and resources can be discarded in the face of present difficulties. Once identified, these strengths can often be tapped to address problems. Similarly, challenges related to spiritual distress can often be traced to past spiritual functioning, as is illustrated in this chapter's case example.

The second question set—present spirituality—deals with clients' present experience of God or the sacred. It includes four subsets to explore various facets of clients' spiritual reality. Substantial overlap exists among

BOX 5.1   CHRONOLOGICAL SPIRITUAL HISTORY

## Past Spirituality

Describe the spiritual/religious tradition you grew up in. How did your family
  express its spirituality?

When did you first personally discover or learn about God?

How did you conceptualize spirituality when you were younger?

How did you express your spirituality?

What sort of spiritual experiences stood out for you when you were growing up?

What spiritual milestones have you experienced during your journey?

## Present Spirituality

### Conceptualizations of God or the Sacred

What do you hold sacred in your life?

How has your understanding or experience of God changed since you were a child?

How have your spiritual beliefs and practices changed since you were a child?

Why are you involved in spirituality?

What do you feel God wants from you?

What do you imagine God feels when he sees you going through this difficult time?

Have there been times where you felt God was absent in your life?

Do you ever experience a different side of the sacred than you are experiencing
  now? What is that like?

Do you ever have mixed thoughts and feelings about God? What are they like?

### Expression and Experience of Spirituality

How would you describe your current spiritual orientation?

How do you experience God in your life?

What has helped nurture your relationship with God?

What has damaged or hindered you spiritually?

When/where do you feel most connected to the sacred?

When/where do you feel the sacred is not present?

What spiritual beliefs do you find especially meaningful?

What spiritual rituals or practices are particularly important to you?

What aspects of your spirituality are particularly uplifting?

When/where do you feel closest to God?

How have your present challenges affected your relationship with God?

BOX 5.1 (CONTINUED)

*Spiritual Efficacy*

Are there ways in which your spirituality has changed your life for the better? Worse?

To what degree has your relationship with God been a source of strength? Pleasure? Meaning? Joy? Intimacy? Connectedness to others? Hope for the future? Confidence in yourself? Compassion for others?

To what degree has your spirituality been a source of pain? Frustration? Guilt? Anger?

Are there ways in which your spirituality has helped you cope with problems?

Are there ways in which your faith has been a source of challenges?

*Religious Environment*

Who supports you spiritually? How so?

Who does not support you spiritually? How so?

Are there ways in which your religious community has been a source of assistance and encouragement?

Are there ways in which your religious community has been a source of problems?

**Future Spirituality**

How do you see yourself changing spiritually in the future?

In what ways do you want to grow spiritually?

How does your spirituality relate to your goals in life?

How does your relationship with God affect your future life plans?

*Source*: Adapted with permission from Pargament & Krumrei (2009)

the questions in the various subsets, in keeping with the fluid nature of spirituality. Nevertheless, grouping the questions together in this manner can help in the administration of an assessment by highlighting different areas of emphasis.

The subset involving conceptualizations of God or the sacred explores current understandings of spirituality and how those understandings have changed or matured since childhood. Questions in this subset can be used to provide a smooth transition to the exploration of current conceptualizations of spirituality. In some cases it is possible to begin the assessment with questions drawn from this subset.

The subset on expressions and experiences of spirituality examines relatively experiential aspects of spirituality. The questions in this subset tend to have a strong emotional tone to them. As such they can provide insight into the powerful affective dimension of clients' relationship with God or the sacred.

The subset on spiritual efficacy examines the functionality of spirituality. These questions reflect the assumption that spirituality is typically a source of strength. But they acknowledge the reality that spirituality can be the source of problems as well. For instance, clients' spirituality can be experienced as a source of stress if their right to express their faith is suppressed or violated.

The subset on religious environment explores the role of social influences in the form of people and religious communities. These communities are also generally perceived to be an asset and a resource. However, in some cases they can be a source of difficulties, as can occur when a conflict exists between congregants.

The final question set in the chronological assessment—future spirituality—examines the role that spirituality plays in future plans. Aspirations for the future are also part of clients' spiritual stories. In the same way that past beliefs can shape present functioning, beliefs about the future can also shape present beliefs and practices (Slife & Williams, 1995).

Thus an exploration of future plans, goals, dreams, and expectations can provide important clinical insights. Existential practitioners, for instance, may find future-oriented questions to be a particularly good fit with their therapeutic perspective. In addition to being helpful in the assessment and goal-formulating process, these questions can be employed in the termination phase as a way of synthesizing progress and transitioning to a discussion of posttreatment dynamics.

Administered appropriately, this chronological model does an effective job of creating an open environment for clients to relate their stories. The chronological, narrative format imposes minimal structure on clients' stories. This process allows for the open-ended co-exploration of clients' spiritual narratives.

Although chronological spiritual histories are often administered in a single session, the questions may also be integrated into the clinical dialogue in a less structured format. In other words, questions may be incorporated into the conversation over the course of treatment when they seem relevant in light of the content being discussed. For example, when exploring potential strategies to ameliorate problems, a solution-focused therapist might use more present- and future-oriented questions to help identify spiritual resources that might be used to address problems. In addition to the practitioner's theoretical orientation, other factors that can shape the administration of the spiritual history include the client's belief system, the clinical setting, and the practitioner's personal preferences and style.

As alluded to above, other methods for conducting a spiritual history have also appeared in the literature. The following approach provides an alternative perspective that may be useful for exploring spirituality in a single session or in a less sequential manner, as clinically relevant issues emerge over the course of treatment.

### Anthropological Spiritual History

An anthropologically based spiritual history is another option for conducting a comprehensive assessment (Hodge, 2001a). This approach retains the basic narrative concept that animates the chronological method. However, it provides some additional structure to assist practitioners in conducting assessments (Hodge & Limb, 2013).

As some commentators have observed, it is anthropology that drives the methodology of spiritual assessment (Bullis, 1996). One's view of human beings determines the domains that are explored during assessment. This understanding often operates at an unconscious level, implicitly shaping the assessment process. An anthropological assessment seeks to make these implicit assumptions about the nature of humanity explicit, highlighting key domains that may be helpful in administering an assessment.

Two question sets (box 5.2) can be used to operationalize an anthropological spiritual history (Hodge, 2001a). The first is referred to as an *initial narrative framework*. The purpose of this set is to provide practitioners with possible questions to help clients tell their stories (Hodge & Limb, 2009).

This framework essentially represents a condensed version of the chronological history described earlier. The same basic approach is used in both. Questions are administered in a generally chronological manner to engender an open-ended co-exploration of clients' spiritual stories.

BOX 5.2   ANTHROPOLOGICAL SPIRITUAL HISTORY

### Initial Narrative Framework

1. Describe the spiritual or religious tradition in which you were raised. How does your family express its spiritual beliefs? How important was spirituality to your family? Extended family?

2. What sort of personal experiences (practices) stand out during your years at home? What made these experiences noteworthy? How have they shaped your life?

3. How have you changed or matured from those experiences? How would you describe your current spiritual orientation? Is spirituality a strength? If so, how?

### Interpretive Anthropological Framework

1. *Cognition*: What are your current spiritual beliefs? What are they based on? What beliefs do you find particularly meaningful? What does your faith say about personal trials? How does this belief help you overcome obstacles? How do your beliefs affect your daily choices? What are your spiritual plans for the future?

2. *Volition*: Are there certain spiritual rituals or practices that help you deal with challenges or problems? How often do you participate in church, youth group, etc.? How are they supportive? Are there spiritually encouraging individuals that you connect with on a regular basis?

3. *Affect*: What aspects of your spiritual life give you pleasure? What role does your spirituality play in handling life's sorrows? Enhancing life's joys? Coping with life's pain? How does your faith give you hope for the future? What do you hope to accomplish in the future?

4. *Communion*: Describe your relationship with God (or the transcendent). What has been your experience of God? How does God communicate with you? How have these experiences encouraged you? Have there been times of deep spiritual intimacy? How does your relationship with God help you face challenges? Get you into trouble? How would God describe you?

5. *Conscience*: How do you determine right and wrong? What are your key values? How does your spirituality help you deal with guilt (sin)? How does forgiveness factor into your life?

6. *Intuition*: To what extent do you experience intuitive hunches (flashes of creative insight, premonitions, nonlocal communication, spiritual insights)? Have these insights been a strength in your life? If so, how?

The distinguishing feature of the anthropological history is the second question set, which is referred to as an *interpretive anthropological framework*. Its purpose is to elicit clinically salient information as clients relate their stories. It is in this framework that anthropological assumptions about the nature of humanity are made explicit. The associated questions potentially allow practitioners to tap a fuller array of information than might occur with a chronological assessment.

These questions can be particularly useful in identifying relevant spiritual information that may emerge in a nonsequential, nonlinear manner during the clinical conversation. The various domains that constitute the framework implicitly highlight areas that may be clinically relevant. Practitioners can explore these areas when these domains may be related to service provision.

The anthropological framework is derived from the work of Nee (1968), a Chinese spirituality writer who conceptualizes the human spirit as an integrative unity composed of communion, conscience, and intuition. All three dimensions interact with and influence one another. Concurrently, they are also interwoven with the three dimensions of personality with which practitioners are familiar: cognition, volition, and affect. As with cognition, volition, and affect, each dimension of the spirit can be defined individually (Hodge & Limb, 2013).

*Communion* refers to spiritually animated relationships. More specifically, it denotes the ability to bond and relate with God and other manifestations of the sacred. This includes relationships with God (as occurs for example in theism), the Creator and Creation (e.g., certain American Indian traditions), a transcendent aspect of the self (e.g., certain streams in the New Age movement), and other manifestations of the sacred.

*Conscience* is conceptualized as the ability to sense right and wrong. Beyond a person's cognitively held values, conscience conveys moral knowledge about the appropriateness of a given set of choices. It can be understood as a subjective ethical guidance system. It informs people about what is virtuous and just, moral and acceptable.

*Intuition* refers to the ability to know—to come up with insights that bypass normal cognitive channels. This dimension includes aspects of what some refer to as nonlocal communication (Mack & Powell, 2005). Examples of the intuitive function of the spirit include flashes of creative insight, sudden impressions to pray for someone, and hunches about a specific course of action. In these and other situations, knowledge is not derived from the application of human rationality but emerges almost spontaneously in one's spirit.

The anthropologically based questions are designed to elicit information about each of the six dimensions, providing a holistic assessment. As clients relate their stories (prompted as necessary by questions drawn from the initial narrative framework), they often touch on dimensions listed in the anthropological framework. Practitioners can interface questions drawn from the anthropological framework into the dialogue to more fully explore clients' reality in the natural flow of the conversation, if a given area is clinically relevant. In short, the narrative questions help clients tell their stories while the anthropological questions assist therapists in eliciting important information as the stories unfold.

Regardless of the approach used to conduct a spiritual history, it is important to reiterate that no single correct format exists for asking questions in practice settings (Pargament, 2007). Assessment is a complex, multilevel process. The spiritual, biological, psychological, and social dimensions of existence are often intertwined. Spirituality and religion, separately or in some combination with these other dimensions, can be related to service provision in complex and critical ways.

In addition, spirituality can emerge as a relevant issue at essentially any time during the course of service provision. Accordingly, practitioners should be ready to explore spirituality when verbal or emotional cues suggest it may be relevant, a topic covered in more depth in chapter 10. Questions drawn from the spiritual history can be adapted and integrated into the clinical conversation as needed.

The case example of Martina, a gregarious, forty-two-year-old Latina mother of three children, depicts the importance of being ready to incorporate assessment questions into the clinical dialogue at any time. Even when the brief assessment suggests that spirituality is unrelated to the presenting problem, it can be an important factor in both problems and solutions.

CASE EXAMPLE    Martina initially sought counseling due to the increasing frequency and intensity of the arguments between herself, and her sixteen-year-old daughter, Sofía. Martina's husband had died suddenly in a car accident a year ago. During the initial brief spiritual assessment, Martina shared that she was Catholic and attended the same parish she grew up in with her parents, who lived a few blocks away. Parishioners had provided material and emotional support to her and her family when her husband died, bringing her meals, sending her cards, and caring for her children. However, given the apparent lack of connection between Martina's faith and her presenting problem, subsequent sessions focused on dealing with the conflict between Martina and Sofía.

In the year since her husband's death, Martina had competently dealt with financial challenges, loneliness, and the pressure of raising three children on her own. However, mounting stress from helping her children with homework, long hours at her job, and conflicts with Sofía, left her feeling empty, tired, and increasingly angry. The therapist provided individual counseling to Martina and family counseling to help Martina establish clearer rules at home, including a set of guidelines specifically tailored for Sofía. The improved family structure helped reduce the arguments at home but did not seem to diminish Martina's exhaustion and chronic anger, which often accentuated her arguments with her daughter.

During an individual session, Martina off-handedly commented on how disappointed God must be with her. Intrigued at the mention of the sacred, her counselor tentatively inquired about Martina's disappointment. Martina explained that she had hoped God would take the suffering she experienced and use it for good, to produce something beautiful in her. Yet instead she felt like she kept failing in her role as mother, daughter, and employee.

In light of the incongruence between Martina's self-assessment as a failure and her apparent competence, the therapist secured Martina's consent to explore her spiritual story. Martina had a long history of faithful attendance at her local parish. Prior to her husband's death, she had enjoyed attending mass several times a week with her mother. She also prayed the rosary every day. However, since her husband's death, Martina's participation in these activities had declined. Then, in a sudden burst of tears, Martina related that she and her husband had had a terrible argument the morning of his car accident. In a pique of anger, she had spoken harshly. Not only was she unable to resolve the fight with her husband before he died, but she was also afraid that her hurtful comments might have contributed to her husband's apparent lack of judgment preceding the accident. God, she felt, couldn't forgive her for what she had done.

In light of Martina's deep relationship with her local parish, her therapist broached the idea of reconnecting with her faith. With the support of her therapist, Martina talked to her priest about the fight with her husband, her questions about God's willingness to forgive, and eventually her ability to receive that forgiveness from both God and herself. Going to confession proved transformative and freeing. As Martina's guilt and grief dissipated, her zest for life began to return, and she was able to manage her emotional responses more productively in her conflicts with Sofía.

This case example illustrates how spirituality can emerge as an important issue at any point during service delivery. Even though the initial presenting problem appeared to be unrelated to spirituality, in actuality it was a key factor in driving the conflict between Martina and her daughter. Addressing her unresolved spiritual issues was central to alleviating the presenting problem.

The case example also highlights the importance of working within one's area of clinical expertise (Plante, 2009). It is widely accepted that practitioners should only provide services that fall within their areas of competence (NASW, 2008). For instance, the Code of Ethics of the American Association for Marriage and Family Therapy (2012) stipulates that marriage and family therapists do not provide services outside the scope of their competence. In keeping with this ethical precept, the therapist in the case study ensured that someone with specific expertise in that area—her local parish priest—provided the spiritual services Martina needed. The case example also implicitly highlights a number of the strengths associated with spiritual histories, which are summarized in box 5.3.

### STRENGTHS

Among the more prominent strengths of spiritual histories is their appeal to highly verbal individuals. Like Martina in the case example, many clients thrive on face-to-face interactions. If such individuals are comfortable

BOX 5.3    STRENGTHS OF SPIRITUAL HISTORIES

Appeal to highly verbal people who enjoy face-to-face interaction.

Are congruent with cultures that value story-telling/oral transmission of knowledge.

Are client centered/directed.

Are a nonstructured, nonlinear approach to assessment.

Are potentially therapeutic.

Are conducive to building a therapeutic alliance.

Are relatively easy to administer.

The concept is readily understood by clients.

Can be integrated into ongoing clinical conversations as needed.

with the direct exploration of their spirituality, this approach can resonate with their personality.

Similarly, spiritual histories may also represent a good fit for clients from cultures that value oral storytelling. For instance, in many American Indian tribes, such storytelling is a culturally familiar way to talk about one's personal experiences (Hodge & Limb, 2010b). Even more introverted clients from such cultures may appreciate an assessment method that is congruent with their cultural values.

Spiritual histories are also highly client-centered (Holloway & Moss, 2010). Clients are free to relate their stories without having to adapt their narratives to fit predetermined frameworks. In contrast, spiritual genograms require clients to fit their spiritual stories into a specific generational framework. The client-centered orientation of spiritual histories implicitly communicates respect for client autonomy.

On a related note, the comparatively nonstructured, nonlinear format allows clients to tell their stories in a natural manner. This results in an assessment that generally feels comfortable for clients, allowing them the freedom to relate their own stories in their own manner. Concurrently, the associated question sets allow practitioners to elicit clinically relevant information as needed, without resorting to the use of what might be considered artificially constructed frameworks (Holloway & Moss, 2010).

This type of storytelling can also be highly therapeutic. The articulation of clients' spiritual narratives can assist in the process of reframing life events (Pargament, 2007). As clients relate their spiritual stories, it can serve to reinforce positive scripts, clarify their identity, and reconnect them with their cultural roots. Thus, in a certain sense, conducting a spiritual history is an intervention in and of itself (Koenig, 2013).

For example, when people are in highly stressful situations, their need for meaning tends to increase. Confusion, uncertainty, and purposelessness accentuate challenges and can even be problems in their own right. Religious worldviews typically provide adherents with a sense of mastery and control (Park, Edmondson, & Hale-Smith, 2013). Accordingly, relating one's spiritual narrative can foster a sense of meaning, purpose, and mastery. This can be therapeutic, especially in stressful circumstances.

In addition, the verbal format is advantageous for building a therapeutic alliance. The face-to-face interaction enables practitioners to communicate acceptance, empathy, and other responses conducive to creating a safe clinical environment. Spiritual histories are comparatively easy to conduct and explain to clients. Indeed, clients typically understand the concept of taking a personal history and see its relevance to service provision.

The questions used to conduct spiritual histories can also be readily integrated into a broader assessment of client functioning. As the case study implies, this provides flexibility in terms of exploring spiritual issues as they arise in the midst of the clinical conversation. These strengths, while substantial, should be considered in light of the limitations associated with spiritual histories, which are summarized in box 5.4.

### LIMITATIONS

Not all clients are verbally oriented or comfortable with the direct exploration of their spiritual narratives (Hodge, 2005a). The use of spiritual histories may be contraindicated with individuals who are more reserved, introverted, or uncomfortable sharing personal, sacred information in a face-to-face setting, perhaps due to cultural norms that favor indirect communication styles. Indeed, client unease in discussing personal topics can be accentuated in such settings. In other words, face-to-face interaction may increase nervousness about discussing sensitive topics such as spirituality.

Some risk also exists that practitioners may offend clients, particularly if the practitioner's level of spiritual competence is marginal. Clients may share spiritual experiences that practitioners perceive to be unusual or abnormal and involuntarily respond inappropriately, damaging the therapeutic relationship. The face-to-face format provides little time or space to manage one's emotional responses.

BOX 5.4    **LIMITATIONS OF SPIRITUAL HISTORIES**

Have minimal appeal for people who are relatively nonverbal.

Face-to-face interaction may increase nervousness about sensitive topics.

Substantial time is required to appropriately conduct a spiritual history.

May cover spiritual terrain that is unrelated to service provision.

Some clients may prefer a more structured or otherwise alternative format.

In the process of exploring clients' spiritual narratives, practitioners can inadvertently inquire about areas that clients desire to remain undisclosed. For instance, even though one in five people reports hearing the voice of God (Stark, 2008), some clients may be embarrassed discussing such experiences for fear of being labeled pathological. Similarly, asking about spiritual ceremonies that people are not allowed to discuss can damage the clinical relationship (Hodge & Limb, 2010a).

Another limitation is the time required to administer a spiritual history. Time is limited in practice settings. Administering a spiritual history appropriately typically requires a substantial investment of time, perhaps especially with clients from cultures that value indirect communication styles. In some cases this limited resource may be better spent exploring other issues and concerns.

On a related note, time may be spent exploring portions of the client's spiritual history that have minimal utility in terms of impacting service provision. Spiritual histories often yield a wealth of knowledge. Practitioners may have difficulty sorting through this information and determining what is clinically relevant. Furthermore, in telling their stories, clients can wander, provide too much information, or provide descriptions of rites of passage rather than focus on the particular beliefs and practices that intersect service provision. Attempting to repeatedly steer the conversation back to clinically pertinent content, or pressuring clients to finish quickly, can impair the therapeutic alliance.

Although spiritual histories are widely used, their limitations preclude their use with certain clients. Other clients may find that the strengths associated with certain diagrammatic approaches provide a better fit with their interests and needs. For instance, spiritual histories may not be a particularly good choice for artistic clients who are interested in more creative approaches. The next chapter discusses a pictorial approach that circumvents many of the limitations associated with spiritual histories while concurrently allowing for a more creative expression of clients' spiritual narratives.

# 6

# Spiritual Lifemaps

IN MANY WAYS, spiritual lifemaps are a diagrammatic alternative to verbally based histories (Hodge, 2005f). At the most basic level, a lifemap represents a pictorial delineation of a person's spiritual journey. A lifemap provides an illustrated account of an individual's relationship with God or the sacred over time. Much like road maps, lifemaps tell us where we have come from, where we are now, and where we are going (Limb & Hodge, 2007).

This method is similar to spiritual development timelines (Canda & Furman, 2010) and spiritual autobiographies (Wiggins, 2009). Indeed, the philosophical roots of lifemaps can be traced back to African spirituality writer Augustine's (354–430/1991) fourth-century text, *Confessions*. In this seminal work, which is widely considered the first autobiographical work in recorded human history, Augustine chronicles his spiritual journey in what has been referred to as an "act of therapy" (Clark, 1993:39).

Indeed, essentially every religious tradition speaks of life as a journey (Pargament et al., 2013). Traditions provide adherents with a map for the paths that should be taken in life. For instance, the eightfold path is a foundational precept of Buddhism, the five pillars of Islam describe the path of living as submission to the will of Allah, and within Taoism, the Tao literally means the way, path, or route. Many people follow the basic path prescribed by these traditions to navigate life's experiences. Others construct their own pathways, drawing from various traditions. In either case, the concept of life as a journey is widely affirmed.

To construct a spiritual lifemap, colored markers and other types of drawing instruments are used to sketch various spiritually significant life events on a large sheet of paper (Limb & Hodge, 2007). Such events are depicted on a path, a roadway, or a single line that represents the client's sojourn. In a manner analogous to spiritual histories, the path typically proceeds chronologically, from birth to the present. The path can also continue on to death and the client's transition to the afterlife.

Hand-drawn symbols, cut-out pictures, and other media can be used to depict key events along the journey. In keeping with the tenets of many religious traditions—which view material existence to be an extension of the transcendent—it is common to incorporate important secular events on the lifemap (e.g., marriage, death, loss of a job). Hills, bumps, potholes, rain, clouds, lightning, and so forth can be used to portray life challenges, including the client's presenting problem, as illustrated by the case example of James, an African American male.

CASE EXAMPLE   Figure 6.1 features a relatively straightforward example of a lifemap. It portrays the journey of a twenty-eight-year-old African American male, James, who recently received an honorable discharge from the military after he lost both legs above the knee from walking on an improvised explosive device. In six months at Walter Reed Medical Center, James underwent multiple surgeries and intensive physical therapy. Despite the love and support from his mother and many friends, James struggled with depression and anger. He sought counseling to address posttraumatic stress disorder issues and the many challenges that lie ahead.

Given James's introverted personality and his artistic abilities, his counselor invited James to construct a spiritual lifemap. The resulting map depicts James's childhood in the city, his father's death when James was twelve, the football coach who mentored him through his tumultuous adolescence, and his decision to become a Christian at sixteen. Also depicted is his discouragement about being passed over for a college football scholarship, the breakup with his girlfriend because of his military enlistment, his fervent prayers during combat, near brushes with death, and his current despair. He depicts his mother's prayers covering him every step along the way.

His counselor used the lifemap to help James reflect on his life, his pit and peak experiences, the lessons he had learned, and the people who had assisted him. James began to see that his life could still have meaning and purpose despite the loss of his legs. The process of creating the lifemap helped to clarify that God had watched over him and guided him through some difficult times in the past. This fostered hope that God was still with him and had a plan for his future, even if that plan was not quite what he had previously expected. The lifemap helped James consider his long-term goals and fostered determination to press ahead in his present mission—learning to walk again. This exercise, coupled with his repeated brushes with death, served to underscore the brevity of life and its divine value, in tandem with strengthening James's desire to make a difference in the world.

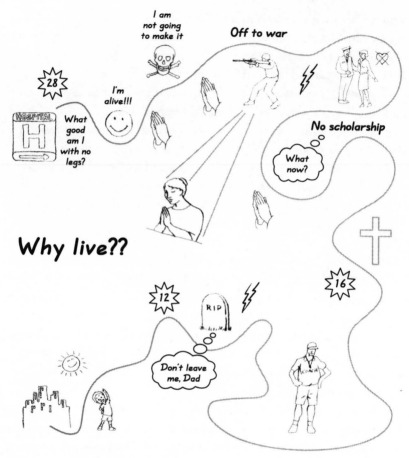

FIGURE 6.1  Spiritual lifemap

## ADMINISTERING A SPIRITUAL LIFEMAP

In terms of administering an assessment using this approach, a number of issues might be considered (Hodge, 2005f). To assist clients with articulating their spiritual journeys, it is helpful to have a supply of various media available. Box 6.1 lists a number of drawing utensils, media, and other supplies that can facilitate the construction of spiritual lifemaps. For example, pictures and text can be cut from old magazines and newspapers and pasted onto the lifemap to illustrate spiritually significant events.

BOX 6.1   SUPPLIES TO FACILITATE THE CONSTRUCTION OF SPIRITUAL
LIFEMAPS

**Drawing Utensils**

Drawing pencils (ideally #1, although #2 is also sufficient)

Erasers

Colored drawing pencils

Fine- and broad-nibbed colored markers

Large and small crayons

**Media**

White and colored paper of various sizes

**Additional Materials**

Scissors

Glue sticks

Rulers

Old magazines and newspapers from diverse sources

To capture the amount of data lifemaps typically elicit, it is usually best to use a large sheet of paper. When faced with a sizable blank sheet of paper, however, some clients experience reluctance to proceed. Unlike James in the case example, many people are not artistically inclined. Such individuals can have difficulty initiating the process or delineating certain events and concepts. In such cases, it is typically appropriate to validate client's emotions, note there is no single correct method for drawing a lifemap, and encourage the client to plunge into the process. It can also be useful to communicate that the central purpose of the project is not to assess artistic ability but to convey and express one's spiritual journey. Thus a map with stick figures is just as valid as one with more elaborate portrayals.

Suggesting options can also be helpful. As illustrated in James's lifemap, a single line is often used to depict one's spiritual journey. One way to proceed is to draw this line on the paper first, break the line into years or decades, and then fill in events along the line. This approach ensures that equal space is allotted to each time period (Canda & Furman, 2010). Alternatively, a more freeform approach can be used, which allows clients the opportunity to devote more space to spiritually significant events. Callouts can be used with both approaches. For instance, another sheet of paper could be added to the lifemap to flesh out a particular event in clients' spiritual journey that is deemed to be particularly significant. Another option for overcoming reluctance is to start with a smaller sheet of paper and then add on to it as space is used up.

To fully operationalize the potential of spiritual lifemaps, it is important to ask clients to delineate the various trials they have encountered along with the resources used to overcome the challenges. Depicting strategies clients have successfully used in the past frequently suggests options for overcoming present struggles (Saleebey, 2013). Similarly, it can be productive to ask clients to list their spiritual assets and resources. While it is appropriate to provide general guidelines and, if asked, specific tips for construction, client creativity and self-expression should be encouraged.

During the creation of a lifemap, practitioners adopt a secondary, supportive role, assisting clients as needed. For example, they might help clients clip pictures from magazines if they elect to use such media (Bushfield, 2009). The goal at this stage in the assessment is to help clients tell their stories while nurturing an affirming, supportive relationship.

After the lifemap has been completed, the central aim is to understand clients' phenomenological reality. Toward this end, practitioners typically ask clients to explain their lifemap (Would you tell me about your spiritual lifemap?). As clients relate their spiritual stories, it is appropriate to express interest, curiosity, and even fascination. Other useful techniques include emphatic replies, minimal verbal prompts (But? And? Yes), and accent responses (in which a word or short phrase is repeated in a questioning tone) (Hepworth et al., 2013). As understanding of clients' worldview is obtained, service provision can be tailored accordingly.

The identification and integration of spiritual strengths into service provision is often a key component of this tailoring process (Snyder et al., 2011). Since current challenges can cause clients to overlook strengths that might be marshaled to address current problems, practitioners should consider how clients approached problems encountered in the past. More specifically, they might ask themselves two questions: (1) How have various assets been used to ameliorate or cope with problems in the past? (2) What types of resources are currently available that might be operationalized to address current challenges?

To answer these questions, practitioners transition from understanding clients' lifemaps to exploring how they have dealt with past trials, as well as their extant strengths. In the case example, James's spiritual strengths helped him to deal with past challenges, such as being passed over for a football scholarship. Accordingly, a practitioner might ask him to elaborate on the difficulties depicted on the lifemap, seek to understand the assets he used to overcome the challenges, and explore how those strategies might be deployed to address current obstacles. To elicit additional information about the process, "how" questions (How did you cope with that event?) and embedded questions (I'm interested in knowing more about what you consider to be your spiritual strengths?) can often be effective.

Box 6.2 lists a number of questions that can be used to identify spiritual assets and resources in four domains (Hodge, 2005f). These strengths-oriented questions can be used to explore clients' perceptions, identifying spiritual assets and resources in four areas: relationship with God (or more broadly the sacred), spiritual beliefs, spiritual rituals or practices, and religious or spiritual community (Hodge, 2005f). Clients frequently view these areas as sources of strength, a perception supported by empirical research (Koenig et al., 2012; Pargament, 2007).

Lifemaps often portray these domains in some manner. Practitioners can use question sets from these or other sources to explore these areas. As is the case with the other question sets featured in this book, the queries for identifying spiritual assets need not be asked in any specific order, nor is it necessary that their exact wording be retained. Rather, the questions should be adapted to reflect clients' value systems and incorporated into the conversation in a natural manner.

In situations where some of the four domains do not appear on the map, practitioners might consider inquiring about them. These four areas are integral to virtually every religious tradition (Pargament, 2013a; Richards & Bergin, 2014; Van Hook et al., 2001). Thus it is likely they have played some role in clients' spiritual journey. In such explorations, tentative phrasing should be used (I was wondering if there might be some spiritual practices you have found helpful over the course of your journey?). It is also helpful to normalize nonresponses, in light of the fact that these questions can intrude on culturally sensitive information that should be kept secret (King & Trimble, 2013).

BOX 6.2    QUESTION SETS FOR IDENTIFYING SPIRITUAL ASSETS
AND RESOURCES

### Relationship with God

How did your relationship with God (or the sacred) help you to address that challenge? What did God teach you about that situation? Have you been able to apply those lessons in other situations going forward? How has God supported you in times of crises? What assets or resources do you draw from your relationship with God?

### Spiritual Beliefs

What does your faith teach about trials? Is there a metaphysical reason for life's challenges? What are your favorite scriptures or precepts? Are there certain scriptures that really speak to you during times of stress? What spiritual precepts have you learned from life's experiences?

### Spiritual Rituals

Are there certain rituals or regular spiritual practices that help you cope with life's trials? Are some rituals particularly effective in certain situations? Are there specific rituals that strengthen your relationship with God?

### Religious Community

What role has your church or spiritual community played during this crisis? Are there relationships in your church community that are particularly supportive? Has there been a spiritual mentor in your life that has been particularly significant? How have these individuals assisted you in coping with challenges?

If subsequent inquiry yields new insights, clients should be given the opportunity to revise their lifemap. In any case, it is important to ensure that the lifemap continues to serve as the focal point of the discussion. Focusing on the physical map helps capitalize on the strengths associated with this approach, which are summarized in box 6.3.

BOX 6.3    STRENGTHS OF SPIRITUAL LIFEMAPS

Allow for creativity and artistic expression.

Honor nonverbal talents and strengths.

Are congruent with cultures that value the use of symbols to convey information.

Are client constructed (implicitly communicate important competencies).

Client controls level of intrusiveness/vulnerability.

Secondary role of therapists allows time to acclimate to clients' worldview.

Visual depiction of life history can foster new insights (e.g., strengths).

Construction process may be cathartic or healing (e.g., develop salutary scripts).

Approach is readily understood by clients.

Can be assigned as therapeutic homework.

**STRENGTHS**

Given the often private nature of spirituality, using a physical object to center discussion around offers some distinct advantages. Face-to-face interaction can increase clients' anxiety when discussing personal topics. Lifemaps, like other diagrammatic approaches to assessment featured in this book, can alleviate this anxiety by shifting the focus from the client to a more neutral object.

As the case example in this chapter suggests, lifemaps are often a particularly suitable choice for creative or artistic clients. Indeed, lifemaps can be created on virtually any media, including canvas, wood, and electronic media with graphic art software. The same can be said regarding the fit of lifemaps with individuals who are not verbally oriented, who are from cultures that honor nonverbal talents and strengths, or who are from cultures that use symbolic and pictorial forms of communication (Hodge & Limb, 2010b). In such cases, lifemaps can enhance client buy-in through the use of an approach that is perceived to be more personally and culturally authentic.

Of the six comprehensive assessment methods, lifemaps are perhaps the most client-directed. The placement of client-constructed media at the center of the assessment involves clients in the clinical process in a meaningful way right from the beginning of service provision. This involvement implicitly conveys some significant therapeutic concepts. Requesting that clients initiate construction of an important clinical module communicates the message that clients are competent, proactive, self-directed, fully engaged participants in the therapeutic process. It is empowering in the sense that it implicitly calls on clients to take responsibility for their personal well-being by actively participating in the process. Additionally, completing the construction of a lifemap sets in place a pattern of successfully tackling and completing tasks from the beginning of service provision.

The high level of client directedness offers clients more control over the degree to which personal information is shared. Since clients are in charge of the construction process, they have more freedom to construct a map that is congruent with their sense of personal vulnerability. For example, sacred ceremonies that should not be shared with outsiders can be left off the map or included in an oblique manner.

The relatively secondary role that practitioners play during assessment also offers important advantages. There is less risk that the therapeutic relationship will be jeopardized owing to comments that are inadvertently offensive, an important consideration given that many practitioners have received minimal training in spiritual competence (Canda & Furman, 2010; Koenig, 2013; Vogel et al., 2013). Space is created for practitioners to learn about clients' spiritual value systems while building rapport by providing an atmosphere that is accepting, nonjudgmental, and supportive during assessment. The secondary role allows time to acclimate to clients' worldviews.

The visual depiction of one's spiritual journey can elicit new clinical insights above and beyond those obtained using spiritual histories (Oakes & Raphel, 2008). Given the amorphous, subjective nature of spirituality, physical depiction can make spiritual strengths more concrete and identifiable. In other words, the process of conceptualizing and charting one's spiritual journey may help to isolate and objectify spiritual assets, which can then be discussed and marshaled to address problems or enhance coping. Similarly, seeing how one used spiritual resources in the past to overcome challenges helps engender confidence that current obstacles can also be overcome.

As suggested by the case example, spiritual lifemaps also aid in the process of spiritual reframing (Pargament, 2007). The process of constructing a map often helps clients see how various components of their spiritual narratives fit together as part of a larger, cohesive story, typically a story with a divine purpose. In James's case, constructing a map allowed him to connect events that previously seemed discordant into a unified sacred narrative that engendered a sense of hope and optimism. In the same way that physical depiction can aid in identifying strengths, it can also facilitate the creation and adoption of new, more salutary personal narratives.

Spiritual lifemaps are often useful when clients are dealing with existential concerns (Bushfield, 2009). For instance, hospitalized clients expressing a spiritual need to conduct a life review may benefit from this approach. Similarly, lifemaps may help alleviate death anxiety among clients in hospice settings, as well as others struggling with anxiety and related concerns (Soenke et al., 2013).

Like other diagrammatic approaches, lifemaps can be used to track progress during counseling, reinforcing positive changes that occur through various pictorial devices. In keeping with this aim, new content can be incorporated into the lifemap. For example, callouts might be added to note significant achievements.

Lifemaps also fit well with interventions drawn from existential therapy that emphasize the brevity of life. Practitioners conversant in this modality may find this approach to be a good fit with their theoretical orientation. For instance, lifemaps can be used to highlight the shortness of life, the ontological reality of choice, and the creation of meaning.

Much like spiritual histories, spiritual lifemaps are usually readily understood by clients. Since they are easy to understand and highly self-directed, clients can often construct them independently. Thus, in contexts where conserving time is crucial, practitioners may assign the creation of a lifemap as clinical homework and then discuss the completed map in the next session. As important as these strengths may be, the use of spiritual lifemaps may be contraindicated in some situations.

### LIMITATIONS

As with all assessment approaches, spiritual lifemaps are also characterized by a number of limitations (see box 6.4). A major drawback is related to clients' level of artistic ability. For clients who see themselves as lacking such ability, the use of lifemaps may actually increase anxiety and stress. This stress may be accentuated if practitioners do not adequately explain the assessment tool and its purpose.

BOX 6.4    LIMITATIONS OF SPIRITUAL LIFEMAPS

Clients may be concerned over perceived lack of artistic skills and/or dislike of
    drawing.
Clients may feel uncomfortable drawing some aspects of their journeys.
Are potentially a poor use of practitioners' time.
Can be time intensive to construct.
Lack generational information.

Similarly, many clients are uninterested in drawing in practice settings. This includes some people with artistic ability. For example, certain individuals may feel uncomfortable depicting their spiritual story on paper, perhaps due to its sacred character (Hodge & Limb, 2010b). Naturally, using an assessment that conflicts with clients' interests is ill advised.

Constructing a lifemap can be a time-intensive process. Some practitioners may feel so removed from the assessment process that the approach makes poor use of their time (Bushfield, 2009). Although lifemaps can often be assigned as homework, this practice forfeits some of the strengths inherent in the approach. For example, practitioners lose the opportunity to create a safe, affirming atmosphere during the assessment, which in turn sets the stage for the subsequent exploration of the lifemap and the transition to developing interventions.

In addition, clients and practitioners may find an alternative approach a better fit with their interests. For example, clients who prefer more direct practitioner/client involvement or more verbal interaction may find the use of a largely nonverbal, pictorial method to be a poor fit with their interests. For such clients, spiritual histories may be a better choice.

In other situations, a clearer understanding of family dynamics is beneficial. Although individually oriented approaches represent important contributions, it should also be acknowledged that each person is imbedded in a particular family structure. With some clients, it can be important to understand the effects of spirituality in greater breadth (i.e., across the wider family system) or in greater depth (i.e., back through the generations). In such settings, the approach discussed in the next chapter might be used.

# 7

# Spiritual Genograms

MUCH LIKE SPIRITUAL HISTORIES, spiritual genograms are frequently employed to conduct comprehensive assessments (McGoldrick, Gerson, & Petry, 2008; Roberts, 2009; Wiggins, 2009; Willow, Tobin, & Toner, 2009). Traditional genograms are common in social work, marriage and family therapy, counseling, and other helping professions. This may help account for the popularity of spiritual genograms, as many practitioners are familiar with their basic construction and use.

Spiritual genograms depict the flow of spirituality across the family system in a manner analogous to traditional genograms (Limb & Hodge, 2010). Through the use of what is essentially a family tree that has been modified to incorporate spiritual information, they help both clients and practitioners understand the flow of historically rooted patterns through time, typically back through three generations (Davis, Lambie, & Ieva, 2011). Spiritual genograms provide a graphic color snapshot of complex intergenerational interactions related to spirituality (Hodge, 2001b).

Regardless of whether individuals negotiate a place for themselves within their family's religious tradition or exercise their right to change traditions, their family of origin continues to inform beliefs and experiences (Limb & Hodge, 2010). For example, grandparents often play a decisive role in shaping the spirituality of their children and grandchildren. In settings where grandparents do not live in the household, they indirectly shape perceptions through the memories they evoke, especially in cases where at least one of the grandparents—typically a grandmother—was noted for piety (Wuthnow, 1999).

To construct spiritual genograms, the basic family system is delineated on a piece of paper, following standard genogram conventions (McGoldrick et al., 2008). In addition to the use of squares for men and circles for women, alternative geometric shapes or figures can be used to depict important people who are not members of the immediate biological family. Triangles, for example, might be used to portray key members of clients' "spiritual family." To indicate a person's religion, colored drawing pencils are used to shade in the squares, circles, and any other geometric figures included on the genogram (Frame, 2003). Various colors are used to signify different affiliations (e.g., red = Catholic, black = southern Baptist, blue = New Age or syncretistic, no color = unknown affiliation).

A change in affiliation is depicted by drawing a circle outside the geometric figure and filling in the space between the circle and the figure with the appropriate color (Hodge, 2001b). The date of the change can also be listed on the diagram beside the larger circle. This helps indicate the stability or fluidity of the person's beliefs over time. Symbols drawn from clients' worldview can be used to signify meaningful events—such as baptisms, confirmations, bar mitzvahs, visions, mission trips, degree of spirituality— as illustrated in the case example of Jacob and Amy, a couple who has been married for eight years.

CASE EXAMPLE   Jacob, age thirty-two, and Amy, age thirty, are both of European American descent. They sought marital counseling because of increasing emotional distance and conflict in their eight-year marriage. Amy reported feeling overly controlled and unsupported in her role as homemaker and primary nurturer of their four children, ages one, three, five, and seven. Initially an enthusiastic convert, Amy felt increasing disenchanted with her new faith and her husband's dedication to his work. Jacob expressed concern over the lack of unity in their values and Amy's declining involvement in the Church of Jesus Christ of Latter-day Saints (LDS). In light of the nature of their present challenges, their therapist administered a spiritual genogram (fig. 7.1).

As demonstrated by the uniform coloring, Jacob's parents and grandparents were committed LDS. In the past both his father and grandfather had served as bishops of their wards in Utah. Like other devout LDS, Jacob had served a two-year mission. Currently he was using his musical talents as the choir director in their local ward. He also enjoyed teaching Sunday School classes to the youth in his ward periodically.

Amy grew up attending the United Methodist Church with her parents and maternal grandparents. Her father, Philip, was raised in the Presbyterian Church and was baptized

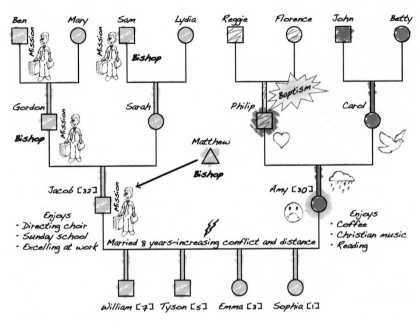

FIGURE 7.1   Spiritual genogram

in the United Methodist Church shortly after proposing to Amy's mother. Jacob and Amy clicked instantly when they met at Arizona State University. They believed they were highly compatible, until they got married.

After a short honeymoon period, the differences in their religious backgrounds became increasingly apparent. As illustrated on the genogram, Amy was used to drinking coffee and enjoyed listening to music and reading books that were popular in the evangelical Christian subculture. In contrast, Jacob followed the value system affirmed by the LDS Church, which abstains from coffee, and viewed Amy as less devout in her beliefs for deviating from these values over time. As a result, Amy felt erroneously judged by Jacob and became increasingly resentful of the long hours he spent at work, as well as the additional time he served in their local ward—time she felt could be better spent helping her with their children at home. Amy frequently felt exhausted caring for their children and had little energy left to teach Sunday School, much to Jacob's chagrin.

The therapist used the genogram to clarify differences, engender empathy, and identify solutions. The genogram illustrated the differences between their religious upbringings and highlighted how the Presbyterian upbringing of Amy's father and the more permeable boundaries of the United Methodist culture shaped Amy's spirituality. Understanding the historical factors that influenced their respective lives helped Jacob and Amy see each other in a new, more empathetic light.

The strengths listed on the genogram served as a starting point for developing solutions. Owing to their shared commitment to spiritual disciplines, the therapist encouraged them to pray individually and together for inspiration about how to become more unified as a couple. The therapist also encouraged them to consult with their local bishop, Matthew, whom Jacob respected. Matthew encouraged Jacob to step down from his demanding role as choir director and consider just singing in the choir until his children were older. He suggested to Amy that she might become more involved in the Women's Relief Society as a way to address some of her felt social needs while helping others. In light of Jacob's commitment to LDS values, the therapist brainstormed with the couple regarding how they could prioritize weekly "Family Home Evenings," given the demands of Jacob's job. As Jacob followed through on the recommendations of the bishop and carved out time each week for his family, Amy felt more emotionally connected with Jacob and "his" church. Her increased interactions with the women in the local ward not only fed her soul but also enhanced her appreciation for spiritual values affirmed by the LDS Church.

### ADMINISTERING A SPIRITUAL GENOGRAM

As with other diagrammatic approaches, creativity should typically be encouraged when creating spiritual genograms. Toward this end, various symbols might be used to denote the degree of commitment. Alternatively, a unique color might be used to represent individuals who are especially devout (Mutter & Neves, 2010). Similarly, a specific color could be used to portray people who affiliate with two traditions simultaneously. It is also possible to incorporate relational information using the guidelines featured in chapter 8. This allows clients to depict the flow of energy or interest between different actors, as portrayed in the case example between Jacob and Matthew.

In conducting assessments using spiritual genograms, a few additional points should be noted (Hodge, 2001b). While it is critical not to stereotype, it can be helpful to have some awareness of common patterns that may warrant exploration. Although these points have applicability to other approaches, they may be particularly relevant to spiritual genograms given their generational emphasis.

Many people change religious affiliations (Ellison & McFarland, 2013). According to research conducted by the Pew Forum on Religion and

Public Life (2009), approximately 50 percent of Americans have changed their affiliation at some point in their lives. Among those who change, most people leave the tradition of their family of origin by age twenty-four. It is not uncommon for these individuals to subsequently switch to a different tradition or reconnect with their original faith at a later point in life. After reaching age fifty, comparatively few people change affiliations.

People switch traditions for a wide variety of spiritual, personal, and social reasons (Chaves, 2011). As illustrated in the case example, major life-cycle events, such as marriage, often spark a shift in affiliations. Those raised in nonreligious families frequently have a spiritual awakening and then join a particular tradition. The converse is true as well: people reject the spirituality of their youth in favor of secularism.

The point is that these transitions can cause conflicts of various types that ripple throughout the family system (Ellison & McFarland, 2013). In the case of Jacob and Amy, for example, their marriage resulted in a clash of two different value systems. Similarly, tension can arise when individuals switch affiliation or transition from a secular family of origin to a religious tradition and vice-versa. Accordingly, changes in affiliation can warrant examination.

It can also be helpful to identify spiritual mentors in the extended family as such individuals can represent untapped resources. Older adults, for instance, are disproportionately likely to affirm the importance of spirituality in their lives, and some commentators speculate that the salience of spirituality increases with age (Newport, 2012). Furthermore, in many communities, elders play an important role in the transmission of spiritual values, and emotionally rich, cross-generational bonds may arise with spiritually receptive grandchildren.

In many religious cultures, the congregational community is viewed as a type of family (Pargament, 2013a). As portrayed in the case example, Jacob's bishop, Matthew, functioned as an important spiritual mentor in his life. Thus when examining potential spiritual mentors, it is helpful to consider clients' immediate families, extended families, and their congregational or spiritual families (Cnaan & Curtis, 2013).

Toward that end, box 7.1 features two question sets that may aid in operationalizing this assessment approach. The first set provides options to facilitate the construction of a spiritual genogram. The questions are grouped somewhat thematically, moving toward increasing degrees of

BOX 7.1    QUESTIONS TO AID IN OPERATIONALIZING SPIRITUAL GENOGRAMS

### Constructing Spiritual Genograms

What type of religious affiliation characterized each member of your family, going back to your grandparents? How meaningful was their relationship with their denomination/faith? Their church (house of worship)? To what extent were their personal beliefs and those of their church/denomination congruent? What was their level of participation? To what extent did they enjoy religious fellowship? Their spiritual lives?

How did they express their spiritual and religious beliefs? What were the particular rituals or sayings that were commonly evidenced? How were spirituality and religion assets in their lives? How did their spirituality intersect with the difficulties they encountered in life? How did their faith help them cope with trials?

What spiritually significant events (transitions/conversions/changes in affiliations/ encounters with transpersonal beings) have occurred in the family? How did these events affect the individuals involved? How did other members react to these changes?

What are the differences (and similarities) among various family members in their beliefs (practices)? How were differences and conflicts managed? Who was the spiritual leader in your family? What role did your grandparents play in your spiritual walk?

What spiritual relationships stand out to you from your childhood years? What are your earliest religious memories? Did your family hold regular devotional times? What types of spiritually based practices occurred at home? Which members of your family have had the most influence on your spiritual walk? Whom do you feel closest to in a spiritual sense?

### Transitioning to Interventions

In relationship to your family, what are your current religious and spiritual beliefs? How have your beliefs (practices/feelings) changed since childhood (adolescence)? How has your family's beliefs and practices affected your present expression of spirituality?

BOX 7.1   (CONTINUED)

To what extent do you experience conflict (fellowship/harmony) with other family members over your spiritual beliefs? What have you accepted and rejected from your family's spiritual history? What prompted these decisions?

What sort of patterns do you see emerging over time? How does your present spirituality intersect with these patterns? How has God worked through your family? How has God worked through your family to touch you?

How does your spirituality assist you in dealing with difficulties? Are there religious practices that help you cope with trials? Does the severity of your problem(s) dissipate or disappear when you engage in certain spiritual practices? What does your faith teach about forgiveness? How have you been able to apply this teaching in your own life?

Are there spiritual strengths in your family's history that you could draw on to help you deal with problems? Are there methods of dealing with problems that you might be able to adapt from others? What sort of insights could you draw from your spiritual genogram that might help you to address your current difficulties?

*Source:* Adapted with permission from Hodge (2003).

personal disclosure. Given the highly personal nature of spirituality, some clients may find it easier answering questions about relatives' beliefs and practices, at least until a degree of trust is established.

After the basic historical components are completed, a transition is made to present dynamics. That is, the focus shifts from family members to clients. In this stage of the assessment, practitioners help clients explore how their past spiritual history has shaped their current spiritual functioning. This exploration also sets the stage for a subsequent discussion of potential interventions. The second set of questions is designed with this purpose in mind, featuring questions that move from personal exploration toward intervention.

### Constructing Spiritual Genograms

What type of religious affiliation characterized each member of your family, going back to your grandparents? How meaningful was their relationship with their church/faith? With members of their church?

To what extent were their personal beliefs consistent with the teachings of their church? What was their level of participation (e.g., serving in the church, regular attendance)? How was religion an asset in their lives? How did their faith or religious beliefs help them make sense of the difficulties they encountered?

What religiously significant events (e.g., baptisms, marriage, changes in affiliations, temple attendance, promptings from the Holy Ghost) have occurred in your family? How did these events affect the individuals involved? How did other members react to these changes?

What were the differences and similarities among various family members in their beliefs and practices? How were differences and conflicts managed? Who was the spiritual leader?

What religious practices or experiences stand out in your childhood years (e.g., prayer, church attendance, scripture reading, family home evening, or other religious practices or ordinances)? Which members of your family have had the most influence on your spiritual development?

### Transitioning to Interventions

How have your beliefs (practices/feelings) changed since childhood (adolescence)? How have past religious patterns in your family shaped your current practice of religion?

How comfortable/content are you with your own level of spirituality and your relationship with Heavenly Father and Jesus Christ? To what extent do you experience conflict and/or harmony with family members over your religious or spiritual

BOX 7.2   (CONTINUED)

beliefs? What have you accepted and rejected from your family's spiritual history? What motivated these decisions?

How does your faith or religious belief help you make sense of trials or difficulties? Are there particular religious practices that you would be comfortable sharing with me that help you deal with challenges (e.g., prayer, temple attendance, scripture reading, family home evening, or other religious practices or ordinances)? Does the severity of your problem(s) decrease when you engage in certain religious or spiritual practices?

Are there religious strengths in your family's history that you can draw on to help you deal with problems? Are there examples of dealing with problems that you might be able to adapt from others? Are there individuals in your ward or branch (e.g., bishop, home or visiting teacher, relief society president) that are especially supportive? What sort of Gospel insights can you draw from your genogram that might help you to address your current difficulties?

Box 7.2 features an analogous set of questions that might be used to operationalize spiritual genograms with LDS clients such as Jacob and Amy. These questions differ from prior question sets featured in this text in one important way. The questions in box 7.1 and in previous chapters were typically tailored to reflect what might be called generic theism, a phrasing designed to be congruent with common understandings of spirituality within the general population at large. Conversely, the LDS-specific questions in box 7.2 have been adapted to reflect typical phrasing within the LDS culture.

For instance, Heavenly Father is used instead of God, the term religion is generally privileged over spirituality, and it is implicitly acknowledged that certain religious practices should not be shared with outsiders (Hodge & Limb, 2013). This illustrates how practitioners might alter terminology to increase its level of cultural congruence. In the same way that the phrasing has been altered to reflect common terms in the LDS culture, the original questions might be adapted to be more culturally congruent with other groups practitioners frequently encounter.

Regardless of how questions are phrased, practitioners should not feel locked into any specific order or question wording. Similarly, questions can be drawn from other sources, including practitioners' accumulated store of clinical wisdom. The key point is that questions, no matter what their source, should be modified and woven into the conversation in a manner that aids in the identification of clinically pertinent information in a spiritually competent manner (Starnino et al., 2012). The strengths that characterize spiritual genograms are discussed in the following section and summarized in box 7.3.

### STRENGTHS

Spiritual genograms are particularly useful when clients present with problems involving family members or family of origin issues (McGoldrick et al., 2008; Walsh, 2013). Couples, for example, often experience challenges that stem from attempting to synthesize differing spiritual value systems. As illustrated by Jacob and Amy, these challenges are frequently accentuated when individuals come from different traditions. Spiritual genograms are particularly well suited for illuminating areas of difference as well as highlighting the respective spiritual strengths each person brings to the relationship (Minatrea & Duba, 2012).

BOX 7.3    STRENGTHS OF SPIRITUAL GENOGRAMS

Depict problems rooted in differing family systems (interfaith couples).

Identify areas of commonality among couples (same-faith couples).

Explore family-of-origin issues.

Illustrate spiritual and religious patterns across generations.

Can identify previously unrecognized strengths in the family system.

Implicitly communicate respect for extended family members.

Can appeal to clients interested in a very structured approach.

Conversely, spiritual genograms can also be used to increase intimacy among couples from the same tradition. Shared understanding plays a key role in fostering high levels of intimacy (Heller & Wood, 2000). Spiritual genograms can help foster such intimacy by fleshing out similarities so that areas of commonality can be enhanced. For example, marital satisfaction might be increased by charting and facilitating joint religious communication and tradition-specific forgiveness processes (David & Stafford, in press).

Similarly, individuals working through issues involving family members or family-of-origin issues may benefit from this approach (Frame, 2003). Examples include people seeking to reconnect with their historical religious or cultural roots; clients differentiating from their family of origin and in doing so choosing different spiritual beliefs or practices; and changes in affiliation that spark family conflict or estrangement.

Another asset associated with this method is its visual orientation (Willow et al., 2009). Spiritual genograms effectively illustrate spiritual patterns. The colorful depiction can spark new insights. As occurred with Jacob and Amy, seeing their different religious backgrounds physically represented helped them understand their present conflicts in a fresh light while also engendering empathy for each other. A picture can convey information that verbal descriptions fail to communicate.

Similarly, the process of charting various family members can help identify previously unrecognized spiritual strengths. For example, a young African American struggling with racism might benefit from learning how the Christian beliefs of elderly grandparents enabled them to deal with similar problems (Oman, 2013). In addition to learning helpful strategies, the relational connection can be empowering (Walsh, 2009).

Systems-oriented practitioners may find that spiritual genograms fit well with their theoretical orientation, as well as opening up new therapeutic options. For example, some therapists have successfully employed spiritual interventions that incorporate God as part of the family system. Substitutive triangles, featuring God as an active participant, are used to minimize conflict by diverting intimacy to God (Frame, 2003).

In some cases spiritual genograms can be advantageous with clients from cultures that value tradition and the wider family system, such as LDS (Walton, Limb, & Hodge, 2011), Latinos (Poole, 1998), and Muslims (Husain & Ross-Sheriff, 2011). They can also be helpful in illuminating cultural differences in family functioning. In much the same way that individuals can affirm value systems that differ from the secular culture, families from various subcultures can also affirm culturally distinct value systems (Wilcox, 2009). Delineating these unique interactions can help practitioners understand these cultural norms and design culturally appropriate interventions.

Like other diagrammatic approaches, spiritual genograms shift the focus from the client to the inanimate object, which can help alleviate client concern about discussing sensitive topics. Spiritual genograms can also appeal to clients who prefer a very structured assessment approach. With other clients, however, the structure can be a shortcoming. This and other, related limitations are summarized in box 7.4 and discussed in more depth in the next section.

### LIMITATIONS

Spiritual genograms employ a specific structure. In turn, the format inherent in genograms places constraints on how clients relate their spiritual stories. A generational framework must be used. For clients who tend to understand spirituality in terms of a personal, chronological spiritual narrative or prefer more creativity and flexibility, this approach may be problematic. Although it is possible to add some creative components to a genogram, the generational structure limits the flexibility of this approach.

Spiritual genograms are also relatively complicated to understand and construct. Consequently, a fair degree of practitioner involvement may

BOX 7.4    LIMITATIONS OF SPIRITUAL GENOGRAMS

Are highly structured; must fit story into a generational format.

Are complex; can be difficult to explain and construct.

Are time consuming to construct, particularly with large families.

May explore dimensions of clients' stories that are unrelated to their presenting problems.

Many indigenous cultures forbid speaking of those who have passed on.

Clients may not connect exploration of past functioning with present problems.

be required to explain and administer the assessment. This mitigates the role of clients in the assessment while implicitly highlighting practitioners' knowledge and capabilities. It also limits practitioners' ability to assign genograms as homework.

Furthermore, it is often difficult to introduce and administer a spiritual genogram in a single session since clients may not have access to the information needed for the construction process (Willow et al., 2009). To fully operationalize the strengths inherent in the approach, it is often necessary to assemble background information on one's family history. It can require a considerable investment of clients' time to collect data on people's religious affiliations, the meanings attached to spirituality in various generations, family strengths and conflicts related to spirituality, the impact of religion on marriages, rituals, celebrations, interpersonal relationships, and other dimensions of family functioning that have flowed across generations.

These problems are compounded when working with more diverse, nonnuclear family structures (McGoldrick et al., 2008). Genograms tend to work best with smaller family units, such as the nuclear family widely affirmed in mainstream discourse. In many cultures, however, large families are normative. In other cultures, extended families tend to be common. In such cases, the construction of spiritual genograms is even more complex and time intensive, if not impossible.

To some extent, the problems can be alleviated by leaving less significant family members out of the genogram. For instance, in the case example, only those family members who were perceived to be particularly instrumental in Jacob and Amy's lives were featured. While this strategy can be helpful in some situations, in others it is less useful as important information is left undepicted.

The historical orientation can result in spending time on dimensions of clients' spirituality that are unrelated to service provision (Hodge, 2005a). In situations where the family system or historical influences are of minor importance, spiritual genograms may have limited utility.

Exploration of historical factors also risks intrusion into sensitive areas. For example, speaking of those who have passed on is forbidden in many American Indian cultures (Hodge & Limb, 2010a). This creates problems as the method itself is arguably culturally incongruent with certain cultures.

In addition, many clients across cultures do not connect past events with current challenges (McGoldrick et al., 2008). In keeping with their generational structure, spiritual genograms shift people's attention from the present to the past. To be sure, this can be helpful in many clinical contexts. Clients, however, do not always see the relationship between historical events and present problems. In such cases, clients can view genogram construction as an inefficient use of time.

Indeed, from clients' perspectives, it is the present challenge that is typically experienced as acutely pressing. Consequently, it is not unreasonable for clients to focus on present solutions to problems that are currently experienced. The time of both practitioners and clients is limited and valuable; why not focus time and energy on the problems at hand? When such sentiments exist, a more present-oriented assessment approach may be especially useful. The next chapter discusses such a method.

# 8

# Spiritual Eco-maps

SPIRITUAL ECO-MAPS REPRESENT A CONCEPTUALLY different approach to assessment relative to the methods discussed in previous chapters (Hodge & Limb, 2009). Spiritual histories, lifemaps, and genograms are all designed to examine some portion of clients' stories as they unfold through time, typically a period ranging from one to three generations. In contrast with these approaches, spiritual eco-maps illustrate clients' current relationships to spiritual systems in their present environment (Hodge, 2000).

Eco-map is short form for ecological map. These maps were originally developed as a way to depict the ecological systems that surround individuals or families (Hartman, 1995). While genograms and other historically oriented approaches represent people *over time*, eco-maps portray them *in space*. In other words, eco-maps focus on the major systems that are currently part of people's lives as well as their relationships to those systems.

Clients' relationships with God, their religious communities, and other dimensions of the sacred are typically experienced as an ongoing reality (Granqvist & Kirkpatrick, 2013). Although the relational dynamics may vary over time, individuals experience their relationships with the transcendent in the present. In other words, people have a currently experienced, ongoing relationship with God and other transcendent dimensions of existence. Spiritual eco-maps spotlight clients' relational dynamics with the sacred as it is experienced in the here and now.

To construct spiritual eco-maps, an individual is depicted in the center of a sheet of paper. Alternatively, a family can be portrayed using standard genogram conventions (Hodge & Williams, 2002). On the outskirts of the paper, surrounding the individual or family system, a series of circles are used to represent significant spiritual systems (Mutter & Neves, 2010).

These spiritual systems can be supplemented by other systems that are also relevant to service provision if a broader assessment is of interest. For instance, one might include systems such as friends, work, school, sports, recreation, and physical health, or various dimensions of these entities. Put differently, it is possible to seamlessly adapt this approach to include a variety of environmental variables that are perceived to be relevant to service delivery, a point illustrated in this chapter's case example.

The central feature of spiritual eco-maps is the relationships between the individual (or family) system and the surrounding spiritual systems. In keeping with the conventions listed in figure 8.1, these relationships are represented with various types of lines and arrows that convey information about the content and character of the relational connection between the systems (Hodge & Limb, 2009). The lines and arrows depict the felt intensity and supportive nature of the various environmental systems.

As with the other diagrammatic approaches, creativity is encouraged. Short, descriptive summaries, significant dates, and other artistic depictions can be used to provide more information about relational dynamics. As illustrated in the case example of Joseph, a twenty-five-year-old American Indian, the heart of the map is the intensity and character of the relationships associated with the environmental systems.

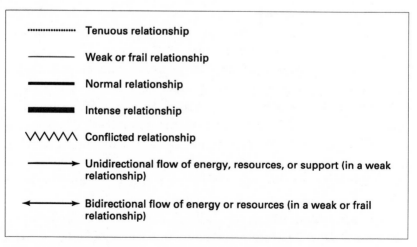

FIGURE 8.1   Depicting relational information in diagrammatic form

CASE EXAMPLE  Joseph, a twenty-five-year old Cherokee male, sought help with a drinking problem. Joseph was a skilled mechanic and was grateful to be employed after struggling for five months to find work. After failing to show up for work three times in a month, his employer had placed him on probation. This event precipitated his decision to seek counseling.

In light of Joseph's interest in spirituality, his counselor suggested they construct a spiritual eco-map together (fig. 8.2). The counselor used the map to assist Joseph in identifying positive and negative relationships with significant systems in his environment, particularly those that fostered or inhibited his alcohol misuse. As illustrated on the map,

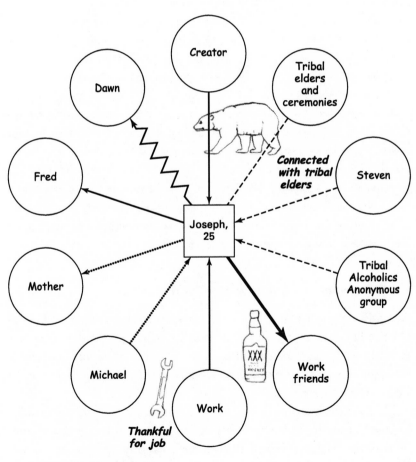

FIGURE 8.2  Spiritual eco-map

Joseph's work relationships often resulted in after-hours socialization at local bars. Similarly, his relationships with Dawn, his ex-girlfriend, and Fred, his critical stepfather, were strained. In turn, the taxing nature of these relationships served to make socializing after work and escaping from such stresses all the more appealing.

In addition to illustrating detrimental relationships, the eco-map portrayed positive relationships that might help Joseph realize his goals. Included among these was his relationship with his older brother, Michael, a recovering alcoholic. His childhood friend, Steven, regularly participated in their tribe's spiritual ceremonies—activities Joseph had enjoyed as a youth but had long since stopped attending.

The physical depiction of the positive and negative energy flows helped clarify both the environmental influences operating in Joseph's life and his options in terms of possible changes. Joseph decided to stop pursuing a renewed relationship with Dawn. He also finalized his decision to move out of his mother's home, decreasing his interactions with his stepfather. Joseph also started attending Alcoholics Anonymous with his brother on the reservation, where most of the attendees shared his spiritual beliefs and values. He also contacted his friend Steven to discuss meeting with the tribal elders and participating in spiritual ceremonies again.

As Joseph reflected on the relational dynamics depicted in his eco-map, he realized his life lacked harmony and balance due in part to the influence of the negative energy sources. In turn, this triggered his drinking. By changing his circle of friends and filling his life with more life-giving people and sacred activities, he could effectively fight the urge to misuse alcohol. To support Joseph in this goal, his counselor periodically administered new eco-maps to document and reinforce his progress in a visual and concrete manner as Joseph worked on de-emphasizing negative relationships and accentuating life-giving relationships to restore harmony and balance with himself and his Creator.

## ADMINISTERING A SPIRITUAL ECO-MAP

Administering spiritual eco-maps is a relatively straightforward process (Mutter & Neves, 2010). After delineating the client (or family) in the center of the paper, practitioners collaborate with clients to identify and depict meaningful spiritual systems. These systems are then placed on the sheet, in a circle around the client.

Ideally clients list the systems that are perceived to be significant (Hodge & Limb, 2009). It can also be helpful, however, to have knowledge of common spiritual systems. Systems that people frequently report include rituals (or spiritual practices), God (or clients' relationship with the transcendent or sacred), faith communities (or religious or spiritual communities), and transpersonal beings. The latter include encounters with beings such as angels, an experience reported by more than half the American public (Stark, 2008).

Box 8.1 features some generic questions that might be used to flesh out perceptions in these four areas (Hodge, 2000). To tease out potentially significant distinctions, practitioners may wish to collaborate with

BOX 8.1    QUESTIONS FOR ADMINISTERING SPIRITUAL ECO-MAPS

**Rituals**

What particular rituals or practices nurture your spirituality/family life? Are there specific symbols that are spiritually significant to you? What rituals/practices facilitate coping with hardship, illness, or trials?

**God/Transcendent**

Describe your relationship to God. Have there been times when you have felt deep intimacy with (distance from) the divine? What facilitates this sense of closeness (distance)? How does the state of your conscience affect your relationship with God? How does your spirituality relate to life's difficulties (joys)? How do you deal with transgressions/misdeeds that violate your conscience? How does your relationship with the transcendent affect your relationship with others? What sort of fruit does it produce? Have you received premonitions or intuition insights from God concerning life events?

**Faith Community**

What is your level of involvement in faith communities (churches, mosques, small groups, synagogues, temples, etc.)? What are their primary religious/spiritual beliefs, and how reflective are they of yours? What sort of atmosphere (e.g., cold, warm, conflicted, open) does your faith community transmit?

**Spirit Beings**

Have you had encounters with transpersonal beings such as angels, demons, or evil spirits? Did you ever feel the intervention of a saint (angel/lower order god) on your behalf? Have you had experiences with relatives who have died? How would you describe these encounters?

clients to break larger systems into smaller systems. For instance, a client might respond that she attends church and her participation represents an important, salutary activity in her weekly schedule. The practitioner might explore which particular aspects of this general participation are perceived to be particularly beneficial (e.g., sacraments, worship, preaching, specific elders and congregants, postservice socializing).

The generic nature of these questions should be underscored. Some questions will be relevant to clients from some religious backgrounds but not clients from other traditions. Accordingly, it is important to integrate questions into the clinical conversation only to the extent they are congruent with clients' cultural worldview. Indeed, the use of some of the questions can be offensive to clients from particular traditions.

Take, for instance, the question about experiences with relatives who have died in the transpersonal beings system. Among certain segments of the general population, after-death communication with a deceased relative is relatively common (Mack & Powell, 2005). Such experiences are often significant events in people's lives and can have important therapeutic implications (Kwilecki, 2011). Thus it is appropriate to inquire about such experiences in certain situations with people from traditions that allow the sharing of such experiences.

Conversely, questions about deceased relatives are inappropriate with clients from some other traditions. Some American Indian cultures prohibit asking about experiences with relatives who have passed, particularly when nontribal members ask such questions (Hodge & Limb, 2010a). Similarly, as mentioned earlier, some tribes proscribe discussing certain rituals with outsiders, even though the rituals are often understood to be instrumental to health and wellness. This highlights the importance of tailoring the protocols used to operationalize an assessment so that they are culturally congruent.

Box 8.2 illustrates what this tailoring might look like when interacting with American Indian clients. The box lists these same four systems featured in box 8.1, modified to be more congruent with common American Indian values. Thus instead of the terms rituals, God, faith communities, and transpersonal beings, the terms ceremonies, Creator, community, and spirit beings are used to describe the underlying systems.

Similarly, the sample questions have been reworked to reflect values widely affirmed among many American Indian tribes. For example, it is

### Ceremonies

Without sharing personal or secret information, can you tell me if there are ceremonies or practices that help keep your family strong and healthy? How often do you participate in these ceremonies? Are there any obstacles that prevent you from participating? Are there customs or symbols that are meaningful during hardship for you? Your family? Your tribe?

### Creator

If it is not too personal, would you mind describing your relationship with the Creator and creation? What effect does your relationship with the Creator have on your relationships with others? Your family? Your enjoyment of life? Your energy? Creativity? When you are out of balance or harmony, are there ceremonies that help restore balance or harmony?

### Community

Do you practice spiritual ways within a community? How often do you participate? Is it a good thing in your life? What is the most important benefit of participating?

### Spirit Beings

If it is OK with you, I would like to ask your permission to talk about spirit helpers or spirit guides. Have you had spiritual experiences that have connected you with spirit helpers or spirit guides? Without sharing personal information, can you share with me some of the ways they have helped you? How often and when do you talk with your ancestors? Would it help if we arranged for a visit from a tribal elder or medicine man?

*Source*: Adapted from Hodge & Limb (2009), with permission from Springer Science and Business Media.

explicitly acknowledged that certain ceremonies are private and should not be shared with nontribal members (or even with many tribal members in some cases). Likewise, the highly sensitive nature of spirit beings within Native Indian cultures is also noted.

In keeping with the diversity that exists within every tradition, it is important to note that the nomenclature used would not resonate with every American Indian. Hundreds of tribes exist in North America, each with their own distinct cultural value system (King & Trimble, 2013). The worldview of individual clients may be influenced by many factors, either alone or in combination with one another. Included among these are acculturation to the dominant secular culture, various forms of Christianity, the pan-American Indian movement, as well as clients' own tribal background. The point is to employ language that is commonly used among American Indians so as to legitimize the spiritual perspective conveyed by this language (Hodge & Limb, 2010a). Using culturally relevant language can also help build therapeutic rapport and assist clients and practitioners in the process of identifying important spiritual systems.

Once all relevant systems have been placed on the map, the relational information is added, as illustrated in the case example. If an eco-map is constructed for a family, then individual lines are typically drawn between each family member and the various spiritual systems in accordance with each person's understanding of the relationship (Hodge & Williams, 2002).

When working with couples and families, a number of options exist in terms of administering the assessment. For example, a couple might be asked to construct an eco-map together, or each person might be asked to develop an individual map. Alternatively, the couple might be asked to construct a map for each other, based on their perception of their spouse's relational connections. The resulting map can then be compared with the map featuring the spouse's own perceptions to identify areas in which perceptions are similar and different.

Relational information can be communicated in a variety of ways. For example, instead of using the thickness of the lines to denote the relative strength of the relationships, it is also possible to vary the number of lines, with more lines indicating stronger, more important relationships (Jung, 2010). Thus a single line would represent a weak relationship, two lines a normal relationship, three lines a strong relationship, four lines a very strong relationship, and so on.

Alternatively, colors might be used instead of thickness or number of lines as a way to indicate the relative strength or importance of various relationships. Colors can also be employed to supplement the information conveyed by the use of different types of lines. For instance, colors might be used to accentuate various features of a map or to designate certain types of relational information (e.g., red to denote a relationship that fosters anger; blue for a connection that engenders creativity).

Regardless of the method used to illustrate the character of the relationships, it is this capability to depict relational information about environmental systems that is responsible for some of this method's unique strengths. These assets are summarized in box 8.3 and discussed in the following section.

### STRENGTHS

As with all diagrammatic approaches, spiritual eco-maps provide an object that can serve as the focal point of discussion, an important consideration for clients hesitant to discuss delicate topics such as spirituality or alcoholism. By virtue of their design, however, eco-maps are especially adept at transferring attention from clients to the diagrammatic assessment. Spiritual eco-maps focus on environmental systems rather than, for example, clients' problems. While other approaches tend to emphasize clients, eco-maps explicitly stress the systems in their environments (Hartman, 1995).

BOX 8.3    STRENGTHS OF SPIRITUAL ECO-MAPS

Relational focus can mitigate concerns about discussing sensitive topics.

Clients generally understand the approach (especially in contrast to genograms).

Highlight potential resources in environment.

Visual presentation can foster self-understanding and clarify choices.

Are quick and relatively easy to construct.

Concepts can be integrated into a broader psychosocial assessment.

Provide a smooth transition to intervention planning.

Document salutary changes and reinforce treatment gains.

Consequently, this method may be particularly beneficial for clients who prefer indirect communication or are reluctant to proceed with a comprehensive assessment due to the sensitive nature of the subject matter.

Spiritual eco-maps are relatively easy to grasp at a conceptual level and visually highlight relationships to diverse environmental systems (Hodge & Limb, 2010b). Clients typically understand the need to examine sources of possible strength in their environments. Since problems are experienced in the present, it seems reasonable to look at the various environmental systems that may be related to current challenges. If clients perceive generational factors to be operative, they can be depicted on eco-maps as an environmental system. However, the resistance that can occur when clients are asked to construct spiritual genograms is often circumvented owing to the present-focused orientation of eco-maps.

The visual presentation of relational information is also a key feature. The physical portrayal of relational information can elicit new insights, identify untapped assets, and clarify choices. For instance, looking at an eco-map that depicts numerous energy-draining relationships can help clients understand why they have trouble making progress. Similarly, observing weak relationships with salutary spiritual systems suggests the possibility of leveraging those assets to address current challenges.

For example, Joseph's depiction of various health-promoting relationships, such as his positive relationship with his childhood friend, Steven, resulted in a decision to strengthen those relationships. For visually oriented people, eco-maps can help clients see their situation in a new light. Patterns become more apparent. Joseph realized that his life lacked balance given the strength of the draining relationships and weak nature of the salutary relationships.

Of the five comprehensive assessment approaches, spiritual eco-maps may take the least amount of time to administer. An eco-map can be constructed in approximately twenty to thirty minutes (Jung, 2010). The efficiency offered by this approach can be an important asset in practice settings where time is particularly constrained.

As illustrated in the case example, eco-maps can also be readily adapted to a broader assessment of psychosocial functioning by adding relevant environmental systems to the map. In this sense they are like spiritual histories. In contrast, the other methods may not be as amenable to being used in this capacity.

Because of their present orientation, spiritual eco-maps can also be effective in planning interventions, tracking changes, and reinforcing treatment gains. Regarding the former, once the eco-map has been completed, it can serve as a springboard for discussion about future changes clients would like to see. For example, the depiction of Joseph's detrimental and salutary relationships provided a natural transition to a discussion about how he would envision those relationships in the future.

Spiritual eco-maps can also be used to track and reinforce changes that occur during counseling. Reinforcing the perception that change is occurring is an important therapeutic concept (Hepworth et al., 2013). Progress, however, is often difficult to quantify. Constructing a new eco-map later in service provision, and comparing it to the original, demonstrates the changes that have occurred in a concrete manner.

Similarly, in the termination phase, eco-maps can be used to conclude service provision on a positive note by reviewing and recording the changes that have occurred. Clients might also be asked to review their spiritual eco-maps on a periodic basis to reinforce the gains they have made and inhibit relapse. Although the focus on present relational dynamics is associated with a number of strengths, some limitations should also be noted when considering this approach. These limitations are summarized in box 8.4 and discussed next.

## LIMITATIONS

Spiritual eco-maps may oversimplify relationships (Hodge & Limb, 2010b). Clients' connections with the spiritual systems in their environments are often complex and multifaceted. Eco-maps may not capture this nuance

BOX 8.4   LIMITATIONS OF SPIRITUAL ECO-MAPS

May oversimplify complex, multifaceted relationships.

May require practitioner assistance to construct, at least initially.

Are somewhat structured, with limited opportunity for creative expression.

Overlook important generational information.

in the same manner as, for example, spiritual histories. Likewise, they may hold relatively little appeal to clients who thrive on direct, face-to-face verbal interaction.

At a conceptual level, the notion of examining current resources to address current problems is typically readily understood. Nevertheless, some clients may experience difficulty constructing spiritual eco-maps. This method does not have the same natural appeal as spiritual lifemaps or histories, which are often quickly understood at an intuitive level because of their congruence with the notion of chronological story telling. Although spiritual eco-maps are relatively quick to construct with some degree of practice, practitioners may need to assist clients in the construction process, at least initially.

As a result, assigning spiritual eco-maps as a form of homework may be problematic. On a continuum of complexity, spiritual eco-maps fall somewhere between lifemaps and genograms. Once clients acclimate to the method, however, it may be possible to assign eco-maps as homework to, for example, document clinical progress.

Spiritual eco-maps allow for a moderate amount of creative expression. This method uses a certain framework to relate clients' spirituality. This approach employs more structure than lifemaps but less than genograms. Consequently, spiritual eco-maps may not appeal to more creative individuals. To some extent, however, this concern can be mitigated by encouraging artistic individuals to express their creativity by adding symbols, color, and other imaginative content to their eco-maps.

Another limitation is the exclusive focus on current relationships to present environmental systems. In some situations this can result in an assessment that overlooks important historical factors. Family history often plays a significant role in shaping clients' lives and their relationships to currently experienced challenges. In such situations, it is often critical to explore generational influences in tandem with present environmental systems. The following chapter discusses an approach that simultaneously assesses both generational and current resources.

# 9

# Spiritual Ecograms

SPIRITUAL ECOGRAMS REPRESENT A RELATIVELY new approach to assessment. They were created to fill the need that existed for an approach that explores current and past influences in a single diagrammatic instrument (Hodge, 2005e). For example, with some clients it is helpful to understand the assets and resources that exist in their present environment as well as in the wider family system going back through three generations. Ecograms address this need, combining the strengths of spiritual eco-maps and spiritual genograms in a single assessment approach (Limb & Hodge, 2011).

Put differently, spiritual ecograms portray information in space and across time (Hodge, 2005e). They depict present information that exists in space, like a spiritual *eco*-map, as well as information that exists across time, like a spiritual geno*gram*. Hence the name ecogram. Historical influences on current systems can be seen as well as current relationships to historical actors. Diverse connections between past and present functioning are illustrated simultaneously.

Although clients' relationship with the sacred is experienced in the present, it is also shaped by historical influences (Granqvist & Kirkpatrick, 2013). People are born into a particular family system, which in turn continues to influence their experience of the present. Clients' spiritual experience in the here and now is related to the historical influences that have affected their lives. It is this holistic interplay between past and present that spiritual ecograms attempt to capture.

Spiritual ecograms look much like an amalgamation of spiritual genograms and eco-maps (Limb & Hodge, 2011). The client appears in approximately the center of the page. The top half of the page charts the client's spiritual history across three generations (see chapter 7). The bottom half of the page features the client's current relationships to spiritual systems (see chapter 8).

Unique to ecograms, however, is the incorporation of the client's history as a spiritual system, alongside other spiritual systems in the client's present environment (Elliott, 2012). As noted above, many of the people and events in an individual's history continue to exhibit a strong influence in the present. Thus, in addition to sketching relationships between the client and spiritual systems that exist in a spiritual eco-map, lines are also drawn connecting the client with various aspects of the family history using the conventions listed in figure 8.1. This allows clients and practitioners to see the connections between past and present functioning on a single sheet of paper. As the case example of fifteen-year-old Ada suggests, this holistic presentation can be highly beneficial in many practice settings.

CASE EXAMPLE   Ada, a fifteen-year-old Asian American Muslim, had sought help from the school nurse for abdominal pains and headaches. In turn, the nurse had referred Ada to the school counselor when she witnessed a group of students teasing Ada for praying discreetly in-between classes and wearing a headscarf.

After spending some time getting to know Ada and her family, the counselor administered an ecogram (fig. 9.1). The counselor selected this approach to understand the role of Islam in Ada's life, communicate respect for Ada's family, and identify potential strengths and challenges. As illustrated on the ecogram, Ada's parents came to America from Pakistan roughly two decades ago along with Ada's paternal grandparents. Since everyone in Ada's family was Muslim, one format was used to denote those who immigrated to America, another to depict family members who remained in Pakistan, and another to portray particularly devout individuals.

Although Ada's paternal grandparents lived in a different part of town, they all attended the same mosque. Ada enjoyed attending the mosque as it provided her with the opportunity to interact with her grandmother, whom she really enjoyed, as well as other devout Muslim teenagers. Unfortunately, the mosque was ninety minutes away by car, which inhibited Ada's family from attending as often as they would like.

Ada's school relationships were far more challenging. Although Ada enjoyed learning, she was quiet and had few friends. On days the cafeteria served hot dogs or other foods containing pork, she often went hungry. She experienced intense internal conflict over participating in physical education classes because of her desire to fit in, on one hand, and her loyalty to her faith and her family's value system, which called for more modest attire relative to her classmates, on the other. As a result of her efforts to live out her spirituality, she was picked on frequently. Ada coped by internalizing the pain and suffering quietly in shame.

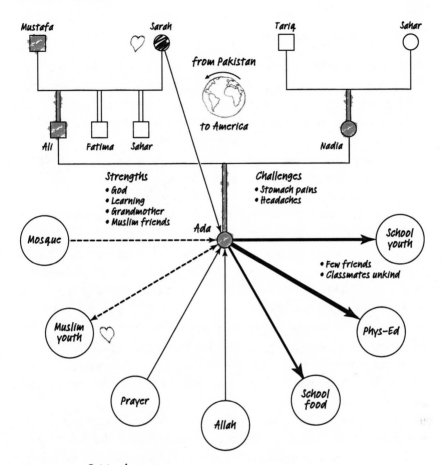

FIGURE 9.1 Spiritual ecogram

The physical depiction of Ada's relationships on the ecogram helped to validate emotions of which she was only partially aware. It also heightened her parents' awareness of the isolation and the challenges she faced at school. As a result, they decided to prioritize attending services at the mosque on a regular basis and encouraged Ada to begin having online video conversations with her grandmother during the week. Ada's counselor arranged for the cafeteria to provide its menu to Ada in advance so she could bring food from home when needed. The counselor also worked with Ada's father to arrange for their imam to come and speak at the school about Islam to help others understand and appreciate the Islamic value system. The counselor also worked collaboratively to develop some Islamically modified CBT self-statements. Ada agreed to incorporate these statements into her prayers throughout the day, an endeavor supported by her parents, her grandmother, and her imam.

## ADMINISTERING A SPIRITUAL ECOGRAM

Administering spiritual ecograms is similar to the process used for spiritual genograms and eco-maps. In other words, the same basic procedures used to construct these pictorial assessments are used to create spiritual ecograms. Interested readers may wish to consult the previous two chapters that dealt with these methods for additional details.

There are, however, a few issues that are unique to ecograms. Of all the approaches presented in this text, spiritual ecograms are perhaps the most complex (Hodge & Limb, 2010b). This can introduce specific challenges to the administration process. For instance, fitting all the information on a single sheet of paper can be problematic.

To address this potential problem, it is helpful to obtain the basic data needed for a particular ecogram before starting construction (McGoldrick et al., 2008). This information helps ensure that space is appropriately allocated on the paper. Key data to procure include (1) the number of times each parent was married, (2) the number of siblings each parent has and their respective birth orders, and (3) the number of significant spiritual systems that exist. Once the bones of the ecogram have been delineated on paper, this skeleton can be fleshed out with the appropriate spiritual and religious content.

The individual client, couple, or family is typically placed slightly below the center of the paper to allow adequate space to chart the flow of spirituality across three generations on the top of the page. It can be helpful to begin filling in the generational information first, to help establish rapport with the client. The assessment then might move to the more personal, present-focused information, which also sets the stage for subsequent discussion of possible interventions.

The degree to which spirituality is employed to help solve problems within the context of counseling depends on a number of factors, including practitioners' level of spiritual competence and their theoretical orientation. As noted previously, practitioners whose work is informed by strengths-based, solution-focused, or brief theoretical frameworks will frequently benefit from exploring how clients' spiritual assets might be deployed to address challenges. Similarly, as the case example illustrates, a comprehensive assessment can help practitioners proficient in CBT identify spiritual precepts and practices that can be incorporated into cognitive behavioral protocols (Hodge & Nadir, 2008; Nielsen, 2004).

CBT is among the most effective treatment modalities for a wide variety of psychological problems (Chorpita et al., 2011; Hollon & Ponniah, 2010). Research also indicates that CBT modified to incorporate clients' spiritual values is highly effective (Hook et al., 2010; Tan, 2013; Worthington, Hook, Davis, & McDaniel, 2011). In spiritually modified CBT, standard cognitive behavioral treatment protocols are modified with spiritual beliefs and practices drawn from clients' spiritual worldviews. The cognitive restructuring techniques and the behavioral assignments are identical to traditional CBT. However, once unproductive beliefs and behaviors are identified, they are replaced with salutary schema and actions drawn from clients' spiritual narratives.

Table 9.1 features some Islamically modified CBT protocols that might be relevant in work with Ada. The table lists four secular self-statements, primarily drawn from the work of Ellis (2000), and the underlying therapeutic concept each statement is designed to address (e.g., needing approval and love). It also delineates the equivalent statements that have been modified to increase their level of cultural congruence with Muslims.

The underlying therapeutic concepts are the same in both sets of statements. In the spiritually modified statements, the secular terminology used to express the concepts has been reworked so that the statements reflect common Islamic values. Put differently, the underlying therapeutic concepts have been repackaged in theistic terminology drawn from Ada's spiritual value system. Further information is available elsewhere on the process of constructing Islamically modified CBT statements (Hodge & Nadir, 2008) and spiritually modified CBT statements in general (Hodge, 2008). Readers may also benefit from obtaining a detailed case example employing this modality (Nielsen, 2004).

Articulating the therapeutic concepts in Islamic terminology increases the likelihood that Ada will successfully incorporate the statements into her personal narrative. The modification process renders the statements more personally meaningful to Ada, her family, and her religious community. In addition to enlisting community support for the implementation of the protocols, this phrasing can help mitigate the stigma associated with seeking help that exists in some cultures (Loewenthal, 2013).

TABLE 9.1    Secular and Islamically Modified CBT Protocols

| SECULAR SELF-STATEMENTS | ISLAMICALLY MODIFIED STATEMENTS |
|---|---|
| **Needing approval and love** | |
| It is highly preferable to be approved of, to be loved by significant people, and to have good social skills. But if I am disapproved of, I can still fully accept myself and lead an enjoyable life. | Although it is nice to have the favor of others, we do not need the approval of others. True satisfaction and solace is found in our relationship with Allah. Our regular remembrance of Allah helps us to know that He loves us. |
| **Self-acceptance** | |
| If I fail at school, work, or some other setting, it is not a reflection on my whole being. (My whole being includes how I am as a friend, daughter, etc., as well as qualities of helpfulness, kindness, etc.) Further, failure is not a permanent condition. | Allah knows us better than we know ourselves. Allah knows our weakness. Allah knows we make mistakes. Consequently, we can take comfort in Allah's mercy and accept ourselves with our strengths and weaknesses. |
| **Self-worth** | |
| I am a worthwhile person with positive and negative traits. | We have worth because we are created in Allah. We are created with strengths and weaknesses. |
| **High frustration tolerance** | |
| Nothing is terrible or awful, only—at worst—highly inconvenient. I can stand serious frustrations and adversity, even though I never have to like them. | Misfortunes and blessings are from Allah. Misfortunes are not terrible or awful, but rather a test. Although adversity may be unpleasant, we can withstand it. Allah tells us that He will not test us beyond what we can bear. By reminding ourselves of Allah's goodness, and engaging in prayer, we can cope with life's challenges. |

*Source*: Hodge & Nadir (2008).

At a broader level, table 9.1 illustrates how interventions can be adapted to increase their relevance to clients. In the same way that the questions used to administer an assessment should be tailored to reflect clients' value systems, the interventions that flow from the assessment can also often be modified (Tan, 2013). Indeed, the information obtained by administering virtually any comprehensive assessment can be used to tailor interventions so as to increase their cultural relevance. Although this strength is not unique to spiritual ecograms, the next section discusses some advantages that are associated with this approach (see box 9.1 for a summary of these advantages).

### STRENGTHS

A central asset of spiritual ecograms is their capability to provide a holistic view of spirituality. Ecograms implicitly acknowledge the interconnected nature of reality and offer clients and practitioners a forum in which to see the larger picture (Elliott, 2012). As part of this process, they integrate historical and present influences, offering a more relationally based understanding of environmental impacts on functioning.

In turn, the depiction of both generational and relational influences can help elicit new understandings, assets, and options (Hodge & Limb, 2010b). All diagrammatic approaches help people see events through fresh eyes via the process of delineating spirituality in a concrete, objective manner. The comprehensive representation afforded by ecograms can, however, be especially effective in sparking new insights.

To follow up on the case example, the ecogram helped Ada to recognize the various emotions she was experiencing at a largely unconscious level. Even though she had many generational sources of support, her present, relational dynamics were far more challenging. The concrete depiction of her difficult relational dynamics validated her suffering and implicitly gave her permission to recognize her previously somatized feelings. Likewise,

BOX 9.1    **STRENGTHS OF SPIRITUAL ECOGRAMS**

Holistic depiction acknowledges the interconnected nature of reality.

Offer clients and practitioners the ability to see the big picture.

Elicit new understandings, assets, and options relative to eco-maps/genograms.

Relational emphasis can mitigate unease discussing spirituality.

Can be used to document therapeutic changes over time.

Communicate respect for the extended family.

Provide additional, present-oriented data with interfaith and same-faith couples.

Present orientation may mitigate client reluctance to explore generational data.

the visual portrayal helped Ada's family understand her situational context in a fuller, more extensive manner relative to other approaches such as spiritual genograms or eco-maps.

A similar dynamic exists regarding the identification of spiritual strengths. Spiritual ecograms illustrate current and historical assets as well as the connections between these resources in clients' lived realities. Visually highlighting spiritual assets in present space and across generations can suggest new options for tackling problems (McGoldrick et al., 2008). In Ada's case the comprehensive portrayal of relational dynamics helped to identify clinical strategies that tapped both present and generational resources, such as attending the mosque on a weekly basis and strengthening Ada's salutary relationship with her grandmother. The visual delineation of a more extensive range of options also helps engender hope that currently experienced challenges can be overcome.

In a manner similar to eco-maps, spiritual ecograms can mitigate client unease with the topic of spirituality. The relational emphasis tends to deflect attention from clients to the spiritual systems in their environment. Ecograms largely replicate this strength while also providing generational data.

Ecograms are also useful for documenting change over time. New ecograms can be constructed to track and reinforce changes. In Ada's case a new ecogram might be constructed in a few months to reinforce the positive changes stemming from the implementation of the various interventions. This provides a way to quantify the changes that are occurring in clients' lives, which is an important therapeutic task (Hepworth et al., 2013). This process could be simplified by leaving out generational information that clients deem extraneous.

Like spiritual genograms, ecograms implicitly communicate respect for the wider family system. This can be important when working with clients from cultures that privilege this value (e.g., Muslims, Hindus, Latter-day Saints). Although charting family history can be time consuming, it can play an important role in establishing rapport. In Ada's case it helped to reassure her family that the counselor valued their involvement and would support, rather than subvert, their faith.

Ecograms can also be productively employed with couples. They can supplement the generational information provided by spiritual genograms through the depiction of relational data that reflect connections to both present and historical systems (McGoldrick et al., 2008). This can provide a richer set of options with various clients, such as interfaith couples struggling with religious differences. Similarly, ecograms can be a good fit for same-faith couples seeking to increase their intimacy by building on areas of shared interests. For example, currently experienced strengths, such as prayer, might be supported by drawing on family traditions that encourage this practice as a means to enhance couples' functioning (Fincham & Beach, 2013).

In addition, the incorporation of relational data can alleviate concerns about the time spent exploring historical information. As noted in chapter 7, some clients are reluctant to spend time examining generational factors since they do not see a connection between past functioning and present problems. This disinclination can exist even when generational factors are clearly related to the challenges clients face. The holistic approach of spiritual ecograms can help reduce this hesitancy by treating the generational components as a set of spiritual systems that are experienced in the present. In this sense, the focus is shifted from generational factors to clients' relationship to spiritual systems in their present environment. As noted in chapter 8, the need to examine present relationships to address currently experienced problems is widely understood.

Owing to their comprehensive nature, spiritual ecograms require a considerable investment of time and thought to construct. Considering all the various aspects of one's spirituality can be an important asset. For example, positive spiritual narratives may be reinforced and spiritual strengths that have previously been overlooked may be identified. The flip side of this strength, however, is a notable shortcoming. These shortcomings are discussed in the next section and summarized in box 9.2.

### LIMITATIONS

Perhaps the most prominent limitation of spiritual ecograms is their complexity (Hodge & Limb, 2010b). Integrating concepts drawn from spiritual genograms and eco-maps into a single diagrammatic instrument is not a simple matter. Indeed, of all the approaches discussed, ecograms may be the most complex. As a result, clients can have difficulty understanding this method. Consequently, practitioners must frequently invest a substantial amount of time explaining and helping construct ecograms. Even under the best of circumstances, the construction process is rather time consuming.

BOX 9.2   LIMITATIONS OF SPIRITUAL ECOGRAMS

Are very complex.

Are difficult to understand and construct.

Speaking of those who have passed on is forbidden in many indigenous cultures.

Limited opportunity exists for creative expression.

Multifaceted relationships may be oversimplified.

May explore dimensions of clients' stories unrelated to presenting problem.

This complexity also limits their use in other ways. For example, as with other diagrammatic approaches, ecograms can be used with individuals, couples, or families (Tanyi, 2006). For instance, an assessment might be administered to each family member and the results compared, a process that helps to illustrate differences in perceptions among members of the family unit. Alternatively, couples or families might complete an assessment jointly, a process that can foster unity and cohesion as family members work together to complete a task. Because of the complexity of ecograms, however, it is often difficult for families, and sometimes even couples, to complete one together (McGoldrick et al., 2008). The problems associated with constructing spiritual genograms are often compounded with ecograms owing to the incorporation of additional data regarding present relational dynamics. In many cases it is difficult to fit all the information on a single sheet of paper in a coherent manner, especially with large families.

Spiritual ecograms share some of the limitations associated with spiritual genograms. For instance, many indigenous cultures prohibit inquiring about people who have passed on, limited opportunity exists for creative expression, and multifaceted relationships may be oversimplified. Likewise, spiritual dimensions that are unrelated to clients' presenting challenges may be explored, misusing time that might be spent more productively on other issues.

Accordingly, other comprehensive approaches may better serve clients and practitioners. For example, spiritual eco-maps require less time to construct and may provide all the information needed. In other situations, practitioners may desire to use the limited amount of page space to amplify the generational dynamics in a spiritual genogram. Lifemaps may provide a better assessment approach with more artistic individuals, and spiritual histories may be better suited for more verbally oriented clients.

Spiritual ecograms, like all the other assessment approaches discussed up to this point, employ what might be called an explicit approach to assessment. Beginning with the iCARING brief assessment, the discussion of each tool has been premised on the assumption that clients are more or less comfortable with an overt or explicit discussion of spirituality or religion. Explicit approaches, however, may not be effective with all clients (McSherry, 2010).

Certain clients are uncomfortable with an explicit discussion of either spirituality or religion. Explicit assessments may be contraindicated with such clients. Yet in some cases successful service provision is contingent on understanding how the sacred manifests in their lives. The next chapter discusses an alternative approach to assessment that offers a more culturally congruent method for conducting assessments with such individuals.

# 10

# Implicit Spiritual Assessment

IMPLICIT SPIRITUAL ASSESSMENTS WERE DEVELOPED to provide an alternative approach to assessment. Traditional assessment methods are predicated on the assumption that clients are generally comfortable talking about spirituality or religion. Accordingly, such approaches may be ineffective with clients who are uncomfortable with spiritual language or who are otherwise hesitant to discuss spirituality overtly. Implicit assessments were developed to meet the need for a valid assessment method for such clients.

This chapter begins by describing an implicit assessment, along with the populations for whom this approach is particularly well suited. The process of administering an implicit assessment is discussed, sample questions are provided to help operationalize this approach, and a case example is used to illustrate how an implicit assessment might be used in clinical settings. The chapter concludes by offering suggestions for integrating an implicit assessment with more traditional assessment approaches.

## WHAT IS AN IMPLICIT ASSESSMENT?

An implicit spiritual assessment employs terminology that is implicitly spiritual in nature to explore content in clients' narratives that is potentially relevant to service provision (Hodge, 2013a). The assessment is driven by existentially oriented questions. These items do not mention spirituality or religion, nor do they refer to prayer, meditation, mindfulness, or other concepts that are associated with various religious traditions. Rather they employ what might be called existential or psycho-spiritual language that suggests the possibility of a higher, transcendent dimension of existence.

Specifically, the assessment centers on concepts such as joy, peace, meaning, passion, purpose, and forgiveness. These and other analogous terms are commonly used in spiritual contexts. For instance, they are often employed to describe the effects or outcomes that flow from an intimate relationship with God or the transcendent (Swinton, 2010). Accordingly, this language conveys rich, emotionally powerful connotations that invite a spiritual exploration (Pargament, 2007).

Such assessments will not resonate with all clients. For some clients, however, they can be instrumental in eliciting clinically relevant information. As such, implicit assessments provide a method to identify and operationalize dimensions of clients' experience that may be critical to effective service provision but would otherwise be overlooked in an explicit spiritual assessment.

Who might benefit from this type of assessment? An implicit assessment can be productively employed with diverse client populations (Canda & Furman, 2010). There are, however, two groups of people for whom implicit spiritual assessments may be particularly useful: (1) those who doubt practitioners' level of spiritual competence, and (2) those who view explicit spiritual language to be irrelevant to their lived realities.

## CONCERNS ABOUT SPIRITUAL COMPETENCE

Some clients question practitioners' ability to address spirituality appropriately (Hodge, 2013b). These individuals are often comfortable using spiritual language but unsure about the degree to which they can trust practitioners with a topic in which they are highly invested (Lewis, 2001). In short, they are hesitant to trust practitioners with a sacred dimension of their being until practitioners have demonstrated an ability to interact with them in a spiritually competent manner (Richards & Bergin, 2005).

This concern is so acute that many people avoid seeking help entirely. Using a national sample of likely voters, researchers have examined the reasons that people elect not to seek professional help for mental and emotional problems (Boorstin & Schlachter, 2000). The most prominent reason cited is the belief that they can handle their problems on their own. The second most common reason was fear that their spiritual values and beliefs would not be respected or taken seriously. Apprehension about practitioners' spiritual competence ranked ahead of financial concerns, the third most prominent reason given for avoiding professional assistance.

Fear that their spiritual beliefs would not be respected was especially pronounced among African Americans and evangelical Christians, two overlapping groups (Boorstin & Schlachter, 2000).

The perceptions of evangelical Christians are commonly examined because they are the largest subculture in the United States (Hodge, 2004a). Ascertaining representative views of smaller subcultures can be difficult owing to sampling problems and related issues. Nevertheless, concerns about lack of spiritual competence also appear to exist among members of many other subcultures, including, for example, traditional Catholics, Latter-day Saints, American Indians, Muslims, Hindus, and Orthodox Jews (Richards & Bergin, 2014).

Why would clients from these traditions be hesitant to discuss spirituality with practitioners? Helping professionals are often assumed to be members of the dominant secular culture (Richards & Bergin, 2005), with its associated beliefs and values (Hodge, 2009). Indeed, the secularization stemming from the European-based Enlightenment has animated discourse in social work (Holloway & Moss, 2010) and most other professions since the beginning of the twentieth century (Smith, 2003a). In many cases this resulted in spirituality being ignored or otherwise marginalized in professional discourse up until very recently (Cnaan, Wineburg, & Boddie, 1999).

Furthermore, a number of leading authorities have framed devout spirituality as a form of psychopathology that helping professionals should actively attempt to mitigate. Included among these individuals are key actors such as Sigmund Freud. Freud, the father of psychoanalysis, is perhaps the most influential person in the history of counseling. In *The Future of an Illusion*, Freud (1964 [1927]) posited that religion represents a form of mental illness, or more specifically an "obsessional neurosis."

Albert Ellis serves as another case in point. Ellis is widely viewed as the founder of the modern CBT movement. In *The Case Against Religion*, Ellis (1980) argued that religion is a form of "emotional illness" that creates and maintains "neuroses and psychoses."

It is important to note that the weight of the empirical evidence eventually caused Ellis (2000) to revise his earlier beliefs. Later in his career he acknowledged that religion is not necessarily linked to pathology. Nevertheless, he maintained his belief in the superiority of his personal atheistic belief system in terms of fostering mental health. Thus, while religion could be associated with wellness, secularist worldviews were still preferred.

Given the views of these and other thought leaders, it is perhaps unsurprising that analysis has revealed various forms of spiritual bias in numerous forums and disciplines. Included among these are the *DSM III-R* (Larson, Milano, & Lu, 1998), social work (Hodge, Baughman, & Cummings, 2006), nursing (McEwen, 2004), medicine (Laird, Marrais, & Barnes, 2007), psychology (Inbar & Lammers, 2012), and other fields (Yancey, 2011). Clients are often acutely aware of these biases, which often unconsciously inform clinical assessments (Aponte, 2009).

Indeed, concerns about practitioners' level of spiritual competence are underscored by the fact that many practitioners appear to have received little, if any, training on spiritual competence as part of their formal education. For instance, most social workers (Canda & Furman, 2010; Sheridan, 2009), counselors (Walker, Gorsuch, & Tan, 2004), psychologists (Shafranske & Cummings, 2013; Vogel et al., 2013), marriage and family therapists (Carlson, Kirkpatrick, Hecker, & Killmer, 2002), physicians, and many other helping professionals (Koenig, 2013) report receiving minimal training in spirituality.

Put differently, a difference in worldviews frequently exists between clients, who tend to affirm theistic spiritualities, and practitioners, who disproportionately affirm secularism or nontheistic spiritualities that share many values with Enlightenment-based secularism (Shafranske & Cummings, 2013). In addition, the paucity of training in spirituality raises the possibility that even the most well-intentioned practitioners may inadvertently communicate disrespect for clients' spiritual beliefs due to lack of knowledge regarding potentially sensitive issues. It is difficult to avoid stepping on rhetorical landmines if one does not know the territory being traversed.

Consequently, some clients may indicate that they are uninterested in discussing spirituality during the initial brief assessment (Richards & Bergin, 2005). Trust may be developed over time, however, as clients interact with practitioners, particularly over controversial topics such as abortion, gender roles, sexual orientation, and parenting practices. As clients sense that practitioners' underlying posture is one of acceptance and respect for diversity, they may revise their initial decision.

An implicit assessment provides a way to gently ease into the topic at a later point in service provision, after rapport and trust have deepened.

An implicit approach provides a forum in which practitioners can communicate interest, openness, receptivity, and respect for clients' beliefs and values (Canda & Furman, 2010). In such instances, when clients question practitioners' level of spiritual competence, an implicit assessment offers a means to build trust and respect regarding spirituality and extend an implied invitation to enter into a more in-depth discussion of the topic. In the next section, a substantially different population who may benefit from an implicit assessment is discussed.

## SPIRITUAL LANGUAGE IS IRRELEVANT

For some clients, the spiritual and religious language used in a brief assessment does not resonate with their worldviews. As noted in chapter 1, many different understandings of spirituality exist (Ammerman, 2013). Some individuals define spirituality in terms of an individual's relationship with the sacred (Pargament, 2013b). The sacred includes God, but it can also include other entities that people imbue with transcendent meaning.

Included under this umbrella are entities that are essentially secular in nature (Crisp, 2010). Examples include nature, sports, gardening, and a myriad of other activities and entities (Pargament, 2007). These entities are not generally viewed as sacred in and of themselves. They can, however, be constructed as sacred. In other words, these entities function in a manner analogous to God in the lives of devout theists, providing certain individuals with a transcendent sense of meaning and purpose.

Clients' relationship with the sacred can have implications for service provision (Crisp, 2010). This is true regardless of how the sacred is conceptualized. As the case example later in this chapter illustrates, even "secular" entities can have significant ramifications for service provision if they are accorded a sacred role in clients' lives (Griffith & Griffith, 2002).

For some individuals in this category, typical spiritual terminology is irrelevant to their lived experience. Spirituality and related terms can seem like a culturally foreign language or artifacts of a culture that was abandoned long ago. Even though secular activities serve what can be considered an essentially spiritual function, these clients may be uncomfortable or even unwilling to discuss these functions in the context of an explicit spiritual assessment.

In such cases an implicit spiritual assessment provides a culturally appropriate vehicle to identify the role of the sacred in clients' lives. Indeed, for such clients, an implicit assessment is virtually the only means through which their understanding of the sacred can be explored. How does one know when to conduct such an assessment? This issue is discussed next.

## TUNING SPIRITUAL RADAR TO DETECT THE SACRED

As implied earlier, assessment is an ongoing process (Ross & McSherry, 2010). Although a brief assessment is typically conducted at the beginning of service provision, practitioners must remain open to revising their initial working hypotheses as additional information is obtained during subsequent encounters. It is important to remain open to the possibility that spirituality plays an important role in clients' lives, even though the initial brief assessment suggests that it is not relevant to service provision.

Toward this end, practitioners' "spiritual radar" should be switched on and appropriately tuned. The aim is to develop sensitivity to interactions that suggest spirituality is a relevant dimension in clients' lives (Griffith & Griffith, 2002). Particularly helpful in this regard are listening for implied spiritual content in clients' stories and attending to changes in clients' emotions as they relate their narratives.

### Language That Alludes to the Spiritual

Practitioners' spiritual radar should be tuned to listen for language that suggests the presence of the sacred. In the same way that explicit spiritual terminology does not resonate with certain clients, some practitioners may not pick up on implicitly spiritual language (Pargament & Krumrei, 2009). Accordingly, it is important to listen for phrasing that suggests the existence of spiritually relevant topics in the course of clinical conversations.

For example, language that parallels spiritual beliefs and behaviors can indicate the existence of the sacred. Beliefs, practices, and experiences may be described that are not explicitly spiritual but reflect an underlying sacred dimension. For instance, clients may participate in certain activities, causes, or events on a regular basis that are perceived to be highly meaningful. Such rituals or ceremonies may serve a sacred purpose in clients' lives, engendering a transcendent sense of meaning and purpose (Crisp, 2010).

Similarly, using major polarities or speaking in extremes may signify the presence of the sacred (Pargament, 2007). Referring to a person as perfect, faultless, or flawless raises the possibility that aspects of the divine are being attributed to the individual. Alternatively, fixating on the negative, as occurs when someone is "demonized," may indicate that the individual has violated what is held sacred.

In sum, practitioners' spiritual radar should be tuned to detect terminology that may signal the presence of the sacred. Clients often describe thoughts, experiences, and feelings that parallel the spiritual. These descriptions can denote the existence of clinically relevant topics that require further exploration, in much the same way that shifts in affect can signal the presence of such topics.

### Shifts in Affect

As clients relate their stories, changes in affect might also be noted. Many individuals experience the sacred primarily through their feelings (Pargament & Krumrei, 2009). Indeed, spiritual experiences can produce especially powerful emotions.

Encounters with the transcendent often engender positive feelings (Lee, Poloma, & Post, 2013). Interactions with the sacred frequently result in feelings of love, joy, excitement; awe, solemnity, reverence; and hope, meaning, and purpose. Although positive emotions are perhaps more common, interactions with the sacred can also yield negative emotions, such as anger, discouragement, and disappointment (Exline et al., 2011). Clients might, for instance, express deep disappointment over being forced to relinquish a sacred activity that nourished their soul as a result of having children, moving to a new geographic location, or becoming bedridden.

Accordingly, practitioners' spiritual radar should be alert for changes in affect during the course of conversation (Griffith & Griffith, 2002). The emergence of an atypical emotion may indicate that a spiritually relevant topic has been touched on. For instance, a hint of emotion in a client who is otherwise depressed—such as a sparkle in the eye or a smile—may indicate the presence of the sacred. Indeed, as the conversation touches on the sacred, clients may not be fully cognizant of their responses or perhaps may even exhibit surprise over their emotional responses.

Understanding what elicits powerful emotions can provide important insights into clients' relationship with the sacred. In addition to watching for these types of emotional displays, practitioners can facilitate this process through active exploration (Crisp, 2010).

### ADMINISTERING AN IMPLICIT SPIRITUAL ASSESSMENT

If practitioners' spiritual radar detects language or changes in affect that suggest spirituality may be related to service provision, it is typically appropriate to explore this possibility in more depth through the administration of an implicit spiritual assessment. It is critical, however, that client autonomy be respected during this process (Hodge, 2013b). Clients' reactions should be carefully monitored to ensure that clients remain supportive of the process throughout the exploration.

To administer an implicit assessment, existentially oriented questions are employed. These questions are designed to elicit content about clients' relationship with the sacred in contexts in which a more direct exploration of spirituality is contraindicated. A number of authors have developed questions for such assessments (Canda & Furman, 2010; Griffith & Griffith, 2002; Hodge, 2013b; Pargament, 2007; Pargament & Krumrei, 2009). The questions, featured in box 10.1, represent an attempt to build on the strengths of this prior work to provide practitioners with options for indirectly exploring the role of spirituality in clients' lives.

The questions are depicted in a manner similar to a traditional chronological spiritual history (see chapter 5). The first question set—past spirituality—explores how the sacred is manifested in the past, providing a context for understanding how it might shape functioning in the present. In a similar manner, identifying coping strategies that have been used in the past suggests options for addressing current problems (Canda & Furman, 2010).

The second set—present spirituality—examines contemporary experiences of the sacred in four areas: conceptualizations of the sacred, expression and experience of the sacred, spiritual efficacy, and spiritual environment. These questions may be particularly helpful in fleshing out clients' understanding of the sacred. For example, given that clients can

BOX 10.1    CONDUCTING AN IMPLICIT SPIRITUAL ASSESSMENT

### Past Spirituality

What gave you joy growing up?

When were you happiest?

When you think back on your younger years, what things gave you a sense of meaning? A sense of purpose? Hope for the future?

What sort of experiences stood out for you when you were growing up?

How did you cope with challenging situations?

Over the course of your life, what accomplishments are you particularly proud of?

### Present Spirituality

*Conceptualizations of the Sacred*

Whom/what do you put your hope in?

Who/what gives you a sense of purpose and meaning in life?

Where do you find a sense of peace (or inspiration)?

Whom/what do you rely on most in life?

For what are you deeply grateful?

To whom/what are you most devoted?

To whom/what do you most freely express love?

Who best understands your situation?

What things are you most passionate about in life?

What causes you the greatest despair/suffering?

*Expression and Experience of Spirituality*

When have you felt most deeply and fully alive?

Where do you find peace?

At the deepest levels of your being, what nurtures or strengthens you?

What pulls you down and discourages you?

What nourishes your soul?

What feeds your spirit?

What helps you feel most aware (or centered)?

What kinds of experiences provide you with the deepest sense of meaning in life?

If you had a magic wand, what would you change to make your life more meaningful?

What rituals/practices are especially important to you?

BOX 10.1 (CONTINUED)

Can you describe recent experiences (e.g., "aha moments") that sparked new insights?

How do you commemorate special occasions/accomplishments?

When in your life have you experienced forgiveness?

What are your deepest regrets?

### Spiritual Efficacy

What sustains you in the midst of your troubles?

What helps you get through times of difficulty (or crisis)?

What sources of strength do you draw on to keep pressing forward?

When you are afraid/in pain, how do you find comfort/solace?

How have difficult situations changed your life for the better? The worse?

What gives you the strength to carry on day after day?

What would you like to be able to let go of in your life?

What has this experience taught you that you wish you had never known?

What have you discovered about yourself that you find most disturbing?

### Spiritual Environment

Who truly understands your situation?

Who supports you in difficult times? How so?

Who does not support you in difficult times? How so?

## Future Spirituality

What are you striving for in your life?

If you only had a year to live, what are the most important things you would like
to accomplish?

What are your goals for the future?

Why is it important that you are here in this world?

What legacy would you like to leave behind in your life?

How would you like people to remember you when you are gone?

become overwhelmed by their presenting problems, the questions in the spiritual efficacy subset may be helpful in identifying salutary practices to assist clients on their journey toward health and wellness (Saleebey, 2013).

The final question set—future spirituality—explores the role of the sacred as it intersects the future. Future aspirations are an important part of clients' sacred narratives. In the same way that past and present beliefs can shape current functioning, clients' beliefs about the future can also shape present behaviors. Accordingly, an exploration of future plans, goals, dreams, and expectations can provide important clinical insights (Hodge, 2005f).

These questions can be integrated into the flow of conversation as warranted on an individualized basis. Although the questions are presented in a chronological manner, this format is frequently unsuitable for conducting implicit assessments. Rather, practitioners should be alert to the possibility that spirituality may be clinically relevant at any time and ask questions that invite a deeper exploration of spirituality when clients' words or emotions allude to the presence of the sacred.

An implicit assessment typically occurs after the administration of a brief assessment has suggested an explicit examination of spirituality is inappropriate (Pargament, 2007). Thus the process differs from the explicit assessment approaches reviewed in previous chapters. In an implicit assessment, questions are selected, adapted, and integrated into the conversation in an individualized manner that makes sense in the context of multiple factors, including the evolving clinical relationship, clients' unique narratives, and practitioners' clinical judgment. To be sure, listening for language that suggests the sacred, attending to emotional shifts, and incorporating implicit spiritual questions into the conversation constitute a complex, multilevel process that varies from individual to individual. Yet as the case example of Emily, a thirty-seven-year-old European American lesbian, illustrates, this process can lead to significant clinical breakthroughs.

CASE EXAMPLE   Emily, a thirty-seven-year-old European American lesbian, was recently referred to counseling by her medical doctor after expressing despair during a follow-up exam for Lyme disease. Emily had always been an active person with an interest in sports and outdoor activities. She met her partner, Angie, on a hiking expedition with an Audubon group in the Rocky Mountains six years ago. With their shared love of adventure and nature, Emily and Angie's relationship developed quickly.

Two years ago, on one of their numerous camping trips, Emily was bitten by a tick and infected with Lyme disease. The accompanying flu-like symptoms of fever, headaches, and vomiting drained Emily of her usual spunk and energy. On many days she was unable to get out of bed and passed the time listlessly watching television. Two years of medical treatment, both conventional and alternative, produced little change. Emily's relationship with Angie was strained, and their financial resources had dwindled as a result of the costs of the alternative treatments. Emily's usual optimism had been replaced with despair and anxiety about her future, including her future with Angie.

A brief assessment was administered at the beginning of therapy. Emily described herself as an agnostic who had gradually drifted away from the Metropolitan Community Church (MCC) over a decade ago and had little present interest in spirituality. Her therapist saw no need to explore her evolution away from the MCC since it seemed unconnected to her presenting problem. Treatment consisted of individual and couples therapy in which Emily and Angie processed the multiple ways Lyme disease was affecting their lives. Naming their losses helped to normalize their grief and decrease the distance that had grown between Emily and Angie.

The sacred emerged as a salient factor, however, when the therapist explored how Emily had coped with the loss of her mother some years ago. Emily shared that when she was upset or frustrated about something in the past, she would go bike riding on a path near her home or explore new trails in the mountains. Emily's voice quickened and her eyes sparkled as she described drinking in the panoramic views, observing the natural rhythms of plant and animal life, and breathing in the fresh air. Subsequent exploration revealed that Emily used to employ specific practices to help feed her spirit. Particularly important to Emily was the practice of journaling. On hikes she would frequently take a notebook along and journal her thoughts as she sat near a river's edge. This practice helped to release negative emotions, clear detrimental thoughts from her mind, and set her heart at peace.

As it became clear that the onset of Lyme disease had largely disconnected Emily from the sacred, therapy turned toward exploring ways in which she could reestablish this relationship. In light of Emily's interest in journaling, the therapist invited Emily and Angie to construct a spiritual lifemap for homework that depicted all the different ways in which Emily used to draw strength from nature over the course of her life. Using the lifemap as a jumping off point in the next session, the therapist brainstormed with Emily and Angie how they could engage in outdoor activities within the constraints imposed by Emily's physical limitations.

Working together, they developed a number of creative strategies, including taking trips to the local botanical garden, walking down the bike path, planting a garden, learning photography, and rejoining the Audubon society. These strategies helped to reengage Emily in the things that gave her passion for life while also shifting her focus away from her pain and fostering intimacy in her relationship with Angie. On days when she wasn't well enough to go on a walk, take a scenic drive, or attend Audubon social activities with Angie, she sat by their garden and journaled. When she could muster the energy, Emily took photographs of nature. In light of this progress, the therapist invited Emily to reflect on her lifemap and possible next steps she might take in her journey. Emily decided to morph her photographs and journal entries into a blog about her experiences with Lyme disease. This lessened her isolation and gave her a sense that she was contributing to others struggling with the disease.

This case example illustrates how the sacred can emerge as a clinically relevant issue at essentially any time during the therapeutic dialogue. This same point about the potential manifestation of the sacred was also noted in the case example featuring Martina in chapter 5. However, in Martina's case, the impromptu emergence of spirituality led to an explicit assessment, in keeping with the traditional Catholic spirituality revealed in the brief assessment.

In the present example, the use of an explicit assessment was contraindicated. The brief assessment indicated that Emily had little interest in discussing spirituality. Yet, as with Martina, the sacred emerged as a critical issue in counseling. An implicit assessment provided a vehicle to access this area in a way that resonated with Emily's worldview. Without this vehicle, spiritual resources instrumental to Emily's wellness may have been inadequately marshaled or even overlooked entirely.

Implicit assessments are administered to facilitate understanding of the intersection between the sacred and wellness. As comprehension is gained, interventions can be tailored accordingly. As Emily's case demonstrates, this process can be facilitated by transitioning from an implicit assessment to a comprehensive assessment.

## MOVING FROM AN IMPLICIT ASSESSMENT
## TO A COMPREHENSIVE ASSESSMENT

Although the administration of an implicit assessment does not always reveal the presence of spirituality as a clinically relevant factor, in many cases it does. In a manner analogous to Emily, some clients report "secular"

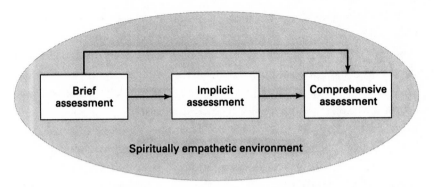

FIGURE 10.1  Integrative assessment model

activities that function as sources of spiritual meaning in their lives (Crisp, 2010). Alternatively, other clients affirm more traditional forms of spirituality that they were initially hesitant to discuss. In both cases it is often helpful to administer a comprehensive assessment to more fully understand the role of spirituality in clients' lived experience.

Figure 10.1 illustrates a model for integrating implicit and explicit spiritual assessments into a unified conceptual framework (Hodge, 2013b). As this figure implies, the creation of a caring, respectful, spiritually empathetic environment is central to the assessment process. The success of the assessment, and indeed the clinical enterprise itself, is contingent on the creation of a supportive atmosphere in which clients' needs and interests are privileged.

The assessment process begins with a brief assessment that explores spirituality in an explicit manner, an endeavor that serves to legitimize the topic of spirituality in practice settings (Mutter & Neves, 2010). If the brief assessment suggests that spirituality may intersect service provision, then practitioners move to a comprehensive assessment, assuming the criteria discussed in chapter 4 for proceeding to such an assessment are satisfied. If the brief assessment indicates spirituality is unrelated to service provision, then practitioners ensure their spiritual radar monitors clients' language and affect, scanning for pointers that indicate the need for an implicit assessment. Such an assessment is conducted if clients' language or emotions suggest the sacred is an important dimension of their lives and practitioners believe this dimension may be related to service provision.

If an implicit assessment indicates that both criteria exist (i.e., the sacred plays an important role and may be related to service provision), then some type of comprehensive approach can often be productively used to flesh out clients' spiritual understanding. This is the case regardless of whether clients are comfortable with traditional spiritual terminology, although some significant caveats should be observed in either case.

For clients whose concerns about practitioner's level of spiritual competence have abated, any of the five comprehensive approaches can likely be used. During this process it is important to ensure that the trust developed over the course of the relationship is maintained by, for example, carefully explaining the rationale and purpose for transitioning to a comprehensive assessment. However, in principle, all comprehensive assessment approaches—spiritual histories, lifemaps, genograms, eco-maps, and ecograms—are relevant in this context.

For clients uncomfortable with spiritual language, the situation is more nuanced. As illustrated in the case example, spiritual lifemaps can readily be used to chart the ways in which clients have connected with the sacred over the course of their lives (Hodge, 2005f). Given their artistic orientation, it is relatively easy to depict activities and events that engendered various sources of transcendent meaning, hope, and purpose at various points in life.

Transcendent sources of strength can also be easily portrayed on eco-maps. To follow up on the case example, the therapist might have asked Emily to create an eco-map as a replacement, or as a supplement, to a lifemap. In this application, Emily might be asked to represent the various ways she connected with nature on the eco-map prior to contracting Lyme disease. The different activities used to nurture her relationship with the sacred could be depicted as spiritual systems around Emily in the center of the paper. The strength or energy Emily used to draw from each system would be represented by different types of lines, in keeping with standard eco-map conventions discussed in chapter 8. Alternatively, Emily and Angie might be represented in the center of the paper, with the various systems arrayed around them, and corresponding lines drawn between the various systems and each individual.

The therapist could then use this eco-map as a starting point for brainstorming about creative ways in which Emily might connect with nature currently. A new eco-map might be constructed illustrating Emily's options in her present condition, as a way to help reinforce the reality of the options, and the hope for a better life they represent. Similarly, a new eco-map might also be constructed featuring both Emily and Angie on a single eco-map, along with their respective relationships to the various systems in their present environment, a process that might help clarify expectations, build unity, and restore intimacy in their relationship.

In sum, spiritual lifemaps and eco-maps can readily be adapted for use with clients who are uncomfortable with spiritual language. Modified in this manner, they are essentially implicit comprehensive assessments. As implied in the case example, the implicit assessment can flow smoothly into a comprehensive assessment that employs the same implicit methodology, at least with these two comprehensive approaches.

Conversely, practitioners should proceed with caution when considering spiritual genograms or ecograms. This is not to say that these approaches should never be used with people uncomfortable with or uninterested in spirituality. In some situations, the depiction of historical information can be clinically important. Take, for instance, a couple composed of a devout New Age adherent and an individual uninterested in spirituality, whose presenting problem involves conflict over the degree to which their children should be exposed to spirituality. In such cases a spiritual genogram or ecogram would likely be helpful in assisting the couple work through their disagreement.

Rather, the point is that the construction of spiritual genograms and ecograms typically involves an explicit discussion of spirituality, manifested either in traditional religious communities (e.g., the Catholic Church) or in alternative religious communities (e.g., the New Age movement). It makes little sense to use an approach that features language that does not resonate with clients' reality. Unless a compelling clinical rationale exists, practitioners are likely better served using an approach that is more congruent with clients' value systems.

In addition to using spiritual lifemaps and eco-maps, practitioners also have the option of conducting a complete spiritual history using an implicit approach. The questions earlier in this chapter can be used to conduct a chronological implicit assessment that explores clients' relationship with the sacred from their family of origin through to their future. Thus, depending on the client, an implicit assessment can flow into a traditional comprehensive assessment or a modified comprehensive assessment, typically in the form of an implicit spiritual lifemap, eco-map, or spiritual history.

Besides discussing implicit assessments, this chapter has presented a conceptual model that integrates implicit and explicit spiritual assessments into a unified framework. Explicit spiritual assessment approaches, such as spiritual genograms and ecograms, represent a good fit for many clients (Canda & Furman, 2010). Others, however, are better served by implicit assessment approaches, expressed in completely verbal forms (an implicit spiritual history) or in diagrammatic forms (an implicit spiritual lifemap or eco-map) (Pargament, 2007). The development of this conceptual assessment toolbox provides the options and flexibility needed to optimize service provision.

It is also possible to draw from different comprehensive methods to develop a composite approach that represents a good fit with clients' unique concerns and interests. Practitioners can pull from various approaches to create new assessment methods. As practitioners gain experience conducting assessments with different approaches, this proficiency aids in creatively adapting and combining various approaches to better address clients' needs, adding to the repertoire of options in one's toolbox.

The development of this assessment toolbox implicitly raises questions about implementation. How, for example, might practitioners go about deciding which comprehensive approach to use in a given situation? The next chapter offers some implementation suggestions, including ideas for selecting between different assessment approaches.

# 11

# Conducting Spiritual Assessments

THE CREATION OF AN EMOTIONALLY safe atmosphere has been emphasized throughout this book. Indeed, a successful assessment is contingent on communicating respect for clients' value systems. Knowledge of clients' worldviews plays an instrumental role in developing spiritual competence, as well as other factors that contribute to the administration of an ethical and effective spiritual assessment. In service of the latter end, this chapter builds on these themes. It begins by suggesting guidelines for selecting between comprehensive approaches, assessing the trustworthiness of the data produced, and using quantitative instruments in clinical settings. Phenomena that can negatively affect the assessment process—namely, biases stemming from spiritual countertransference, and what might be called faux spiritual direction—are discussed next. The chapter concludes by noting the importance of collaborating with clergy as well as the benefits practitioners can derive from such partnerships.

## SELECTING AN ASSESSMENT APPROACH

Selecting a comprehensive assessment approach can be difficult. Few clear-cut rules exist for selecting between different methods. Typically a number of intertwined factors are considered in making a choice (McSherry, 2010). These factors include (1) practitioners' available time, training, and theoretical orientation; (2) clients' cultural influences, personal preferences, and the nature of their presenting problem; and (3) the strengths and limitations of the respective comprehensive approaches.

In weighing various factors, it is important to select an approach that results in a valid assessment. Validity refers to the accuracy of the information obtained during assessment (Babbie, 2013). Put differently, it refers to the trustworthiness of the data.

While the protocols for evaluating the trustworthiness of information derived through quantitative assessment instruments are widely agreed on, the situation is more fluid for qualitative approaches (Denzin & Lincoln, 2013). One understanding of validity that may be useful in selecting an assessment approach is the concept of social validity (Wolf, 1978). The following content on social validity flows into a discussion of clinically relevant timeframes, which can be an important factor in enhancing social validity.

### Social Validity

Social validity refers to the degree to which members of a particular social group or culture believe that a given protocol is valid, relevant, and consistent with their norms and aspirations (Lindo & Elleman, 2010). Cultural validity is another name for this construct. Thus higher levels of congruence with a group's values are equated with higher levels of social or cultural validity. In turn, higher social validity enhances the probability that the protocol will be successfully implemented.

In practice settings, social validity refers to the degree to which clients perceive the assessment is appropriate, acceptable, and relevant to their life situation (Hodge & Limb, 2011). Higher levels of social validity enhance the trustworthiness of the results. In other words, if clients perceive the assessment approach is congruent with their values and relevant to their treatment goals, then the information from the assessment is more likely to be accurate and clinically pertinent.

At present, limited research exists on the social validity of various comprehensive assessment approaches with different groups (Hodge & Limb, 2011). Consequently, professional judgment is typically used to determine social validity. Information obtained through the general intake process, including the brief spiritual assessment, is often helpful in this regard. These data can be used to tentatively suggest and discuss various assessment options with clients.

To facilitate this process, boxes 11.1 and 11.2 summarize, respectively, the strengths and limitations of the five explicit comprehensive approaches

BOX 11.1    STRENGTHS OF COMPREHENSIVE ASSESSMENT APPROACHES

### Spiritual Histories

Appeal to highly verbal people who enjoy face-to-face interaction.

Are congruent with cultures that value story-telling/oral transmission of knowledge.

Are client centered/directed.

Provide a nonstructured, nonlinear approach to assessment.

Are potentially therapeutic.

Are conducive to building a therapeutic alliance.

Are relatively easy to administer.

Clients readily understand the concept.

Can be integrated into ongoing clinical conversations as needed,

### Spiritual Lifemaps

Allow for creativity and artistic expression.

Honor nonverbal talents and strengths.

Are congruent with cultures that value the use of symbols to convey information.

Are client constructed (implicitly communicate important competencies).

Client controls level of intrusiveness/vulnerability.

Secondary role of therapists allows time to acclimate to clients' worldview.

Visual depiction of life history can foster new insights (e.g., strengths).

Construction process may be cathartic or healing (e.g., develop salutary scripts).

Clients readily understand the approach.

Can be assigned as therapeutic homework.

### Spiritual Genograms

Depict problems rooted in differing family systems (interfaith couples).

Identify areas of commonality among couples (same-faith couples).

Explore family-of-origin issues.

Illustrate spiritual and religious patterns across generations.

Can identify previously unrecognized strengths in the family system.

Implicitly communicate respect for extended family members.

Can appeal to clients interested in a very structured approach.

BOX 11.1 (CONTINUED)

### Spiritual Eco-maps

Relational focus can mitigate concerns about discussing sensitive topics.

Clients generally understand the approach (especially in contrast to genograms).

Highlight potential resources in environment.

Visual presentation can foster self-understanding and clarify choices.

Are quick and relatively easy to construct.

Concepts can be integrated into a broader psychosocial assessment.

Provide smooth transition to intervention planning.

Document salutary changes and reinforce treatment gains.

### Spiritual Ecograms

Holistic depiction acknowledges the interconnected nature of reality.

Offer clients and practitioners the ability to see the big picture.

Elicit new understandings, assets, and options relative to eco-maps/genograms.

Relational emphasis can mitigate unease discussing spirituality.

Can be used to document therapeutic changes over time.

Communicate respect for the extended family.

Provide additional, present-oriented data with interfaith and same-faith couples.

Present orientation may mitigate client reluctance to explore generational data.

BOX 11.2

## LIMITATIONS OF COMPREHENSIVE ASSESSMENT APPROACHES

### Spiritual Histories

Have minimal appeal for people who are relatively nonverbal.

Face-to-face interaction may increase nervousness about sensitive topics.

Require substantial time to appropriately conduct.

May cover spiritual terrain that is unrelated to service provision.

Some clients may prefer a more structured or otherwise alternative format.

BOX 11.2 (CONTINUED)

### Spiritual Lifemaps

Clients may be concerned over perceived lack of artistic skills and/or dislike of drawing.

Clients may feel uncomfortable drawing some aspects of their journeys.

Are potentially a poor use of practitioners' time.

Can be time intensive to construct.

Lack generational information.

### Spiritual Genograms

Are highly structured; must fit story into a generational format.

Are complex; can be difficult to explain and construct.

Are time consuming to construct, particularly with large families.

May explore dimensions of clients' stories that are unrelated to their presenting problems.

Many indigenous cultures forbid speaking of those who have passed on.

Clients may not connect exploration of past functioning with present problems.

### Spiritual Eco-maps

May oversimplify complex, multifaceted relationships.

May require practitioner assistance to construct, at least initially.

Are somewhat structured, with limited opportunity for creative expression.

Overlook important generational information.

### Spiritual Ecograms

Are very complex.

Are difficult to understand and construct.

Speaking of those who have passed on is forbidden in many indigenous cultures.

Limited opportunity exists for creative expression.

Multifaceted relationships may be oversimplified.

May explore dimensions of clients' stories unrelated to presenting problem.

discussed in chapters 5 through 9. This collective presentation helps to highlight the unique features of each method relative to other approaches. Developing a working familiarity with these strengths and limitations can help in the process of selecting an assessment method by highlighting pertinent areas to explore with clients.

In some cases the choice of an assessment approach will be readily apparent. For example, relatively nonverbal clients who are creatively oriented often view a spiritual lifemap as an assessment model that is congruent with their beliefs and values. In other situations selecting a socially valid approach can be more difficult.

For instance, respect for the extended family is a common value among both LDS and American Indians. This might be taken to imply that spiritual genograms would be an appropriate choice for clients from these cultures, particularly given widespread practitioner familiarity with the underlying method (McGoldrick et al., 2008). This premise, however, was not fully supported in research examining the social validity of the five comprehensive assessment tools. While spiritual genograms were held to be the most congruent of the five with the LDS value system (Limb, Hodge, Ward, & Alboroto, under review), they were ranked lowest regarding the American Indian value system (Hodge & Limb, 2011). This finding underscores the importance of making tentative suggestions and coselecting an approach that both clients and practitioners find acceptable.

It should be noted that the strengths and limitations listed are generalities and accordingly may not be applicable to all clients. Some people, for example, readily understand spiritual genograms and are able to construct their own as homework, while others have trouble grasping the concept of spiritual eco-maps. As a result, it is perhaps most helpful to understand the characteristics listed in the boxes in a more provisional sense, as areas of potential strengths and limitations that may be relevant to specific, individual clients. In addition to considering the strengths and limitations, it can also be helpful to consider the timeframe covered by the assessment.

### Clinically Relevant Timeframes

Clinically relevant timeframes contribute to perceptions of social validity. The accuracy of the information gathered during assessment can be enhanced if the assessment focuses on a period of time that is of clinical interest. If the assessment covers a timeframe that is largely unrelated to the problem at hand, the trustworthiness of the assessment may be compromised.

Figure 11.1 depicts an assessment decision tree organized by time. After a brief assessment is conducted, the first decision is whether a comprehensive assessment is warranted. If a determination is made that an in-depth assessment is unwarranted at this point, then practitioners move on to other concerns while remaining open to the possibility of administering an implicit assessment or otherwise revisiting the topic later in the course of service provision. This process was demonstrated in the case examples used to illustrate spiritual histories in chapter 5 and implicit spiritual assessments in chapter 10.

If a comprehensive assessment is called for, then the next consideration is the importance of history in clients' presenting challenge. In many situations, intergenerational or historical factors will tend to drive the decision-making process. For example, spiritual genograms or ecograms may be an appropriate choice for interfaith couples experiencing conflicts stemming from differing value systems in their respective family histories, same-faith couples attempting to build intimacy by identifying and building on areas of spiritual commonalities, and individuals seeking to understand or differentiate from established spiritual patterns in their families of origin (Frame, 2003; McGoldrick et al., 2008).

If historical factors are not particularly relevant to clients' concerns, then a more present-oriented approach may be appropriate. To decide among spiritual histories, lifemaps, or eco-maps, consideration might be given to the relevance of present relationships versus life history in addressing the presenting challenge. In situations in which present relationships are of primary importance, eco-maps may be a good choice since they focus on clients' present relationships to spiritual systems in their current environments, are relatively easy to grasp conceptually, are quick to construct, and, if needed, can be integrated into a broader assessment of functioning. Clients generally understand the need to explore their current relationships to problems they are currently experiencing, which in turn enhances social validity (McGoldrick et al., 2008).

If the brief assessment indicates that some degree of life history may be significant, then either spiritual histories or lifemaps might be used. At one level, this represents a choice between a completely verbal approach and a diagrammatic approach. However, as the strengths and limitations

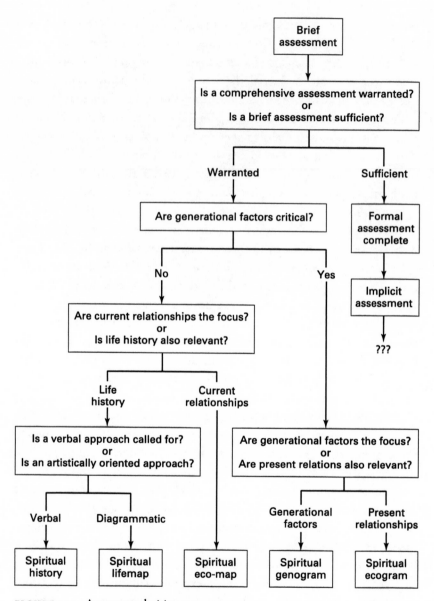

FIGURE II.I  Assessment decision tree

boxes suggest, other factors should be considered as well (e.g., clients' interest in drawing, the ability to assign as homework). Once a comprehensive approach has been selected, the information obtained during the assessment should be evaluated.

### ASSESSING TRUSTWORTHINESS

Assessing the trustworthiness of the information obtained during the administration of a comprehensive assessment is a complex task that typically involves the consideration of numerous factors. In broad relief, it involves attending to clients' words, feelings, and actions (Jordan & Franklin, 2011). These observations are integrated with the data obtained through the broader assessment of functioning. In turn, this provides a framework for assessing the trustworthiness of the data from the assessment. Of particular importance in this process are the issues of coherence, collaboration, and falsification.

Regarding coherence, attention is focused on the degree to which metaphors, pictures, and patterns elicited during the assessment make sense as a part of a larger narrative (Pargament & Krumrei, 2009). If clients' spiritual stories are rational, logical, and consistent within the context of their worldviews, then the trustworthiness of the information is enhanced. It is important to note that the standard for assessing the logical consistency of clients' stories is not practitioners' worldviews. Rather, the yardstick for measuring coherence is clients' worldviews. Trustworthiness is enhanced if clients' narratives are coherent within the framework of their own worldviews.

Another factor to consider is the extent to which collaboration occurs with clients in the discussion and interpretation of the problem. Collaboration in this area often enhances the ability of practitioners to assess the accuracy of information related to spirituality. These interactions provide an important window on clients' feelings, beliefs, and behaviors in an area in which practitioners have some degree of expertise. If the discussion and interpretation of the presenting challenge engenders confidence, this suggests that confidence in clients' spiritual narratives is also warranted.

Falsification is another key principle in assessing trustworthiness (Popper, 1963). As clients relate their spiritual journey, practitioners develop their own understanding of these stories. Attempting to falsify these preconceived initial interpretations helps to enhance trust in the interpretations that survive the falsification process. Concepts such as God, Creator, born-again, charismatic, and witness of the spirit can mean dramatically different things to different people, even people within the same subtradition. Checking out alternative understandings aids in the process of establishing the accuracy of clients' narratives. In addition to verbal exploration, quantitative instruments can also be useful in this task.

### QUANTITATIVE SPIRITUAL ASSESSMENT

Quantitative instruments can provide an important source of supplementary information (Wolfer, 2012). More than one hundred measures have been developed to assess various dimensions of spirituality and religion (Hill & Hood, 1999). Although few of these instruments have been standardized for use in clinical settings, they can be employed to add richness and depth to qualitative assessments (Draper, 2012).

Before using quantitative instruments, a number of factors should be considered. Specifically, an instrument's validity and language should be assessed in light of clients' value systems and capabilities. Possible limitations of such instruments are reviewed below.

#### Validity Limitations

The validity of a particular instrument with a given client population should be assessed prior to using the instrument (Hill & Edwards, 2013). Constructs such as spirituality are defined and operationalized by those with some degree of power and represent their interests or, more broadly, their worldview (Foucault, 1984). The values held by the social scientists who operationalize constructs are implicitly manifested in the specific instruments they create. In short, instruments reflect the values of their creators, rather than those of clients. This sets up a potential difference in value systems between the values reflected in the instrument and those affirmed by clients, which can lead to biased outcomes.

Kohlberg's (1981) widely cited theory of moral development serves as a case in point. As Gilligan (1993) illustrated, the masculine values that characterize dominant discourse biased Kohlberg's theory against women, resulting in females recording lower levels of moral development relative to males. Similarly, Richards and Davison (1992) illustrated how the secular values that inform the dominant discourse resulted in theists recording lower levels of moral development relative to secularists.

The same types of biases exist in spirituality instruments (Watson, 2008). Take, for instance, an instrument that measures spirituality with items such as "I exercise regularly" and "I feel sexually fulfilled" (Whitfield, 1984). Such instruments have limited validity with celibate Catholic sisters who forsake systematic exercise programs to spend more time in prayer and service to the poor out of love for God. In an analogous manner, instruments that operationalize spirituality with items that reflect common Catholic tenets can have limited utility with other groups.

Consequently, each instrument should be carefully examined to ensure that it accurately measures the construct that it purports to measure (Hill & Edwards, 2013). Every instrument reflects a certain set of culturally based suppositions about the nature of spirituality. To obtain an accurate assessment, the values of the instrument's designers and those of the client's must be congruent (Gartner, 1996). Another factor that can affect the validity of quantitative assessments is the language used to operationalize the assessment.

### Language Limitations

The language used in the questions that comprise a scale should also be examined prior to using an instrument. Because of a complex set of interrelated environmental problems, many people have not had the opportunity to develop high levels of language proficiency. This is particularly the case for people from low socioeconomic backgrounds and/or nondominant cultures, the very people for whom spirituality is often most salient.

The prevalence of limited language proficiency is extensive. Some 25–35 percent of adults are functionally illiterate, and a similar percentage have marginal levels of literacy (Vezeau, 2012). According to some estimates, only 20 percent of the public have literacy levels sufficient to perform complex reading and computational tasks.

Many quantitative instruments employ a relatively sophisticated vocabulary and complicated question phrasing (Hodge & Gillespie, 2005). For instance, to avoid response set-bias—the tendency to agree with a set of positively worded questions—negatively worded questions are commonly used. Furthermore, some questions call for potential respondents to disagree with a negatively worded question (e.g., "I never spend time in private spiritual thought and meditation"). Thus people must disagree with a negatively phrased item to be classified as spiritual. Such phrasing, in which respondents have to conceptualize a double negative, increases the probability of incorrect responses.

Another concern is the implicit messages communicated. Using instruments in which clients struggle to comprehend the question phrasing, and how to respond appropriately, does little to foster their self-perceptions as capable, competent individuals. In some cases the use of such instruments can even impair the therapeutic alliance. Thus it is important to consider both the underlying worldview that informs the instrument at a conceptual level and the language employed to express the concepts. If these two guidelines are satisfied, then a quantitative instrument might be employed.

### Potentially Useful Quantitative Measures

Table 11.1 identifies four quantitative instruments that may have utility with some clients. These measures were selected for a number of reasons. They are all publicly available, can be administered in a short period of time and, perhaps most important, have been widely recommended in the literature. Specifically, they are widely perceived to tap constructs that have been cited as important in practice settings. The various constructs assessed include spiritual motivation (Hodge, 2003b), religious commitment (Worthington et al., 2003), spiritual/religious coping styles (Pargament, Smith, Koenig, & Perez, 1998), and ten spiritual and religious domains that are frequently related to health and wellness (Fetzer Institute, 1999). Other, more extensive compilations of quantitative measures are available elsewhere (Hill & Hood, 1999; Pargament, 2007).

The Intrinsic Spiritual Scale (ISS) (Hodge, 2003b) is designed to assess the degree to which spirituality functions as an individual's master motivation in life, among both theistic and nontheistic populations, both within and outside of religious traditions. The ISS is based on Allport and Ross's (1967) intrinsic measure, one of the most widely used measures in the psychology of religion. Although Allport and Ross's measure has been used as a proxy for spirituality, it is limited by the fact that it employs explicitly Christian, theistic, and religious language. The ISS modifies this measure to tap spirituality as an individually oriented construct that is distinct

TABLE 11.1 Quantitative Measures for Assessing Different Dimensions of Spirituality and Religion

| CONSTRUCT | MEASURE AND NUMBER OF ITEMS | SUBSCALES (IF RELEVANT) | SAMPLE ITEM |
|---|---|---|---|
| Spiritual motivation | Intrinsic Spirituality Scale (Hodge, 2003) ($N = 6$) | Unidimensional measure of spiritual motivation | *Growing spiritually is more important than anything else in my life.* |
| Religious commitment | Religious Commitment Inventory (Worthington et al., 2003) (N = 10) | Unidimensional measure of religious commitment | *I enjoy spending time with others of my religious affiliation.* |
| Spiritual/religious coping | Brief RCOPE (Pargament et al., 1998) ($N = 14$) | Positive coping ($n = 7$)<br>Negative coping ($n = 7$) | *Sought God's love and care*<br>*Felt punished by God for my lack of devotion* |
| Health-related spiritual and religious domains | Brief Measure of Religiousness/ Spirituality (Fetzer Institute, 1999) (N = 33) | Daily spiritual experiences ($n = 6$) | *I feel deep inner peace or harmony* |
| | | Beliefs and values ($n = 2$) | *I believe in a God who watches over me.* |
| | | Forgiveness ($n = 3$) | *I know that God forgives me.* |
| | | Private religious activities ($n = 5$) | *How often do you read the Bible or other religious literature?* |
| | | Spiritual/religious coping ($n = 7$) | *I look to God for strength, support, and guidance.* |
| | | Religious support ($n = 4$) | *If you were ill, how much would the people in your congregation help you out?* |
| | | Organizational religiousness ($n = 2$) | *How often do you go to religious services?* |

from religion. Spirituality is defined as an individual's relationship to God or whatever is perceived to represent ultimate transcendence in the eyes of the respondent.

The Religious Commitment Inventory (RCI) (Worthington et al., 2003) serves as a counterpart to the ISS. Whereas the ISS measures personal spiritual motivation, the RCI measures religious commitment, which is defined as the degree to which people adhere to their religious values, beliefs, and practices and use them in daily living. The RCI is designed to assess religious commitment across numerous faiths, including Buddhism, Christianity, Hinduism, and Islam.

The Brief RCOPE measures two distinct spiritual/religious coping styles (Pargament et al., 1998). Positive coping is assumed to reflect a secure relationship with God, while negative coping is posited to reflect a more tenuous relationship with God. These two coping styles tend to be associated with various health outcomes. Although this measure has been widely used, it assumes theistic belief and some degree of involvement with religion, particularly diverse Christian traditions.

The Brief Multidimensional Measure of Religiousness and Spirituality was developed by the Fetzer Institute (1999) in collaboration with the National Institute on Aging (NIA). In addition to single-item measures that tap religious affiliation and self-ascribed levels of spirituality and religiousness, this instrument includes ten short measures. These brief measures are designed to assess discrete domains that are theoretically related to health and wellness among adults of all ages (Idler et al., 2003). Some of these domains mirror the dimensions measured by the other three instruments. In instances where practitioners are interested in exploring one of these dimensions, the use of slightly longer scales may produce more valid information. On the other hand, the Brief Multidimensional Measure has been incorporated in the 1998 GSS, enabling comparisons with the general population. Perceptions regarding spirituality and religion tend to be relatively stable among the public, which suggests that comparisons with these data still have some utility.

### Utilizing Quantitative Measures in Practice

It is often challenging to obtain an accurate understanding of sensitive issues. Clients' stories may, for example, be unintentionally refracted by various psychodynamic factors. In turn, these stories are interpreted through practitioners' own subjective cognitive grid. Indeed, to some extent, communication is always partial, even among people sharing similar cultural backgrounds, socioeconomic status, life experiences, and spiritual beliefs.

Quantitative measures can provide a complementary source of information, which can help ensure that practitioners and clients are on the same page (Pargament & Krumrei, 2009). The four instruments reviewed above can potentially be used to disconfirm and confirm hypotheses, monitor changes over time, and check biases. For the measures included in the Brief Multidimensional Measure, it is possible to tentatively compare clients' responses with those of a normative sample.

For example, practitioners might wonder about clients' level of spiritual motivation or their commitment to their religion. As alluded to in chapter 4, this information could be important in determining whether to transition from a brief assessment to a comprehensive assessment. Similarly, a supplementary source of data about clients' level of spiritual motivation or religious commitment is often helpful in deciding whether to employ spiritual interventions such as spiritually modified CBT, passage meditation, or mindfulness meditation (Koenig et al., 2012). In such cases, the Intrinsic Spiritual Scale and Religious Commitment Inventory might be used to check perceptions developed through the qualitative assessment.

Various measures might also be administered at systematic intervals to monitor changes over the course of counseling. For example, clients might be asked to complete the Brief RCOPE to help understand their use of positive or negative coping methods over time. These data provide a window onto clients' use of spirituality to deal with problems. Increases in negative coping, perhaps accentuated by psychological or environmental stressors, might also suggest the need for collaboration with clergy, a topic discussed in more detail later in this chapter. Alternatively, information obtained by the Brief RCOPE can help assess the effectiveness of spiritual interventions in ameliorating problems.

Measures can be grouped and administered as needed. For instance, the measure of religious support might be abstracted from the Brief Multidimensional Measure and used to independently assess the degree of congregational benefits and problems. Population means and standard deviations for the four questions that comprise this scale are publicly available, enabling practitioners to check their perceptions regarding what is normative with scores from the general public (Fetzer Institute, 1999; Idler et al., 2003). The administration of this short scale, which takes approximately ninety seconds to complete, can be used to complement the information obtained through clinical observations and interviews (Wolfer, 2012).

This ability to disconfirm and confirm hypotheses is predicated, as noted above, on the existence of a high degree of worldview congruence. If the worldviews of clients and the instruments' designers are incompatible, the measures can produce inaccurate results. In the same way that differences in worldviews can affect quantitative measures, they can also play a similar role in fostering bias through spiritual countertransference.

### SPIRITUAL COUNTERTRANSFERENCE

It is widely recognized that unresolved negative emotions can damage clinical relationships through countertransference biases (Hepworth et al., 2013). This phenomenon distorts perceptions, creates blind spots, and engenders detrimental emotional responses. For example, practitioners whose parents' divorce was experienced traumatically can unconsciously attempt to resolve the extant pain through their present work with conflicted couples.

In the same way, negative feelings about past spiritual events can result in spiritual countertransference (Vogel et al., 2013). Practitioners can act out their unresolved feelings regarding spiritual events in their backgrounds with their present clients. In other words, practitioners may unconsciously, or even consciously, use the clinical relationship to address their own unresolved spiritual needs to the detriment of their clients.

Spiritual countertransference may be particularly pronounced when encountering clients from traditions practitioners have rejected. People leave the religious traditions of their family of origin for a wide variety of reasons (Chaves, 2011; Pew Forum on Religion and Public Life, 2009). In some cases, childhood religious traditions are experienced negatively. For example, 20 percent of social workers report negative feelings regarding their childhood religious experiences, which were typically theistic (Hodge, 2003a). Similarly, a quarter of psychologists report they used to believe in God but have rejected theism (Shafranske & Cummings, 2013).

In such cases the process of administering an assessment can trigger spiritual countertransference biases. The unresolved sentiments associated with negative childhood experiences may be elicited in much the same way that practitioners from a divorced family may experience countertransference biases when working with couples considering a divorce. Animosities rooted in childhood experiences may be projected on to clients, resulting in a less empathic posture and increased negative appraisals.

Practitioners may attempt to pathologize clients' values, implicitly frame them as unhelpful, or attempt to convert them to secular values. The latter dynamic might occur by sharing religious perspectives that are more congruent with the values affirmed in secular discourse. These violations of client autonomy may be especially prone to manifest when clients hold theistic values that conflict with those affirmed in the dominant secular culture, such as those related to gender roles, parenting practices, sexual orientation, and abortion (see chapter 4 for examples of potential areas of conflict with Muslim clients).

Accordingly, it is critical to identify and manage spiritual countertransference (Wiggins, 2009). In some cases practitioners will be able to address their biases to such an extent that effective service provision is possible. In other cases referral is necessary (Yarhouse & Johnson, 2013). Indeed, until practitioners work through their negative sentiments, they should generally avoid working with clients who trigger countertransference biases. This helps to safeguard client welfare and ensure that clients receive services that respect their spiritual values and are aligned with their treatment goals.

To protect clients, some practitioners with strong moral views should not attempt to provide services to certain clients. For instance, practitioners who are morally committed to egalitarian gender roles should carefully consider their ability to work with Muslims and other couples who affirm complementary gender roles (Fife & Whiting, 2007). Counselors who believe that complementary beliefs are morally wrong and destructive to healthy interpersonal relationships may not be able to work effectively with couples who hold such beliefs. In such cases the conflict in value systems may preclude practitioners' from providing effective, client-centered services. In other cases practitioners' moral beliefs may interact with spiritual countertransference, a situation that calls for careful self-analysis.

Introspection plays a key role in managing spiritual countertransference. Engaging in self-examination helps to identify unusual emotional responses (Furness & Gilligan, 2010). For example, attending to situations that engender a sense of personal discomfort can aid in identifying and managing biases. Similarly, self-administering the various diagrammatic assessments can help practitioners work through various experiences that might trigger detrimental responses (Willow et al., 2009).

Another strategy for dealing with spiritual countertransference is consultation (Plante, 2009). Emotional responses can be processed with trusted colleagues and supervisors. Similarly, outside observers are often better positioned to identify blind spots, process the results of self-assessments, and suggest alternative perspectives.

It is important, however, that such professional sounding boards have sufficient levels of spiritual competence in the client's tradition. Otherwise, a danger exists that bias will be accentuated rather than mitigated. This may be particularly likely if both supervisor and supervisee share comparable experiences and value systems. A different type of threat to the assessment process stemming from similar worldviews is discussed in the next section.

### FAUX SPIRITUAL DIRECTION

Spiritual countertransference is most likely to occur when a difference in spiritual worldviews exists between practitioners and clients. However, when practitioners and clients affirm the same worldview, the integrity of the assessment process can be compromised by a different dynamic (Hodge, 2005f). This phenomenon might be called faux spiritual direction.

Spiritual direction can be understood as a conversationally based activity that focuses on people's relationship with God (Barry & Connolly, 2009). It is often particularly relevant when people are experiencing various types of life challenges. Spiritual directors typically discuss these challenges in the process of assisting people to grow closer to God through the experiences.

Many similarities exist between counseling and spiritual direction (Hodge, Bonifas, & Chou, 2010). Practitioners and spiritual directors utilize similar skill sets, such as empathy and reflective listening. Life challenges are commonly addressed in both settings, as is people's spirituality. Neither profession sanctions preaching, advice giving, or authoritarian relationships. Both counseling and spiritual direction are essentially egalitarian and growth-oriented in nature.

Owing to these similarities, the boundaries between the two positions can become ambiguous (Sperry, 2013). When discussing spirituality,

TABLE 11.2    Areas of Emphasis in Counseling and Spiritual Direction

| COUNSELING | SPIRITUAL DIRECTION |
|---|---|
| Addresses psychological problems. | Addresses spiritual growth. |
| Clients are typically in emotional distress. | Clients often exhibit wellness. |
| Focuses on symptom amelioration. | Focuses on link between life experience and clients' relationship with God. |
| Concentrates on emotional, cognitive, and behavioral dimensions. | Concentrates on the spiritual dimension (e.g., spiritual experiences). |
| Is empathic to clients' emotions. | Is empathic to the Spirit of God. |
| Typically employs therapies developed and validated within positivistic scientific tradition (e.g., cognitive behavioral therapy). | Typically uses strategies developed and validated over centuries of experience in a given religious tradition (e.g., spiritual exercises such as meditation). |
| Aims to enhance client autonomy. | Aims to enhance surrender to God's will. |
| May help clients adjust to societal norms. | Helps clients adjust to spiritual norms. |
| Is characteristically fee-based. | Is characteristically offered without cost. |
| End goal is psychological wellness or enhanced functioning. | End goal is spiritual transformation. |

*Source*: Adapted from Hodge, Bonifas, & Chou (2010)

practitioners may inadvertently fall into the role of a spiritual director. The risk of this occurring is perhaps especially pronounced when practitioners are highly invested in spirituality and share clients' spiritual worldview. In such cases, practitioners may recommend personally preferred spiritual practices, discount others, or fail to explore viable options that are consistent with clients' spiritual values but conflict with those favored by practitioners.

Table 11.2 depicts areas of emphasis in counseling and spiritual direction. The distinctions that tend to characterize both approaches are delineated. In this way, the table helps to clarify the often ambiguous boundaries between counseling and spiritual direction.

Perhaps the primary distinction to bear in mind is that the overarching aim of a comprehensive assessment is to elicit information about spirituality only to the extent that such information is relevant to service provision (Sperry, 2013). To be clear, this does not preclude practitioners from exploring issues related to clients' spiritual growth. In some cases spiritual growth may be intertwined with symptom amelioration (Sullivan, 2009). The focus, however, should be on assisting clients achieve their clinical goals, which typically entails coping with or ameliorating some type of problem or challenge.

In a manner analogous to spiritual countertransference, faux spiritual direction shifts the focus away from clients' treatment goals. Practitioners' interests subtly take center stage in both situations. However, instead of attempting to work out unresolved issues, as occurs in spiritual counter-transference, in faux spiritual direction practitioners attempt to direct clients' spiritual growth. In both cases client autonomy is compromised.

The same methods used to identify and manage spiritual countertrans-ference bias are also pertinent here (Furness & Gilligan, 2010). Self-exam-ination and consultation can help practitioners remain focused on the intersection between client spirituality and service delivery. In other words, the goal should be to maximize health and wellness (Koenig, 2013). Spiri-tual growth should not be explored for its own sake. Rather, the emphasis is on service provision. Exploration of spirituality that goes beyond this is likely inappropriate.

As noted in chapter 5, working within the boundaries of one's areas of professional competence is a common ethical requirement (NASW, 2008:1.04a). For most practitioners, engaging in spiritual direction falls outside the parameters of their areas of proficiency. In the same way that social workers should, for example, refrain from giving medical direction, providing spiritual guidance should also be avoided. Clients' interests are typically served by offering services within the boundaries of one's area of professional competence. If the exploration of spirituality cannot be linked to a clinical goal that falls within the purview of a practitioners' professional competence, then collaboration with, or referral to, clergy is typically appropriate.

## COLLABORATION WITH CLERGY

Clergy can be an important resource (Yarhouse & Johnson, 2013). As experts on spirituality, they are ideally positioned to collaborate with prac-titioners in addressing clients' spiritual issues. As noted above, clients' inter-ests are typically best served by working within the parameters of one's area of professional competence. Clergy's expertise in spirituality equips them to address spirituality in a competent manner.

It is important to note, however, that a clear demarcation of professional responsibilities between practitioners and clergy can be relatively complex in many situations (Taylor, Woodward, Chatters, Mattis, & Jackson, 2011). For instance, clients wrestling with spiritual issues, perhaps related to their clergy, may desire a neutral environment in which to process the issues. In other situations, clients may want to discuss spiritually based interpersonal conflicts, value incongruence, or other concerns in an impartial setting (Loewenthal, 2013). While acknowledging this complexity, the limits of one's professional expertise should always be borne in mind, and steps should be taken to collaborate with clergy to the fullest extent possible.

When considering collaboration with clients' clergy, consent should be secured from clients before proceeding (Koenig, 2013). As implied above, people may not want their clergy involved in some situations. In such contexts, obtaining supervision from someone with a high level of spiritual competence with the client's spiritual value system is appropriate. Another option is to develop relationships with a variety of clergy in the community who can serve as sources of information and guidance.

Practitioners can benefit from clergy's expertise in numerous ways (Plante, 2013). For example, clergy can help link clients with assets and resources in their congregations, enhance practitioners' level of spiritual competence, and assist in the selection and construction of interventions that resonate with clients' spiritual beliefs and values. Indeed, clergy, who are typically emotionally removed from clients' problems, can often provide helpful insights into salutary spiritual beliefs and practices that clients may have overlooked.

Clergy can also help determine the normative status of spiritual beliefs and behaviors. This can be particularly helpful when practitioners are unsure about clients' reports. This can occur with some degree of frequency when interacting with clients from traditions in which practitioners have marginal levels of spiritual competence.

Take, for instance, clients who report a spiritual justification for actions practitioners believe are counterproductive to treatment or even harmful. An example might be husbands who provide a spiritual rationale for treating their wives in a manner that seems detrimental in the eyes of practitioners (Fife & Whiting, 2007). It can be difficult for practitioners to assess the reality of the situation, perhaps particularly if they personally hold egalitarian beliefs. Attempting to discern what is normative within a given cultural value system is an especially complex task when one's personal value system provides few points of contact.

In such situations, clergy can be helpful. They are ideally situated to assist practitioners sort through what is appropriate and inappropriate within the context of clients' value systems (Plante, 2009). To follow up on the example above, clergy can acquaint practitioners with normative guidelines for behavior within complementary marriages. In situations where a husband's actions are inappropriate, clergy can sketch out spiritual rationales for alternative behaviors.

When seeking such input, it is important that clergy share the same theological orientation as clients. Practitioners should not assume that clergy and clients share the same value system simply because they share the same denominational affiliation. Views within a given tradition can vary, sometimes dramatically, driven by factors such as the degree of acculturation to the dominant secular worldview. To ensure that services are client-centered, clergy must share the same basic worldview as the client.

Many clergy are open to working with practitioners in collaborative relationships (Galek, Flannelly, Koenig, & Fogg, 2007; Harr, Openshaw, & Moore, 2006; Oppenheimer, Flannelly, & Weaver, 2004). Toward this end, practitioners can facilitate positive relationships by interacting with clergy as co-equals and acknowledging their status as professionals. This includes recognizing the importance of spirituality as a distinct dimension of human existence on a par with emotional/cognitive dimensions and exhibiting deference to clergy's specialized spiritual knowledge.

Forming collaborative relationships with clergy typically requires a commitment of time and energy (Plante, 2013). This investment pays off over time, however, by positioning practitioners to provide more effective, client-centered services. Indeed, this is the overarching aim of this book—to equip practitioners to more effectively assist clients in the process of realizing their strengths and aspirations. In keeping with this goal, the final chapter summarizes the key points and suggests additional strategies to accomplish this aim.

# Summary of Key Points and Future Directions

ASSESSMENT PLAYS A CRITICAL ROLE in service provision since it lays the foundation for subsequent decisions that shape the services clients receive. To help practitioners conduct spiritual assessments in an ethical and professional manner, this book has presented a number of key themes. If these themes are mastered and incorporated into clinical work, then salutary outcomes can be expected. Clients will, for example, be protected from coercion, their problems ameliorated, and their health and wellness enhanced.

This chapter reviews some of the major themes presented throughout this text. After summarizing key points, ideas for future directions are offered in the areas of research, practice, and education, which will assist readers in taking the concepts to the next level.

## THE TERRAIN COVERED

Of the various points covered, a number are particularly salient. Among these are the conceptual rationale for a universal spiritual assessment, the two-stage approach to assessment, the development of a comprehensive assessment toolbox, and the notion of an implicit assessment as an alternative to explicit assessment approaches. Together these themes provide a way of thinking about the assessment process as an integral component of service delivery.

## The Foundation

There are important reasons why practitioners should make space in their busy schedules for the administration of a spiritual assessment. Professional ethics codes typically mention spirituality or religion as an area that should be taken into account during service provision. Similarly, religious freedom is a fundamental human right that should be respected in interactions with clients.

In keeping with the status of spirituality as an important human right, clients often want to incorporate their spiritual beliefs and practices into the clinical dialogue. This is particularly true for traditionally disenfranchised populations, such as African Americans, women, and older adults (Boorstin & Schlachter, 2000). In addition to being an important ethical value, respecting client autonomy plays an instrumental role in fostering salutary outcomes.

Clients often want to have their spiritual values taken into account during service provision because they believe spirituality is intertwined with health. Indeed, a substantial body of empirical research suggests that spirituality is an important strength (Koenig et al., 2012). These spiritual assets and resources can often be operationalized to foster coping, ameliorate problems, and enhance wellness in clinical settings.

Spirituality is also intertwined with health in other ways, such as the degree to which services are congruent with clients' spiritual value systems. If services are incongruent, then, at best, clients are less likely to adhere to treatment protocols and, at worse, harm may be perpetuated. Alternatively, interventions that resonate with clients' spiritual values are more likely to be adopted and faithfully implemented, speeding recovery and wellness.

In light of these facts, many accrediting bodies and professional organizations recommend tailoring services to incorporate clients' spiritual values. For instance, the Joint Commission, the National Cancer Institute, and NASW all recommend the administration of a spiritual assessment. To support this recommendation, these organizations often cite operationalizing clients' human rights, autonomy, strengths, and so forth.

Spiritual assessment addresses these concerns. The routine administration of a spiritual assessment provides a practical, concrete mechanism to (1) ensure compliance with professional ethics codes, (2) show respect for clients' basic human rights, (3) honor client autonomy, (4) identify strengths that can be used to facilitate coping and wellness, (5) provide culturally relevant services, and (6) adhere to professional standards for good practice articulated by various accrediting bodies and professional organizations. These six rationales provide a conceptual foundation for the use of a two-stage assessment model in practice settings.

### Two-Stage Assessment Model

To minimize the demands on practitioners' time, spiritual assessment is commonly conceptualized as a two-stage process. A brief assessment is administered initially, followed—but only if clinically warranted—by an in-depth, comprehensive assessment. A universally administered brief assessment helps to legitimize the topic of spirituality in clinical discourse while concurrently providing practitioners with the background information needed to determine whether spirituality may potentially be related to service provision.

A brief assessment typically leads to one of two immediate outcomes: the administration of a comprehensive assessment or the conclusion of the formal assessment process. In the former case, a comprehensive assessment is conducted, assuming that practitioners have sufficient levels of spiritual competence in the clients' spiritual value system, clients consent to the process, and their spirituality potentially intersects service provision.

### Comprehensive Assessment Toolbox

Practitioners can administer any one of at least five conceptually distinct comprehensive assessment approaches. These approaches include spiritual histories, spiritual lifemaps, spiritual genograms, spiritual eco-maps, and spiritual ecograms. By developing familiarity with these different methods, practitioners can select the assessment tool that best fits the unique needs of their clients.

No single assessment approach is suitable in all contexts (Ross & McSherry, 2010). Clients' cultural backgrounds, desires, and concerns vary, as do practice settings, the nature of presenting problems, practitioners' theoretical orientations, and the amount of time available for assessment. By developing an assessment toolbox, it is possible to move beyond a one-size-fits-all approach so that the interests of practitioners and clients are taken into account. Selecting an appropriate tool that reflects clients' proclivities enhances the trustworthiness of the resulting data and provides a smooth transition to subsequent interventions.

Alternatively, the results of a brief assessment can lead to the conclusion of the formal assessment process. In some cases clients' spirituality is unrelated to service provision or they are uninterested in proceeding with a comprehensive assessment. In such cases the formal assessment process ends. Used in this manner, the two-stage model helps to conserve practitioners' time while simultaneously ensuring that clinically relevant spiritual needs, concerns, and aspirations are adequately addressed.

### Implicit Assessment

While the explicit assessment process may end, it is still advisable to continue to monitor clients' language and affect for signs that suggest the presence of spirituality. Some clients are uncomfortable with an explicit discussion of spirituality until sufficient levels of spiritual competence have been demonstrated and trust has been established. Other clients view traditional spiritual terminology as a culturally foreign language or relics of a long abandoned value system. With clients from either group, an implicit assessment provides a vehicle to explore the clinical relevance of spirituality in a culturally appropriate manner.

As is the case with other clinical interactions, administering an assessment competently requires a certain set of skills and aptitudes, including self-awareness. Practitioners should be alert for biases that can negatively affect the assessment process, such as bias stemming from spiritual countertransference or faux spiritual direction. Collaborating with clergy can play an important role in identifying misconceptions and ensuring that services are congruent with clients' spiritual values. In the next section, some ideas are offered to build on these concepts.

### FUTURE DIRECTIONS

A key theme throughout this book has been the interplay between clients' and practitioners' worldviews. It is widely acknowledged that the effectiveness of service provision is contingent on tailoring interactions and protocols so that they are congruent with clients' value systems (Sue & Sue, 2013).

This is an especially salient concern with spirituality, as unrecognized differences in value systems can bias service provision.

Going forward, a number of strategies can be implemented to address this issue. Below, some options are presented in the areas of research, practice, and education. The overarching aim of these overlapping options is to enhance current and future practitioners' ability to conduct spiritual assessments competently, particularly in cross-cultural contexts. Given the present state of the literature, research can play an important role in this process.

### Research

Additional research is needed to validate comprehensive assessment approaches with various populations. Limited information exists on the validity of all diagrammatic assessments (Jordan & Franklin, 2011). For instance, little research has been conducted assessing the validity of traditional genograms and eco-maps. Even less research exists on approaches specifically designed to assess spirituality.

Drawing from the concept of social validity, some initial work has been done to validate the approaches discussed in this text with American Indians and Latter-day Saints. A degree of preliminary validity with American Indians has been established for the following approaches: brief assessments (Hodge & Limb, 2010c), spiritual histories (Hodge & Limb, 2009), spiritual lifemaps (Limb & Hodge, 2007), spiritual genograms (Limb & Hodge, 2010), spiritual eco-maps (Hodge & Limb, 2009), and spiritual ecograms (Limb & Hodge, 2011). With the LDS population, similar work has been carried out to validate spiritual histories (Hodge & Limb, 2013) and spiritual lifemaps (Limb, Hodge, Leckie, & Ward, 2013).

Researchers might build on these efforts with these and other populations. Ideally the tools discussed in this text should be validated with all major cultures (Jordan & Franklin, 2011). The approaches might be assessed for cultural congruence at the conceptual level and culturally relevant question sets developed where the concept is adequately congruent with a given culture.

The resulting findings can aid in the selection and implementation of various tools. While certain approaches may appear to have some degree of face validity with a given population, subsequent research has not always confirmed these initial suppositions. As noted previously, spiritual genograms are highly congruent with LDS culture but markedly less so with American Indian culture, despite the affirmation of the extended family and historical tradition among both populations. Validation studies can clarify such distinctions and preferences resulting in more effective and ethical assessments. In a related manner, similar studies might be conducted in various clinical venues.

### Practice

In many cases, the nature of the practice setting drives the assessment. The issues explored in marriage and family therapy, for example, tend to differ from those explored in hospice work. Knowing the tools, questions, and procedures that are most relevant in a particular setting can facilitate the assessment process.

Toward this end, focus groups might be convened in specific settings to explore clients' preferences regarding these issues. For example, focus groups might be used to develop a unique set of questions that speak to the issues raised in a given practice context (Timmins & Kelly, 2008). Having a working set of questions helps save time by providing practitioners with items that can then be adapted in work with individual clients.

Another issue that could benefit from additional attention is the implementation process. Despite the role assessment plays in effective service provision, spiritual assessments are not administered to every client (Koenig, 2013). Also troubling is research suggesting that disparities in spiritual care exist. African Americans, for example, may be asked about their spirituality less frequently than European Americans (Williams et al., 2011).

Accordingly, research might be conducted with the aim of facilitating the administration of spiritual assessments. For instance, Bushfield (2009) evaluated the introduction, demonstration, and use of spiritual lifemaps in hospice work. This phenomenological study identified barriers that inhibit the use of lifemaps in hospice settings as well as strategies for circumventing the challenges. Similar translational research might be conducted with various tools in diverse settings to help ensure that all clients receive appropriate services.

Other strategies can also be implemented to enhance practitioners' ability to administer spiritual assessments effectively. For instance, practitioners might take an inventory of the religious demographics of their clients,

BOX 12.1     SUPPLEMENTAL RESOURCES ON SPIRITUAL COMPETENCE

### Spiritual Competence with Different Populations and Faith Traditions

Koenig, H. G. (Ed.). (1998). *Handbook of religion and mental health.* San Diego: Academic Press. [See section 4 on religious perspectives on mental health.]

Koenig, H. G. (2013). *Spirituality in patient care: Why, how, when, and what* (3rd ed.). West Conshohocken, Penn.: Templeton Press. [See chapter 13 on specific religions. The content is oriented toward service delivery in hospitals and similar healthcare settings.].

Pargament, K. I. (Ed.). (2013). *APA Handbook of psychology, religion, and spirituality.* Washington, D.C.: American Psychological Association. [See volume 1, chapters 27-41, for information on working with different populations and faith traditions.]

Richards, P. S., & Bergin, A. E. (Eds.). (2014). *Handbook of psychotherapy and religious diversity* (2nd ed.). Washington, D.C.: American Psychological Association. [Provides information on the intersection between spirituality and therapy among different ethnic groups and faith traditions.]

Van Hook, M., Hugen, B., & Aguilar, M. A. (Eds.). (2001). *Spirituality within religious traditions in social work practice.* Pacific Grove, Calif.: Brooks/Cole. [Primarily focuses on providing practice-oriented information about a diverse array of faith traditions.]

### Diverse Clinical Cases Involving Spirituality

Richards, P., & Bergin, A. E. (Eds.). (2004). *Casebook for a spiritual strategy in counseling and psychotherapy.* Washington, D.C.: American Psychological Association. [Depicts examples of therapists, with various theoretical orientations, working with clients from different theistic traditions.]

Scales, T. L., Wolfer, T. A., Sherwood, D. A., Garland, D. R., Hugen, B., & Pittman, S. W. (Eds.). (2002). *Spirituality and religion in social work practice: Decision cases with teaching notes.* Alexandria, Va.: Council on Social Work Education. [Features decision cases—ethically complex clinical cases that ask individuals to make and justify a course of action.]

as well as the wider catchment area they serve. The idea is to identify the most common spiritual groups. While time constraints make it difficult to develop high degrees of spiritual competence with every group, it is feasible to do so with the comparably fewer groups that are frequently encountered.

Toward this end, some of the resources listed in box 12.1 may be useful. The top half of the box features books that delineate important commonalities in diverse religious traditions. Understanding the beliefs and behaviors that serve to distinguish various traditions helps practitioners conduct spiritual assessments and, more generally, work with clients' spirituality in an ethical and professional manner.

Practitioners might start with the groups they encounter most frequently in clinical settings. To develop expertise regarding a given group, it is important to read multiple sources. Every author brings a unique lens to the subject. To obtain a well-rounded perspective on widely affirmed values within a given tradition, it is important to read different authors. This should include accounts written by cultural insiders, as well as those written by sympathetic outsiders. Web sites developed by various traditions can also be excellent sources of information.

The bottom half of the box features two different compilations of case studies. The cases feature a variety of practice settings as well as clients from diverse religious traditions. Reading these case studies can help practitioners get a sense of how the information gleaned from an assessment can be incorporated into treatment with clients and practitioners from different perspectives. In turn, such information helps equip practitioners to administer spiritual assessments more effectively by providing snapshots of how the whole process fits together.

This is likely to be especially true with the Richards and Bergin (2004) text, which tends to feature cases that chronicle the entire clinical history from in-take to termination. The cases featured in the second book have a somewhat different pedagogical purpose, as will be discussed in the following section. Although the following content is geared toward educators, practitioners might also benefit from some of the ideas.

### Education

A number of options might be used in educational settings to help equip future practitioners conduct assessments with various populations. For instance, students might practice using diagrammatic assessments with case examples involving spirituality. Cases might be taken from the texts featured in the resource list or other sources.

Scales and associates (2002) have compiled a series of diverse case studies that feature different practice settings. These cases are designed to enhance students' ability to engage in ethical and professional practice in the area of spirituality. To accomplish this, students read a rich, ethically complex case and formulate a preliminary opinion about how practitioners should proceed. In a subsequent session, instructors facilitate a discussion, guided by teaching notes contained in the text, that illustrates the strengths and limitations associated with various courses of action.

Many of the cases featured in the book can also be used to develop skills in the area of spiritual assessment. Instructors might select an appropriate case and facilitate a discussion about which diagrammatic approach would represent the best option given the parameters of the case. Students might then be asked to complete a diagrammatic assessment based on the information presented in the case, supplemented, if necessary, by additional information provided by the instructor. A subsequent discussion might focus on the possible interventions that might flow from the assessment and their respective strengths and limitations.

This same basic procedure could also be employed with films featuring spiritual characters. Movies that could be used include *The Color of Paradise* (Islam), *Children of Heaven* (Islam), *Miss Rose White* (Judaism), and *Harvest of Fire* (Amish). Students might watch such films and then depict key information using a diagrammatic assessment tool, perhaps as a homework assignment. In a subsequent class, the instructor might note points of similarity and difference between the various completed assessments in relation to the information featured in the movie.

In a manner analogous to case studies, such films can also be used to facilitate spiritual competence. After viewing the film, completing a diagrammatic assessment on one of the primary characters, and exploring assessment-related issues, the discussion might transition to issues related to spiritual competence. For instance, regarding the film *Harvest of Fire*, issues that might be explored include the distinctive features of the Amish culture, the rationale for the practice of shunning, how this practice is similar to or different from the practices used by other (mainstream) groups to police their social boundaries, and the ways in which the protagonist exemplifies the use of spiritual competency in her work with the Amish and in her confrontation with the film's villain.

Such exercises tend to be most effective when the characters are portrayed in a realistic, strengths-based manner. Unfortunately, it is difficult to find films that portray devout people of faith in an accurate and representative manner. If instructors possess sufficient levels of spiritual competence, negative portrayals of people of faith can be deconstructed to illustrate secular biases in a manner that engenders empathy and creates understanding regarding why people of faith are often hesitant to trust helping professionals. This is often a difficult task to accomplish, however, and risks reinforcing preexisting biases.

Students might also be asked to conduct a self-assessment using the various diagrammatic tools. Willow, Tobin, and Toner (2009) discuss the process and outcomes that result from asking students to conduct a self-assessment using spiritual genograms. Once the genogram is completed, individuals then reflect on and discuss it. The study indicates that the exercise helped participants increase their level of spiritual competence, identify countertransference biases, and enhance their ability to administer spiritual genograms.

Another option is to have students administer spiritual assessments to each other, although ground rules regarding confidentiality and trust must be clearly established before proceeding. In this exercise, people form dyads and take turns conducting an assessment. The person on the receiving end of the assessment takes mental notes regarding the strengths and weaknesses of the process. The participants then switch roles. After both assessments have been conducted, the participants share their impressions of the process with each other, noting what went well and what might be improved. The students then develop a list of nonpersonal information that is shared with the rest of the class so that others can learn from their experiences.

This exercise can be used with all the approaches presented in this book. In addition to equipping students to effectively administer assessments, the exercise fosters an experiential understanding of the various strengths and limitations of the tools. This better positions students to select between different comprehensive assessment approaches.

Learning games represent another option to help students understand the strengths and limitations of different assessment tools. For example, instructors might obtain one of the free *PowerPoint Jeopardy* templates available online. Categories could be created for each assessment approach, along with a respective list of *Jeopardy*-type questions that are ordered to reflect increasing levels of difficulty. Once the game is created, students can be divided up into a number of small groups who compete against each other in a game of *PowerPoint Jeopardy*. The instructor hosts the game, asks the questions, and underscores important pedagogical points along the way. Such learning games can be a constructive way to summarize and reinforce key concepts at the end of a course or course module on spiritual assessment.

## CONCLUSION

For many clients, spirituality is the central, animating motivation of their lives. Health and spirituality are intertwined in often complex ways that are not readily apparent. For such clients, a spiritual assessment must be conducted to optimize services. The assessment provides the information needed to tailor service provision so that it helps rather than hinders clients on their journey toward wellness.

As practitioners across the helping professions have recognized this reality, interest in spiritual assessment has increased. In response to this growing awareness, this book has sought to identify and clarify best practices in the assessment of spirituality. Practitioners who implement these practices in their clinical work will help clients realize their strengths and achieve their goals. And that is an end worth striving for.

# REFERENCES

Ai, A. L. (2002). Integrating spirituality into professional education: A challenging but feasible task. *Journal of Teaching in Social Work*, *22*(1/2), 103–30.

Allport, G. W., & Ross, M. J. (1967). Personal religious orientation and prejudice. *Journal of Personality and Social Psychology*, *5*(4), 432–43.

American Association for Marriage and Family Therapy. (2012). *Code of Ethics*. Retrieved 7/20/2013 from http://www.aamft.org/imis15/content/legal_ethics/code_of_ethics.aspx.

American Psychiatric Association. (2013). *Diagnostic and statistical manual of mental disorders, 5th edition*. Washington, D.C.: Author.

American Psychological Association (APA). (2002). *American Psychological Association ethical principles of psychologists and code of conduct*. Retrieved 5/15/2010 from http://www.apa.org/ethics/code/index.aspx.

American School Counselor Association (ASCA). (2010). *Ethical Standards for School Counselors*. Retrieved 8/28/2011 from http://www.schoolcounselor.org/files/EthicalStandards2010.pdf.

Ammerman, N. T. (2013). Spiritual but not religious? Beyond binary choices in the study of religion. *Journal for the Scientific Study of Religion*, *52*(2), 258–78.

Anandarahah, G., & Hight, E. (2001). Spirituality and medical practice: Using the HOPE questions as a practical tool for spiritual assessment. *American Family Physician*, *63*(1), 81–88.

APA Presidential Task Force on Evidence-Based Practice. (2006). Evidence-based practice in psychology. *American Psychologist*, *61*(4), 271–85.

Aponte, H. J. (2009). *Spiritual resources in family therapy* (F. Walsh, Editor) (2nd ed., pp. 125–40). New York: Guilford Press.

Arnold, R. M., Avants, S. K., Margolin, A. M., & Marcotte, D. (2002). Patient attitudes concerning the inclusion of spirituality into addiction treatment. *Journal of Substance Abuse Treatment*, *23*, 319–26.

Astrow, A. B., Wexler, A., Texeira, K., He, M. K., & Sulmasy, D. P. (2007). Is failure to meet spiritual needs associated with cancer patients' perceptions of quality of care and their satisfaction with care? *Journal of Clinical Oncology*, 25(36), 5753–57.

Augustine. (354–430/1991). *Confessions* (H. Chadwick, Trans.). New York: Oxford University Press.

Babbie, E. (2013). *The practice of social research* (13th ed.). Belmont, Calif.: Wadsworth.

Balboni, M. J., Sullivan, A., Amobi, A., Phelps, A. C., Gorman, D. P., Zollfrank, A., et al. (2013). Why is spiritual care infrequent at the end of life? Spiritual care perceptions among patients, nurses, and physicians and the role of training. *Journal of Clinical Oncology*, 31(4), 461–67.

Balboni, T. A., Vanderwerker, L. C., Block, S. D., Paulk, M. E. L., Christopher S., Peteet, J. R., & Prigerson, H. G. (2007). Religiousness and spiritual support among advanced cancer patients and associations with end-of-life treatment preferences and quality of life. *Journal of Clinical Oncology*, 25(5), 555–60.

Balboni, T., Balboni, M., Paulk, M. E., Phelps, A., Wright, A., Peteet, J., et al. (2011). Support of cancer patients' spiritual needs and associations with medical care costs at the end of life. *Cancer*, 117(23), 5383–91.

Balboni, T. A., Paulk, M. E., Balboni, M. J., Phelps, A. C., Loggers, E. T., Wright, A. A., et al. (2010). Provision of spiritual care to patients with advanced cancer: Associations with medical care and quality of life near death. *Journal of Clinical Oncology*, 28(3), 445–52.

Barry, W. A., & Connolly, W. J. (2009). *The practice of spiritual direction* (2nd ed.). New York: HarperOne.

Boorstin, B., & Schlachter, E. (2000). *American Association of Pastoral Counselors and Samaritan Institute report*. Washington, D.C.: Greenberg Quinlan Research.

Borneman, T., Ferrell, B., & Puchalski, C. M. (2010). Evaluation of the FICA tool for spiritual assessment. *Journal of Pain and Symptom Management*, 40(2), 163–73.

Bullis, R. K. (1996). *Spirituality in social work practice*. Washington, D.C.: Taylor & Francis.

Bushfield, S. (2009). Use of spiritual life maps in a hospice setting. *Journal of Religion, Spirituality & Aging*, 22, 254–70.

Canda, E. R. (1997). Spirituality. In R. L. Edwards (Editor), *Encyclopedia of social work* (19th ed., pp. 299–309). Washington, D.C.: NASW Press.

———. (2008). Human needs: Religion and spirituality. In T. Mizrahi & L. E. Davis (Editors), *Encyclopedia of social work* (20th ed., pp. 413–18). Washington, D.C.: Oxford University Press.

Canda, E. R., & Furman, L. D. (2010). *Spiritual diversity in social work practice: The heart of helping* (2nd ed.). New York: Oxford University Press.

Canda, E. R., Nakashima, M., & Furman, L. D. (2004). Ethical considerations about spirituality in social work: Insights from a national qualitative survey. *Families in Society, 85*(1), 27–35.

Carlson, T. D., Kirkpatrick, D., Hecker, L., & Killmer, M. (2002). Religion, spirituality, and marriage and family therapy: A study on family therapists' beliefs about the appropriateness of addressing religious and spiritual issues in therapy. *American Journal of Family Therapy, 30*, 157–71.

Catterall, R., Cox, M., Greet, B., Sankey, J., & Griffiths, G. (1998). The assessment and audit of spiritual care. *International Journal of Palliative Nursing, 4*(4), 162–68.

Cederbaum, J., & Klusaritz, H. A. (2009). Clinical instruction: Using the strengths-based approach with nursing students. *Journal of Nursing Education, 48*(8), 422–28.

Chandler, E. (2012). Religious and spiritual issues in DSM-5: Matters of the mind and searching of the soul. *Issues in Mental Health Nursing, 33*, 577–82.

Chaves, M. (2011). *American religion: Contemporary trends.* Princeton, N.J.: Princeton University Press.

Chorpita, B. F., Daleiden, E. L., Ebesutani, C., Young, J., Becker, K. D., Nakamura, B. J., et al. (2011). Evidence-based treatments for children and adolescents: An updated review of indicators of efficacy and effectiveness. *Clinical Psychology: Science and Practice, 18*(2), 154–72.

Clark, G. (1993). *Augustine, the confessions.* New York: Cambridge University Press.

Clark, P. A., Drain, M., & Malone, M. P. (2003). Addressing patients' emotional and spiritual needs. *Joint Commission Journal on Quality and Safety, 29*(12), 659–70.

Clarke, J. (2009). A critical view of how nursing has defined spirituality. *Journal of Clinical Nursing, 18*(12), 1666–73.

Cnaan, R. A., & Curtis, D. W. (2013). Religious congregations as voluntary associations: An overview. *Nonprofit and Voluntary Quarterly, 42*(1), 7–33.

Cnaan, R. A., Wineburg, R. J., & Boddie, S. C. (1999). *The newer deal: Social work and religion in partnership.* New York: Columbia University Press.

Cohen, J., & Cohen, P. (1983). *Applied multiple regression/correlation analysis for the behavioral sciences* (2nd ed.). Hillsdale, N.J.: Lawrence Erlbaum.

Cook, C. C. H. (2011). *Recommendations for psychiatrists on spirituality and religion.* Retrieved 6/1/2013 from http://rcpsych.ac.uk/pdf/PS03_2011.pdf.

Crabtree, S. A., Husain, F., & Spalek. (2008). *Islam and social work: Debating values, transforming practice.* Bristol, U.K.: Policy Press.

Crisp, B. R. (2010). *Spirituality and social work.* Farnham, Surrey, U.K.: Ashgate Publishing.

David, P., & Stafford, L. (In press). A relational approach to religion and spirituality in marriage: Religious communication in marital satisfaction. *Journal of Family Issues.*

Davis, K. M., Lambie, G. W., & Ieva, K. P. (2011). Influence of familial spirituality: Implications for school counseling professionals. *Counseling and Values, 55*(2), 199–209.

DeFrain, J., & Asay, S. M. (2007). Strong families around the world. *Marriage & Family Review, 41*(1/2), 1–10.

Denzin, N. K., & Lincoln, Y. S. (Editors). (2013). *The landscape of qualitative research* (4th ed.). Thousand Oaks, Calif.: Sage Publications.

Derezotes, D. S. (2006). *Spiritually oriented social work practice.* Boston: Pearson Education.

Dermatis, H., Guschwan, M. T., Galanter, M., & Bunt, G. (2004). Orientation toward spirituality and self-help approaches in the therapeutic community. *Journal of Addictive Diseases, 23*(1), 39–54.

Dershowitz, A. M. (2004). *Rights from wrongs: A secular theory of the origins of rights.* New York: Basic Books.

Doherty, W. J. (2009). *Spiritual resources in family therapy* (F. Walsh, Editor) (2nd ed., pp. 215–28). New York: Guilford Press.

Dolgoff, R., Harrington, D., & Loewenberg, F. M. (2012). *Ethical decisions for social work practice* (9th ed.). Belmont, Calif.: Brooks/Cole.

Draper, P. (2012). An integrative review of spiritual assessment: Implications for nursing management. *Journal of Nursing Management, 20,* 970–80.

Eck, D. L. (2001). *A new religious America.* New York: HarperCollins.

Elliott, N. (2012). Can spiritual ecograms be utilized in mental health services to promote culturally appropriate family and couples therapy with indigenous people? *First People Child & Family Review, 7*(1), 118–26.

Ellis, A. (1980). *The case against religion: A psychotherapist's view and the case against religiosity.* Austin: American Atheist Press.

———. (2000). Can rational emotive behavior therapy be effectively used with people who have devout beliefs in God and religion? *Professional Psychology: Research and Practice, 31*(1), 29–33.

Ellison, C. G., & McFarland, M. J. (2013). The social context of religion and spirituality in the United States. In K. I. Pargament (Editor), *APA handbook of psychology, religion, and spirituality: Vol. 1. Context, theory, and research* (pp. 21–50). Washington, D.C.: American Psychological Association.

Exline, J. J., Park, C. L., Smyth, J. M., & Carey, M. P. (2011). Anger toward God: Social-cognitive predictors, prevalence, and links with adjustment to bereavement and cancer. *Journal of Personality and Social Psychology, 100*(1), 129–48.

Fetzer Institute. (1999). *Multidimensional Measurement of Religiousness/Spirituality for Use in Health Research* (A Report of the Fetzer Institute/National Institute on Aging Working Group). Retrieved 11/18/2013 from http://www.fetzer.org/resources/multidimensional-measurement-religiousnessspirituality-use-health-research.

Fife, S. T., & Whiting, J. B. (2007). Values in family therapy practice and research: An invitation for reflection. *Contemporary Family Therapy, 29*(1/2), 71–86.

Fincham, F. D., & Beach, S. R. H. (2013). Can religion and spirituality enhance prevention programs for couples? In K. I. Pargament (Editor), *APA handbook of psychology, religion, and spirituality: Vol. 2. An applied psychology of religion and spirituality* (pp. 461–79). Washington, D.C.: American Psychological Association.

Fitchett, G. (1993). *Assessing spiritual needs.* Minneapolis: Augsburg.

―――― (2012). Next steps for spiritual assessment in healthcare. In M. R. Cobb, C. M. Puchalski & B. Rumbold (Editors), *Oxford textbook of spirituality in healthcare* (pp. 299–303). New York: Oxford University Press.

Foucault, M. (1984). *The Foucault reader* (P. Rabinow, Editor). New York: Pantheon Books.

Frame, M. W. (2003). *Integrating religion and spirituality into counseling.* Pacific Grove, Calif.: Brooks/Cole.

Freud, S. (1964 [1927]). *The future of an illusion, civilization and its discontents and other works* (J. Strachey, Trans.) (Vol. 21). London: Hogarth Press.

Furness, S., & Gilligan, P. (2010). *Religion, belief and social work: Making a difference.* Bristol, U.K.: Policy Press.

Galek, K., Flannelly, K. J., Koenig, H. G., & Fogg, S. L. (2007). Referrals to chaplains: The role of religion and spirituality in healthcare settings. *Mental Health, Religion & Culture, 10*(4), 363–77.

Gall, T. L., Malette, J., & Guirguis-Younger, M. (2001). Spirituality and religiousness: A diversity of definitions. *Journal of Spirituality in Mental Health, 13*, 158–81.

Gallup, G. J., & Jones, T. (2000). *The next American spirituality: Finding God in the twenty-first century.* Colorado Springs: Victor.

Ganatra, H. A., Zafar, S. N., Qidwai, W., & Rozi, S. (2008). Prevalence and predictors of depression among an elderly population of Pakistan. *Aging & Mental Health, 12*(3), 349–56.

Gardner, F. (2011). *Critical spirituality: A holistic approach to contemporary practice.* Farnham, Surrey, U.K.: Ashgate Publishing.

Gartner, J. D. (1996). Religious commitment, mental health, and prosocial behavior: A review of the empirical literature. In E. P. Shafranske (Editor), *Religion and the clinical practice of psychology* (pp. 187–214). Washington, D.C.: American Psychological Association.

Gellner, E. (1992). *Postmodernism, reason and religion.* New York: Routledge.

Geppert, C., Bogenschutz, M. P., & Miller, W. R. (2007). Development of a bibliography on religion, spirituality, and addiction. *Drug and Alcohol Review, 26*(4), 389–95.

Gil, D. G. (1998). *Confronting injustice and oppression: Concepts and strategies for social workers.* New York: Columbia University Press.

Gilbert, M. (2000). Spirituality in social work groups: Practitioners speak out. *Social Work with Groups, 22*(4), 67–84.

Gilligan, C. (1993). *In a different voice: Psychological theory and women's development.* Cambridge, Mass.: Harvard University Press.

Granqvist, P., & Kirkpatrick, L. A. (2013). Religion, spirituality, and attachment. In K. I. Pargament (Editor), *APA handbook of psychology, religion, and spirituality: Vol. 1. Context, theory, and research* (pp. 139–55). Washington, D.C.: American Psychological Association.

Gray, M. (2008). Viewing spirituality in social work through the lens of contemporary social theory. *British Journal of Social Work, 38,* 175–96.

Griffith, J. L., & Griffith, M. E. (2002). *Encountering the sacred in psychotherapy.* New York: Guilford Press.

Grim, B. J., & Finke, R. (2010). *The price of freedom denied: Religious persecution and conflict in the twenty-first century.* New York: Cambridge University Press.

Hamilton, J. B., Sandelowski, M., Moore, A. D., Agarwal, M., & Koenig, H. G. (2013). "You need a song to bring you through": The use of religious songs to manage stressful life events. *Gerontologist, 53*(1), 26–38.

Hamilton, J. L., & Levine, J. P. (2006). Neo-pagan patients' preferences regarding physician discussion of spirituality. *Family Medicine, 38*(2), 83–84.

Harr, C., Openshaw, L., & Moore, B. (2006). Moving toward effective interdisciplinary collaborations to address spirituality: Chaplains' perspectives on working with social workers. *Arete, 30*(1), 101–11.

Hartman, A. (1995). Diagrammatic assessment of family relationships. *Families in Society, 76*(2), 111–22.

Hathaway, W. L., & Ripley, J. S. (2009). Ethical concerns around spirituality and religion in clinical practice. In J. D. Aten & M. M. Leach (Editors), *Spirituality and the therapeutic process: A comprehensive resource from intake to termination* (pp. 25–52). Washington, D.C.: American Psychological Association.

Heller, P. E., & Wood, B. (2000). The influence of religious and ethnic differences on martial intimacy: Intermarriage versus intramarriage. *Journal of Marital and Family Therapy, 26*(2), 241–52.

Henery, N. (2003). The reality of visions: Contemporary theories of spirituality in social work. *British Journal of Social Work, 33,* 1105–13.

Hepworth, D. H., Rooney, R. H., Rooney, G. D., & Strom-Gottfried, K. (2013). *Direct social work practice: Theory and skills* (9th ed.). Belmont, Calif.: Brooks/Cole.

Hill, P. C., & Edwards, E. (2013). Measurement in the psychology of religiousness and spirituality: Existing measures and new frontiers. In K. I. Pargament (Editor), *APA handbook of psychology, religion, and spirituality: Vol. 1. Context, theory, and research* (pp. 51–77). Washington, D.C.: American Psychological Association.

Hill, P. C., & Hood, R. W. (Editors). (1999). *Measures of religiosity.* Birmingham, Ala.: Religious Education Press.

Hodge, D. R. (2000). Spiritual ecomaps: A new diagrammatic tool for assessing marital and family spirituality. *Journal of Marital and Family Therapy, 26*(2), 217–28.

———. (2001a). Spiritual assessment: A review of major qualitative methods and a new framework for assessing spirituality. *Social Work, 46*(3), 203–14.

———. (2001b). Spiritual genograms: A generational approach to assessing spirituality. *Families in Society, 82*(1), 35–48.

———. (2003a). The challenge of spiritual diversity: Can social work facilitate an inclusive environment? *Families in Society, 84*(3), 348–58.

———. (2003b). The intrinsic spirituality scale: A new six-item instrument for assessing the salience of spirituality as a motivational construct. *Journal of Social Service Research, 30*(1), 41–61.

———. (2004a). Developing cultural competency with evangelical Christians. *Families in Society, 85*(2), 251–60.

——. (2004b). Spirituality and people with mental illness: Developing spiritual competency in assessment and intervention. *Families in Society,* 85(1), 36–44.

——. (2005a). Developing a spiritual assessment toolbox: A discussion of the strengths and limitations of five different assessment methods. *Health and Social Work,* 30(4), 314–23.

——. (2005b). Epistemological frameworks, homosexuality, and religion: How people of faith understand the intersection between homosexuality and religion. *Social Work,* 50(3), 207–18.

——. (2005c). Social work and the house of Islam: Orienting practitioners to the beliefs and values of Muslims in the United States. *Social Work,* 50(2), 162–73.

——. (2005d). Spiritual assessment in marital and family therapy: A methodological framework for selecting between six qualitative assessment tools. *Journal of Marital and Family Therapy* 31(4), 341–56.

——. (2005e). Spiritual ecograms: A new assessment instrument for identifying clients' spiritual strengths in space and across time. *Families in Society,* 86(2), 287–96.

——. (2005f). Spiritual life maps: A client-centered pictorial instrument for spiritual assessment, planning, and intervention. *Social Work,* 50(1), 77–87.

——. (2006). A template for spiritual assessment: A review of the JCAHO requirements and guidelines for implementation. *Social Work,* 51(4), 317–26.

——. (2008). Constructing spiritually modified interventions: Cognitive therapy with diverse populations. *International Social Work,* 51(2), 178–92.

——. (2009). Secular privilege: Deconstructing the invisible rose-tinted sunglasses. *Journal of Religion and Spirituality in Social Work: Social Thought,* 28(1/2), 8–34.

——. (2011a). Alcohol treatment and cognitive behavioral therapy: Enhancing effectiveness by incorporating spirituality and religion. *Social Work,* 56(1), 21–31.

——. (2011b). Using spiritual interventions in practice: Developing some guidelines from evidence-based practice. *Social Work,* 56(2), 149–58.

——. (2013a). Assessing spirituality and religion in the context of counseling and psychotherapy. In K. I. Pargament (Editor), *APA Handbook of psychology, religion, and spirituality: Vol. 2. An applied psychology of religion and spirituality* (pp. 93–123). Washington, D.C.: American Psychological Association.

——. (2013b). Implicit spiritual assessment: An alternative approach for assessing client spirituality. *Social Work,* 58(3), 223–30.

Hodge, D. R., Baughman, L. M., & Cummings, J. A. (2006). Moving toward spiritual competency: Deconstructing religious stereotypes and spiritual prejudices in social work literature. *Journal of Social Service Research, 32*(4), 211–32.

Hodge, D. R., Bonifas, R. P., & Chou, R. J. (2010). Spirituality and older adults: Ethical guidelines to enhance service provision. *Advances in Social Work, 11*(1), 1–16.

Hodge, D. R., & Bushfield, S. (2006). Developing spiritual competence in practice. *Journal of Ethnic and Cultural Diversity in Social Work, 15*(3/4), 101–27.

Hodge, D. R., & Gillespie, D. F. (2005). Phrase completion scales. In K. Kempf-Leonard (Editor), *Encyclopedia of Social Measurement* (Vol. 3, pp. 53–62). San Diego: Academic Press.

Hodge, D. R., & Horvath, V. E. (2011). Spiritual needs in health care settings: A qualitative meta-synthesis of clients' perspectives. *Social Work, 56*(4), 306–16.

Hodge, D. R., & Limb, G. E. (2009). Spiritual histories and Native Americans: A mixed method validation study. *Journal of Social Service Research, 35*(4), 285–96.

———. (2010a). Conducting spiritual assessments with Native Americans: Enhancing cultural competence in social work practice courses. *Journal of Social Work Education, 46*(2).

———. (2010b). A Native American perspective on spiritual assessment: The strengths and limitations of a complementary set of assessment tools. *Health & Social Work, 35*(2), 121–31.

———. (2010c). Native Americans and brief spiritual assessment: Examining and operationalizing the Joint Commission's assessment framework. *Social Work, 55*(4), 297–307.

———. (2011). Spiritual assessment and Native Americans: Establishing the social validity of a complementary set of assessment tools. *Social Work, 56*(3), 213–23.

———. (2013). Spiritual histories and Latter-day Saints: A mixed method preliminary validation study. *Advances in Social Work, 14*(2), 379–94.

———. (2009). Establishing the preliminary validity of spiritual eco-maps with Native Americans. *Clinical Social Work Journal, 37*(4), 320–31.

Hodge, D. R., & McGrew, C. C. (2006). Spirituality, religion and the interrelationship: A nationally representative study. *Journal of Social Work Education, 43*(3), 637–54.

Hodge, D. R., & Nadir, A. (2008). Moving toward culturally competent practice with Muslims: Modifying cognitive therapy with Islamic tenets. *Social Work*, *53*(1), 31–41.

Hodge, D. R., & Williams, T. R. (2002). Assessing African American spirituality with spiritual eco-maps. *Families in Society*, *83*(5/6), 585–95.

Hollon, S. D., & Ponniah, K. (2010). A review of empirically supported psychological therapies for mood disorders in adults. *Depression Anxiety*, *27*(10), 891–932.

Holloway, M., & Moss, B. (2010). *Spirituality and social work*. London: Palgrave Macmillan.

Hood, R. W., & Francis, L. J. (2013). Mystical experience: Conceptualizations, measurement, and correlates. In K. I. Pargament (Editor), *APA handbook of psychology, religion, and spirituality: Vol. 1. Context, theory, and research* (pp. 391–405). Washington, D.C.: American Psychological Association.

Hook, J. N., Worthington, E. L., Davis, D. E., Jennings, D. J., Gartner, A. L., & Hook, J. P. (2010). Empirically supported religious and spiritual therapies. *Journal of Clinical Psychology*, *66*(1), 46–72.

Huguelet, P., Mohr, S., Betrisey, C., Borras, L., & Gillieron, C. (2011). A randomized trial of spiritual assessment of outpatients with schizophrenia: Patients' and clinicians' experience. *Psychiatric Services*, *62*(1), 79–86.

Husain, A., & Ross-Sheriff, F. (2011). Cultural competence with Muslim Americans. In D. Lum (Editor), *Culturally competent practice: A framework for understanding diverse groups and justice issues* (4th ed., pp. 358–89). Belmont, Calif.: Brooks/Cole.

ICN. (2006). *Code of Ethics for Nurses*. Retrieved 5/14/2011 from http://www.icn. ch/about-icn/code-of-ethics-for-nurses/.

Idler, E. L., Musick, M. A., Ellison, C. G., George, L. K., Krause, N., Ory, M. G., et al. (2003). Measuring multiple dimensions of religion and spirituality for health research. *Research on Aging*, *25*(4), 327–65.

Inbar, Y., & Lammers, J. (2012). Political diversity in social and personality psychology. *Perspectives on Psychological Science*, *7*(5), 496–503.

International Federation of Social Workers (IFSW). (2004). *Ethics in Social Work Statement of Principles*. Retrieved 2/18/2013 from http://ifsw.org/policies/statement-of-ethical-principles/.

Jafari, M. F. (1993). Counseling values and objectives: A comparison of Western and Islamic perspectives. *American Journal of Islamic Social Sciences*, *10*(3), 326–39.

James, W. (1902/1985). *The varieties of religious experience*. Cambridge, Mass.: Harvard University Press.

Johnson, K. S., Elbert-Avila, K. I., & Tulsky, J. A. (2005). The influence of spiritual beliefs and practices on the treatment preferences of African Americans: A review of the literature. *Journal of the American Geriatrics Society, 53*, 711–19.

Joint Commission. (2010). *Advancing effective communication, cultural competence, and patient- and family-centered care: A road map for hospitals*. Oakbrook Terrace, Ill.: Joint Commission.

———. (2012). *Hospital accreditation standards 2012*. Oakbrook Terrance, Ill.: Joint Commission.

Jones, R. P., Cox, D., & Navarro-Rivera, J. (2013). *2013 Hispanic values survey*. Washington, D.C.: Public Religion Research Institute.

Jordan, C., & Franklin, C. (Editors). (2011). *Clinical assessment for social workers: Quantitative and qualitative methods* (3rd ed.). Chicago: Lyceum.

Jung, L. A. (2010). Identifying families' supports and other resources. In R. A. McWilliam (Editor), *Working with families of young children with special needs* (pp. 9–26). New York: Guilford Press.

Kang, J., Shin, D. W., Choi, J. Y., Park, C. H., Baek, Y. J., Mo, H. N., et al. (2012). Addressing the religious and spiritual needs of dying patients by health care staff in Korea: Patient perspectives in a multi-religious Asian country. *Psycho-Oncology, 21*, 274–381.

King, J., & Trimble, J. E. (2013). The spiritual and the sacred among North American Indians and Alaska Natives: Mystery, wholeness, and connectedness in a relational world. In K. I. Pargament (Editor), *APA handbook of psychology, religion, and spirituality: Vol. 1. Context, theory, and research* (pp. 565–80). Washington, D.C.: American Psychological Association.

Koenig, H. G. (Editor). (1998). *Handbook of religion and mental health*. San Diego: Academic Press.

———. (2011). *Spirituality and health research: Methods, measurement, statistics and resources*. West Conshohocken, Penn.: Templeton Press.

———. (2013). *Spirituality in patient care: Why, how, when, and what* (3rd ed.). West Conshohocken, Penn.: Templeton Press.

Koenig, H. G., King, D., & Carson, V. B. (2012). *Handbook of religion and health* (2nd ed.). New York: Oxford University Press.

Koenig, H. G., McCullough, M. E., & Larson, D. B. (2001). *Handbook of religion and health*. New York: Oxford University Press.

Kohlberg, L. (1981). *The philosophy of moral development: Moral stages and the idea of justice.* San Francisco: Harper & Row.

Kristeller, J. L., Rhodes, M., Cripe, L. D., & Sheets, V. (2005). Oncologist assisted spiritual intervention study (OASIS): Patient acceptability and initial evidence of effects. *International Journal of Psychiatry in Medicine, 35*(4), 329–47.

Kuhn, T. S. (1970). *The structure of scientific revolutions* (2nd ed.). Chicago: University of Chicago Press.

Kwilecki, S. (2011). Ghosts, meaning, and faith: After-death communications in bereavement narratives. *Death Studies, 35*(3), 219–43.

Laird, L. D., Marrais, J. D., & Barnes, L. L. (2007). Portraying Islam and Muslims in MEDLINE: A content analysis. *Social Science & Medicine, 65,* 2425–39.

Larimore, W. L., Parker, M., & Crowther, M. (2002). Should clinicians incorporate positive spirituality into their practices? What does the evidence say? *Annals of Behavioral Medicine, 24*(1), 69–73.

Larson, D., Milano, G. M., & Lu, F. (1998). Religion and mental health: The need for cultural sensitivity and synthesis. In S. O. Okpaku (Editor), *Clinical methods in transcultural psychiatry* (pp. 191–210). Washington, D.C.: American Psychiatric Association.

Leach, M. M., Aten, J. D., Wade, N. G., & Hernandez, B. C. (2009). Noting the importance of spirituality during the clinical intake. In J. D. Aten & M. M. Leach (Editors), *Spirituality and the therapeutic process: A comprehensive resource from intake to termination* (pp. 75–92). Washington, D.C.: American Psychological Association.

Lee, M. T., Poloma, M. M., & Post, S. G. (2013). *The heart of religion: Spiritual empowerment, benevolence, and the experience of God's love.* New York: Oxford University Press.

Lewis, M. M. (2001). Spirituality, counseling, and the elderly: An introduction to the spiritual life review. *Journal of Adult Development, 8*(4), 231–40.

Limb, G. E., & Hodge, D. R. (2007). Developing spiritual lifemaps as a culture-centered pictorial instrument for spiritual assessments with Native American Clients. *Research on Social Work Practice, 17*(2), 296–304.

———. (2010). Helping child welfare workers improve cultural competence by utilizing spiritual genograms with Native American families and children. *Children and Youth Services Review, 32*(2), 239–45.

———. (2011). Utilizing spiritual ecograms with Native American families and children to promote cultural competence in family therapy. *Journal of Marital and Family Therapy, 37*(1), 81–94.

Limb, G. E., Hodge, D. R., Leckie, R., & Ward, P. (2013). Utilizing spiritual lifemaps with LDS clients: Enhancing cultural competence in social work practice. *Clinical Social Work.*

Limb, G. E., Hodge, D. R., Ward, P., & Alboroto, R. (Under review). A LDS perspective on spiritual assessment: Examining the strengths and limitations of a complementary set of assessment tools.

Lindo, E. J., & Elleman, A. M. (2010). Social validity's presence in the field-based reading intervention research. *Remedial and Special Education, 31*(6), 489–99.

Loewenthal, K. M. (2013). Religion, spirituality, and culture: Clarifying the direction and effects. In K. I. Pargament (Editor), *APA handbook of psychology, religion, and spirituality: Vol. 1. Context, theory, and research* (pp. 239–55). Washington, D.C.: American Psychological Association.

Lyotard, J.-F. (1979/1984). *The postmodern condition: A report on knowledge* (G. Bennington & B. Massumi, Trans.). Minneapolis: University of Minnesota Press.

Mack, J., & Powell, L. (2005). Perceptions of non-local communication: Incidences associated with media consumption and individual differences. *North American Journal of Psychology, 7*(2), 279–94.

Mathai, J., & North, A. (2003). Spiritual history of parents of children attending a child and adolescent mental health service. *Australasian Psychiatry, 11*(2), 172–74.

McEwen, M. (2004). Analysis of spirituality content in nursing textbooks. *Journal of Nursing Education, 43*(1), 20–30.

McGoldrick, M., Gerson, R., & Petry, S. S. (2008). *Genograms: Assessment and intervention* (3rd ed.). New York: Norton.

McSherry, W. (2010). Spiritual assessment: Definitions, categorizations and features. In W. McSherry & L. Ross (Editors), *Spiritual assessment in healthcare practice* (pp. 57–78). Keswick, U.K.: M&K Publishing.

Melton, J. G. (2009). *The encyclopedia of American religions* (8th ed.). Detroit: Gale Research.

Miller, D. W. (2001, May 12). Programs in social work embrace the teaching of spirituality. *Chronicle of Higher Education,* The Faculty, A12. Retrieved 11/24/2003 from http://chronicle.com/prm/weekly/v47/i36/36a01201.htm.

Miller, G. (2003). *Incorporating spirituality in counseling and psychotherapy.* Hoboken, N.J.: Wiley.

Minatrea, N. B., & Duba, J. D. (2012). Counseling interfaith couples. In P. A. Robey, R. E. Wubbolding, & J. Carlson (Editors), *Contemporary issues in couples counseling: A choice theory and reality therapy approach* (pp. 129–41). New York: Taylor & Francis.

Moss, B. (2005). *Religion and spirituality*. Lyme Regis, U.K.: Russell House.

Mutter, K. F., & Neves, C. M. (2010). A dialogical model for engaging spirituality in therapy. *Clinical Social Work Journal, 38*, 164–73.

Narayanasamy, A. (2010). Recognising spiritual needs. In W. McSherry & L. Ross (Editors), *Spiritual assessment in healthcare practice* (pp. 37–55). Keswick, U.K.: M&K Publishing.

National Association of Social Workers (NASW). (2001). *Standards for Cultural Competence in Social Work Practice*. Retrieved 2/23/2013 from http://www.socialworkers.org/practice/standards/NASWCulturalStandards.pdf.

———. (2005). *NASW Standards for Social Work Practice in Health Care Settings*. Retrieved 7/14/2013 from http://www.naswdc.org/practice/standards/naswhealthcarestandards.pdf.

———. (2008). *Code of Ethics*. Retrieved 1/14/2014 from http://www.socialworkers.org/pubs/code/code.asp.

National Cancer Institute (NCI). (2012). *Spirituality in cancer care*. Retrieved 6/18/2013 from http://www.cancer.gov/cancertopics/pdq/supportivecare/spirituality/HealthProfessional/page1/AllPages.

———. (2013). *NCI mission statement*. Retrieved 6/18/2013 from http://www.cancer.gov/aboutnci/overview/mission.

National Institute for Clinical Excellence. (2004). *Improving supportive and palliative care for adults with cancer*. Retrieved 2/23/2013 from http://www.nice.org.uk/nicemedia/live/10893/28816/28816.pdf.

Nee, W. (1968). *The spiritual man*. (Vols. 1–3). New York: Christian Fellowship Publishers.

Nelson-Becker, H. (2005). Religion and coping in older adults: A social work perspective. *Journal of Gerontological Social Work, 45*(1/2), 51–67.

Nelson-Becker, H., Nakashima, M., & Canda, E. R. (2007). Spiritual assessment in aging: A framework for clinicians. *Journal of Gerontological Social Work, 48*(3/4), 331–47.

Nesvag, J., Diesen, I., Solheim, D., de Jimenez, I. G., & Osttveit, J. (2001). *Freedom of religion: A report with special emphasis on the right to choose religion and registration systems*. Oslo, Norway: Forum 18.

Newport, F. (2012). *God is alive and well: The future of religion in America*. New York: Gallup Press.

Nielsen, S. L. (2004). A Mormon rational emotive behavior therapist attempts Qur'anic rational emotive behavior therapy. In P. S. Richards & A. E. Bergin (Editors), *Casebook for a spiritual strategy in counseling and psychotherapy* (pp. 213–30). Washington, D.C.: American Psychological Association.

Oakes, K. E., & Raphel, M. M. (2008). Spiritual assessment in counseling: Methods and practice. *Counseling and Values, 52,* 240–52.

Oman, D. (2013). Spiritual modeling and the social learning of spirituality and religion. In K. I. Pargament (Editor), *APA handbook of psychology, religion, and spirituality: Vol. 1. Context, theory, and research* (pp. 187–204). Washington, D.C.: American Psychological Association.

Oppenheimer, J. E., Flannelly, K. J., & Weaver, A. J. (2004). A comparative analysis of the psychological literature on collaboration between clergy and mental-health professionals—perspectives from secular and religious journals: 1970–1999. *Pastoral Psychology, 53*(2), 153–62.

Ortega, R. M., & Faller, K. C. (2011). Training child welfare workers from an intersectional cultural humility perspective: A paradigm shift. *Child Welfare, 90*(5), 27–49.

Paley, J. (2008). Spirituality and secularization: Nursing and the sociology of religion. *Journal of Clinical Nursing, 17*(2), 175–86.

———. (2009). Keep the NHS secular. *Nursing Standard, 23*(43), 26–27.

Pargament, K. I. (1997). *The psychology of religion and coping.* New York: Guilford Press.

———. (2007). *Spiritually integrated psychotherapy: Understanding and addressing the sacred.* New York: Guilford Press.

——— (Editor). (2013a). *APA Handbook of psychology, religion, and spirituality.* Washington, D.C.: American Psychological Association.

———. (2013b). Searching for the sacred: Toward a nonreductionistic theory of spirituality. In K. I. Pargament (Editor), *APA handbook of psychology, religion, and spirituality: Vol. 1. Context, theory, and research* (pp. 257–73). Washington, D.C.: American Psychological Association.

Pargament, K. I., & Krumrei, E. J. (2009). Clinical assessment of clients' spirituality. In J. D. Aten & M. M. Leach (Editors), *Spirituality and the therapeutic process: A comprehensive resource from intake to termination* (pp. 93–120). Washington, D.C.: American Psychological Association.

Pargament, K. I., Mahoney, A., Exline, J. J., Jones, J. W., & Shafranske, E. P. (2013). Envisioning an integrative paradigm for the psychology of religion and spirituality. In K. I. Pargament (Editor), *APA Handbook of psychology, religion, and spirituality: Vol. 1 Context, theory, and research* (pp. 3–19). Washington, D.C.: American Psychological Association.

Pargament, K. I., Smith, B. W., Koenig, H. G., & Perez, L. (1998). Patterns of positive and negative coping with major life stressors. *Journal for the Scientific Study of Religion, 37*(4), 710–24.

Park, C. L., Edmondson, D., & Hale-Smith, A. (2013). Why religion? Meaning as a motivation. In K. I. Pargament (Editor), *APA handbook of psychology, religion, and spirituality: Vol. 1. Context, theory, and research* (pp. 157–71). Washington, D.C.: American Psychological Association.

Pattison, S. (2013). Religion, spirituality and health care: Confusions, tensions, opportunities. *Health Care Analysis, 21*(3), 193–207.

Pearce, M. J. (2013). Addressing religion and spirituality in health care systems. In K. I. Pargament (Editor), *APA handbook of psychology, religion, and spirituality: Vol. 2. An applied psychology of religion and spirituality* (pp. 527–41). Washington, D.C.: American Psychological Association.

Pearce, M. J., Coan, A. D., Herndon, J. E., Koenig, H. G., & Abernethy, A. P. (2012). Unmet spiritual care needs impact emotional and spiritual well-being in advanced cancer patients. *Supportive Care in Cancer, 20*(10), 2269–76.

Pearlin, L. (2002). Some institutional and stress process perspectives on religion and health. *Psychological Inquiry, 13*(3), 201–38.

Pew Forum on Religion and Public Life. (2009). *Faith in flux: Changes in religious affiliation in the U.S.* Retrieved 7/22/2013 from http://www.pewforum.org/ uploadedfiles/Topics/Religious_Affiliation/fullreport.pdf.

Plante, T. G. (2009). *Spiritual practices in psychotherapy.* Washington, D.C.: American Psychological Association.

———. (2013). Consultation with religious institutions. In K. I. Pargament (Editor), *APA handbook of psychology, religion, and spirituality: Vol. 2. An applied psychology of religion and spirituality* (pp. 511–26). Washington, D.C.: American Psychological Association.

Poole, D. L. (1998). Politically correct or culturally competent? *Health and Social Work, 23*(3), 163–66.

Popper, K. (1963). *Conjunctures and refutations: The growth of scientific knowledge.* New York: Routledge & Kegan Paul.

Praglin, L. J. (2004). Spirituality, religion, and social work: An effort towards interdisciplinary conversation. *Journal for Religion and Spirituality in Social Work, 23*(4), 67–84.

Propst, L. R. (1996). Cognitive-behavioral therapy and the religious person. In E. P. Shafranske (Editor), *Religion and the clinical practice of psychology* (pp. 391–407). Washington, D.C.: American Psychological Association.

Pruyser, P. (1976). *The minister as diagnostician.* Philadelphia: Westminister Press.

Puchalski, C. M. (2001). The role of spirituality in health care. *Proceedings (Baylor University Medical Center), 14*(4), 352–57.

Reamer, F. G. (2006). *Social work values and ethics* (3rd ed.). New York: Columbia University Press.

Reichert, E. (2003). *Social work and human rights: A foundation for policy and practice.* New York: Columbia University Press.

Reinert, K. G., & Koenig, H. G. (2013). Re-examining definitions of spirituality in nursing research. *Journal of Advanced Nursing, 69*(12), 2622–34.

Richards, P. S., & Bergin, A. E. (Editors). (2004). *Casebook for a spiritual strategy in counseling and psychotherapy.* Washington, D.C.: American Psychological Association.

———. (2005). *A spiritual strategy for counseling and psychotherapy* (2nd ed.). Washington, D.C.: American Psychological Association.

———. (Editors). (2014). *Handbook of psychotherapy and religious diversity* (2nd ed.). Washington, D.C.: American Psychological Association.

Richards, P. S., & Davison, M. L. (1992). Religious bias in moral development research: A psychometric investigation. *Journal for the Scientific Study of Religion, 31*(4), 467–85.

Richards, P. S., Rector, J. M., & Tjeltveit, A. C. (1999). Values, spirituality, and psychotherapy. In W. R. Miller (Editor), *Integrating spirituality into treatment* (pp. 133–60). Washington, D.C.: American Psychological Association.

Roberts, J. (2009). *Spiritual resources in family therapy* (F. Walsh, Editor) (2nd ed., pp. 359–78). New York: Guilford Press.

Roland, A. (1997). How universal is psychoanalysis? The self in India, Japan, and the United States. In D. Allen (Editor), *Culture and self* (pp. 27–39). Boulder, Colo.: Westview Press.

Rose, E. M., Westefeld, J. S., & Ansley, T. N. (2001). Spiritual issues in counseling: Clients' beliefs and preferences. *Journal of Counseling Psychology, 48*(1), 61–71.

———. (2008). Spiritual issues in counseling: Clients' beliefs and preferences. *Psychology of Religion and Spirituality, S*(1), 18–33.

Ross, L. (2008). Commentary on Paley J (2008) spirituality and secularization: Nursing and the sociology of religion. *Journal of Clinical Nursing*, *17*, 2793–2800.

Ross, L., & McSherry, W. (2010). Considerations for the future of spiritual assessment. In W. McSherry & L. Ross (Editors), *Spiritual assessment in healthcare practice* (pp. 161–71). Keswick, U.K.: M&K Publishing.

Saleebey, D. (Editor). (2013). *The strengths perspective in social work practice* (6th ed.). Upper Saddle River, N.J.: Pearson.

Scales, T. L., Wolfer, T. A., Sherwood, D. A., Garland, D. R., Hugen, B., & Pittman, S. W. (Editors). (2002). *Spirituality and religion in social work practice: Decision cases with teaching notes*. Alexandria, Va.: CSWE.

Shafranske, E. P. (2005). The psychology of religion in clinical and counseling psychology. In R. F. Paloutzian & C. L. Park (Editors), *Handbook of the psychology of religion and spirituality* (pp. 496–514). New York: Guilford Press.

Shafranske, E. P., & Cummings, J. P. (2013). Religious and spiritual beliefs, affiliations, and practices of psychologists. In K. I. Pargament (Editor), *APA handbook of psychology, religion, and spirituality: Vol. 2. An applied psychology of religion and spirituality* (pp. 23–41). Washington, D.C.: American Psychological Association.

Sheridan, M. (2009). Ethical issues in the use of spiritually based interventions in social work practice: What we are doing and why. *Journal of Religion and Spirituality in Social Work*, *28*(1/2), 99–126.

Slife, B. D., & Williams, R. N. (1995). *What's behind the research? Discovering the hidden assumptions in the behavioral sciences*. Thousand Oaks, Calif.: Sage Publications.

Smith, C. (2003a). *The secular revolution*. Berkeley: University of California Press.

———. (2003b). Theorizing religious effects among American adolescents. *Journal for the Scientific Study of Religion*, *42*(1), 17–30.

Smith, E. J. (2006). The strength-based counseling model. *Counseling Psychologist*, *34*(1), 13–79.

Smith, J. I. (1999). *Islam in America*. New York: Columbia University Press.

Smith, T. W. (2002). Religious diversity in America: The emergence of Muslims, Buddhists, Hindus, and others. *Journal for the Scientific Study of Religion*, *41*(3), 577–85.

Smith, T. W., Marsden, P. V., Hout, M., & Kim, J. (2013). *General Social Surveys, 1972–2012 [machine-readable data file]*. Storrs, Conn.: Roper Center for Public Opinion.

Snyder, C. R., Lopez, S. J., & Pedrotti, J. T. (2011). *Positive psychology: The scientific and practical explorations of human strengths* (2nd ed.). Thousand Oaks, Calif.: Sage Publications.

Soenke, M., Landau, M. J., & Greenberg, J. (2013). Sacred armor: Religion's role as a buffer against the anxieties of life and the fear of death. In K. I. Pargament (Editor), *APA handbook of psychology, religion, and spirituality: Vol. 1. Context, theory, and research* (pp. 105–22). Washington, D.C.: American Psychological Association.

Solhkhah, R., Galanter, M., Dermatis, H., Daly, J., & Bunt, G. (2008). Spiritual orientation among adolescents in a drug-free residential therapeutic community. *Journal of Child & Adolescent Substance Abuse, 18*(1), 57–71.

Sperry, L. (2013). Distinctive approaches to religion and spirituality: Pastoral counseling, spiritual direction, and spiritually integrated psychotherapy. In K. I. Pargament (Editor), *APA handbook of psychology, religion, and spirituality: Vol. 2. An applied psychology of religion and spirituality* (pp. 223–38). Washington, D.C.: American Psychological Association.

Stark, R. (2008). *What Americans really believe: New findings from the Baylor surveys of religion.* Waco, Tex.: Baylor University Press.

Starnino, V. R., Gomi, S., & Canda, E. R. (2012). Spiritual strengths assessment in mental health practice. *British Journal of Social Work,* pp. 1–19.

Stoll, R. I. (1979). Guidelines for spiritual assessment. *American Journal of Nursing, 79*(9), 1574–77.

Suarez, Z. E., & Lewis, E. A. (2013). Spirituality and culturally diverse families: The intersection of culture, religion, and spirituality. In E. P. Congress & M. J. Gonzalez (Editors), *Multicultural perspectives in social work practice with families* (3rd ed., pp. 231–44). New York: Springer Publishing.

Sue, D. W., Arredondo, P., & McDavis, R. J. (1992). Multicultural counseling competencies and standards: A call to the profession. *Journal of Counseling and Development, 70*(4), 477–86.

Sue, D., & Sue, D. (2013). *Counseling the culturally diverse: Theory and practice* (6th ed.). Hoboken, N.J.: Wiley.

Sullivan, W. P. (2009). Spirituality: A road to mental health or mental illness. *Journal of Religion and Spirituality in Social Work, 28*(1/2), 84–98.

Swinton, J. (2010). The meanings of spirituality: A multi-perspective approach to "the spiritual." In W. McSherry & L. Ross (Editors), *Spiritual assessment in healthcare practice* (pp. 17–35). Keswick, U.K.: M&K Publishing.

Tan, S.-Y. (2013). Addressing religion and spirituality from a cognitive-behavioral perspective. In K. I. Pargament (Editor), *APA handbook of psychology, religion, and spirituality: Vol. 2. An applied psychology of religion and spirituality* (pp. 169–87). Washington, D.C.: American Psychological Association.

Tanyi, R. A. (2006). Spirituality and family nursing: Spiritual assessment and interventions for families. *Journal of Advanced Nursing, 53*(3), 287–94.

Taylor, R. J., Woodward, A. T., Chatters, L. M., Mattis, J. S., & Jackson, J. S. (2011). Seeking help from clergy among Black Caribbean in the United States. *Race and Social Problems, 3*(4), 241–51.

Thyer, B., & Myers, L. (2010). The quest for evidence-based practice: A view from the United States. *Journal of Social Work, 11*(1), 8–25.

Timmins, F., & Kelly, J. (2008). Spiritual assessment in intensive and cardiac care nursing. *Nursing in Critical Care, 13*(3), 124–31.

United Nations. (1948/1998). *Universal Declaration of Human Rights*. Retrieved 2/27/2006 from http://www.un.org/Overview/rights.html.

United Nations Association in Canada. (1995). *Human rights: Questions and answers*. Retrieved 6/18/2004 from http://www.unac.org/rights/actguide/questions.html.

Van Hook, M., Hugen, B., & Aguilar, M. A. (Editors). (2001). *Spirituality within religious traditions in social work practice*. Pacific Grove, Calif.: Brooks/Cole.

Vezeau, T. (2012). Low literacy and vulnerable clients. In M. de Chesnay & B. A. Anderson (Editors), *Caring for the vulnerable* (3rd ed., pp. 59–76). Burlington, Mass.: Jones & Bartlett Learning.

Vogel, M. J., McMinn, M. R., Peterson, M. A., & Gatherecoal, K. A. (2013). Examining religion and spirituality as diversity training: A multidimensional look at training in the American Psychological Association. *Professional Psychology: Research and Practice, 44*(3), 158–67.

Walker, D. F., Gorsuch, R. L., & Tan, S.-Y. (2004). Therapists' integration of religion and spirituality in counseling: A meta-analysis. *Counseling and Values, 49*, 69–80.

Walsh, F. (2009). *Spiritual resources in family therapy* (F. Walsh, Editor) (2nd ed., pp. 31–61). New York: Guilford Press.

———. (2013). Religion and spirituality: A family systems perspective in clinical practice. In K. I. Pargament (Editor), *APA handbook of psychology, religion, and spirituality: Vol. 2. An applied psychology of religion and spirituality* (pp. 189–205). Washington, D.C.: American Psychological Association.

Walton, E., Limb, G. E., & Hodge, D. R. (2011). Developing cultural competency with Latter-day Saint clients: A strengths-based perspective. *Families in Society*, *92*(1), 50–54.

Watson, P. J. (2008). Faithful translation and postmodernism: Norms and linguistic relativity within a Christian ideological surround. *Edification*, *2*(1), 5–18.

Whitfield, C. L. (1984). Stress management and spirituality during recovery: A transpersonal approach. Part 1: Becoming. *Alcoholism Treatment Quarterly*, *1*(1), 3–54.

Wiggins, M. I. (2009). Therapist self-awareness of spirituality. In J. D. Aten & M. M. Leach (Editors), *Spirituality and the therapeutic process: A comprehensive resource from intake to termination* (pp. 53–74). Washington, D.C.: American Psychological Association.

Wilcox, W. B. (2009). How focused on the family? Evangelical Protestants, the family, and sexuality. In S. Brint & J. R. Schroedel (Editors), *Evangelicals and democracy in America:* (pp. 251–75). New York: Russell Sage Foundation.

Williams, J. A., Meltzer, D., Arora, V., Chung, G., & Curlin, F. A. (2011). Attention to inpatients' religious and spiritual concerns: Predictors of association with patient satisfaction. *Journal of General Internal Medicine*, *26*(11), 1265–71.

Willow, R. A., Tobin, D. J., & Toner, S. (2009). Assessment of the use of spiritual genograms in counselor education. *Counseling and Values*, *53*(3), 214–33.

Wolf, J. T. (2004). Teach, but don't preach: Practical guidelines for addressing spiritual concerns of students. *Professional School Counseling*, *7*(5), 363–66.

Wolf, M. M. (1978). Social validity: The case for subjective measurement. *Journal of Applied Behavior Analysis*, *11*(2), 203–14.

Wolfer, T. A. (2012). Religion, spirituality, health, and social work. In S. Gehlert & T. Browne (Editors), *Handbook of health social work* (2nd ed., pp. 263–90). Hoboken, N.J.: Wiley.

Wong, Y.-L. R., & Vinsky, J. (2009). Speaking from the margins: A critical reflection on the "spiritual-but-not-religious" discourse in social work. *British Journal of Social Work*, *39*, 1343–59.

World Health Organisation (WHO). (1990). *World Health Organisation expert committee: Cancer pain relief and palliative care*. Retrieved 1/23/2013 from http://whqlibdoc.who.int/trs/WHO_TRS_804.pdf.

Worthington, E. L., Hook, J. N., Davis, D. E., & McDaniel, M. A. (2011). Religion and spirituality. In J. C. Norcross (Editor), *Psychotherapy relationships that work: Evidenced-based responsiveness* (pp. 402–19). New York: Oxford University Press.

Worthington, E. L., Wade, N. G., Hight, T. L., McCullouogh, M. E., Berry, J. T., Ripley, J. S., et al. (2003). The religious commitment inventory—10: Development, refinement, and validation of a brief scale for research and counseling. *Journal of Counseling Psychology, 50*(1), 84–96.

Wuthnow, R. (1999). *Growing up religious.* Boston: Beacon Press.

———. (2007). *After the Baby Boomers: How twenty- and thirty-somethings are shaping the future of American religion.* Princeton, N.J.: Princeton University Press.

Yancey, G. (2011). *Compromising scholarship: Religious and political bias in American higher education.* Waco, Tex.: Baylor University Press.

Yarhouse, M. A., & Johnson, V. (2013). Values and ethical issues: The interface between psychology and religion. In K. I. Pargament (Editor), *APA handbook of psychology, religion, and spirituality: Vol. 2. An applied psychology of religion and spirituality* (pp. 43–70). Washington, D.C.: American Psychological Association.

Note: Page numbers followed by *b* refer to boxes; those followed by *f* refer to figures; and those followed by *t* refer to tables.

CPSIA information can be obtained
at www.ICGtesting.com
Printed in the USA
LVOW07*1005201117
556991LV00002B/4/P